Atomic Junction

After Atomic Junction, along the Haatso-Atomic Road there lies the Ghana Atomic Energy Commission, home to Africa's first nuclear program after independence. Traveling along this road, Abena Dove Osseo-Asare gathers together stories of conflict and compromise on an African nuclear frontier. She speaks with a generation of African scientists who became captivated with "the atom" and studied in the Soviet Union to make nuclear physics their own. On Pluton Lane and Gamma Avenue, these scientists displaced quiet farming villages in their bid to establish a scientific metropolis, creating an epicenter for Ghana's nuclear physics community. By placing interviews with town leaders, physicists, and local entrepreneurs alongside archival records, Osseo-Asare explores the impact of scientific pursuit on areas surrounding the reactor, focusing on how residents came to interpret activities on these "Atomic Lands." This combination of historical research and personal and ethnographic observations shows how Ghanaians now stand at a crossroads, where some push to install more reactors, whilst others merely seek pipe-borne water.

ABENA DOVE OSSEO-ASARE is Associate Professor in the Department of History at the University of Texas at Austin, holds a secondary appointment as an Associate Professor in the Department of Population Health at UT's Dell Medical School, and is a serving member of the editorial boards of *Endeavour* and *Social History of Medicine*. She is the author of *Bitter Roots: The Search for Healing Plants in Africa* (2014), which was awarded the Melville J. Herskovits Prize in African Studies and the American Historical Association Pacific Coast Branch Book Prize.

Atomic Junction

Nuclear Power in Africa after Independence

ABENA DOVE OSSEO-ASARE

University of Texas at Austin

CAMBRIDGE
UNIVERSITY PRESS

University Printing House, Cambridge CB2 8BS, United Kingdom

One Liberty Plaza, 20th Floor, New York, NY 10006, USA

477 Williamstown Road, Port Melbourne, VIC 3207, Australia

314–321, 3rd Floor, Plot 3, Splendor Forum, Jasola District Centre,
New Delhi – 110025, India

79 Anson Road, #06-04/06, Singapore 079906

Cambridge University Press is part of the University of Cambridge.

It furthers the University's mission by disseminating knowledge in the pursuit of
education, learning, and research at the highest international levels of excellence.

www.cambridge.org
Information on this title: www.cambridge.org/9781108471244
DOI: 10.1017/9781108557955

First published 2019

Printed in the United Kingdom by TJ International Ltd, Padstow Cornwall

A catalogue record for this publication is available from the British Library

Library of Congress Cataloging-in-Publication Data
Names: Osseo-Asare, Abena Dove Agyepoma, author.
Title: Atomic junction : nuclear power in Africa after independence /
Abena Dove Osseo-Asare, University of Texas, Austin.
Description: Cambridge, United Kingdom; New York,
NY, USA: Cambridge University Press, [2019] |
Includes bibliographical references.
Identifiers: LCCN 2019019451 | ISBN 9781108471244 (hardback) |
ISBN 9781108457378 (pbk.)
Subjects: LCSH: Nuclear engineering – Ghana – History – 20th century.
Classification: LCC TK9119.G45 O87 2019 | DDC 621.4809667–dc23
LC record available at https://lccn.loc.gov/2019019451

ISBN 978-1-108-47124-4 Hardback
ISBN 978-1-108-45737-8 Paperback

Have no fear for atomic energy
'Cause none of them can stop the time
Bob Marley, Redemption Song
(Island Records, 1980)

Contents

Figures

Preface: Nuclear Reveries

I first learned about Ghana's nuclear ambitions from my father and his friends. I half-remember an evening in State College, Pennsylvania when I was a child. Ghana had fallen into the grip of yet another military dictatorship and many of the country's intellectuals had taken flight to distant, snowy lands. My father taught materials science and engineering at Pennsylvania State University. That night, some Ghanaian researchers and their families had come for dinner and I overheard a heated discussion as I fell asleep. The next day, my father was laughing. He could not believe that with all of the economic and political problems at home, some of his friends were still fixated on bringing nuclear reactors to Ghana to generate electricity. I learned early on that African countries had the intellectual capacity – the first scientists and mathematicians I met were from Rwanda, Kenya, Nigeria, and Ghana – to have nuclear dreams. But, with near-famine conditions across the continent in the early 1980s, it seemed unethical to devote finite financial resources to such an expensive vision. My childhood visits to Ghana were tinged with shock at visible food scarcity, crumbling infrastructure, and beaten-down cars.

Many years later, I spent a summer back in Ghana with my brother Dankwa in 2004. He was staying at a friend's house in Haatso, a suburb outside of the capital city, Accra. I had lived in Accra on previous occasions, but I had never stayed in this part of the city. Haatso and its environs were in transition. Wealthy families were building large, impressive mansions. Many of these lavish homes were incomplete. Inside the dark structures, often lacking pipe-borne water or electricity, families came to "squat." They strung up vibrant fabric curtains to demarcate their makeshift homes, burning mosquito coils all night to keep the insects at bay.

I often found myself passing along the Haatso-Atomic Road, which terminated in a nexus of roadways popularly called "Atomic Junction." Along the way, sharply pointed iron fixtures emerged from tall grasses, shielding a long winding boulevard onto the hidden campus of the Ghana Atomic Energy Commission. Drivers of minibuses crammed with passengers whizzed through Haatso, Madina, and surrounding suburbs announcing their destination, "Atomic, Atomic, Atomic." Local entrepreneurs had added "Atomic" to the names of the pharmacy, clinic, gas station, and other businesses nearby. Slowly, the adjective "Atomic" had become a geographic designator for an emerging suburb, evoking the dawn of an African nuclear age.

What was the Ghana Atomic Energy Commission, and what did people do there? I began discussing my interest in the organization with family and friends, at church, and over meals. In 2006, after posing dutifully in photographs with my new husband for family at Christmastime, I stayed in Accra a couple of extra weeks and arranged to meet with some of the scientists who worked at the Ghana Atomic Energy Commission. On my first day, I watched as the driver of the taxi I had hired went in circles in his bid to find the place. "The Commission, the Commission, it is a law firm, correct?" he asked nervously. When we finally reached the gates, he was shocked when I mentioned to the guard that I had an appointment with the Director and he opened the gates. We were in.

One thing I hoped to do was take a look at the reactor itself. At the center of the pretty campus with rolling lawns and trim hedges there stood a tall-story building with no glass over the windows. It was completely empty inside, with wind and dust blowing through. I soon learned that the reactor was not in this ghostly, uncompleted structure, even though many outside the gates thought it was. Rather, I was told to check for a small single-story building off to the side.

Along the path to this unassuming office block, I met a slim man named Kofi Anim-Sampong. I gave him my card and he started to laugh. Was I the same Osseo-Asare as the family living in Pennsylvania? He had done a short course on nuclear engineering there and recalled fondly the soups my mother prepared for him during his stay. He had been so surprised that a white lady could manufacture such excellent Ghanaian food! How were my parents? What brought me to the Commission that day? In fact, he was the scientist in charge of the reactor and would be happy to give me a look round and introduce me to his team.

Inside, I put on a badge to monitor radiation exposure. We stepped across the hall to meet several technicians working with computers

Figure 0.1 Kofi Anim-Sampong (r) and colleague with the GHARR-1
(*Source*: author photo)

connected to the reactor. "How did Ghana get a reactor, again?"
I queried my host. "It was provided by China in 1994 – see, the manuals
the men are looking through are mostly in Chinese." He kindly took
me inside to look at the reactor itself. The walls were built so that they
would fall in such a way as to contain radiation should there be an
accident there. The reactor was in the floor, behind a round metal wall
with the Commission motif similar to the ones on the campus gates
above the word "GHARR-1," for Ghana Research Reactor Number
One. It looked like a bunch of tubes connected to metal boxes floating
in a little pond. We took a few photos, me alone in a turquoise-and-
brown striped shirt I got at Urban Outfitters in Harvard Square before
my holiday trip leaning against the gate, a couple of us together, the
scientists in white lab coats (Figure 0.1). Afterwards, we had lunch
in the staff cafeteria across the lawn. I learned that day that nuclear
power could be simultaneously secretive and very mundane.

As this book details, Ghanaian scientists have nurtured nuclear
dreams since the middle of the twentieth century. They transformed a
rural farming community into the hub of Ghana's nuclear enterprise.

The creation of the Atomic-Haatso Road, culminating in the Atomic Junction interchange, carved out a new path for physicists to reach the laboratories of the Ghana Atomic Energy Commission. From here, these scientists moved around the world, seeking access to nuclear technology. They initially learned physics in Russian and courted the Soviet Union, then Germany, then the United States, then China for a reactor. During the long wait for a fission facility, the Commission sent out technicians to monitor radiation at X-ray machines around the country. And they became favored representatives from Africa at inspections of the International Atomic Energy Agency throughout the world.

Meanwhile, the neighborhoods along the Haatso-Atomic Road expanded to breaking point, building up pressure at the perimeter of the expansive grounds for the Commission that first President Kwame Nkrumah's regime expropriated in the 1960s. This pressure culminated most recently in an actual explosion. At Atomic Junction itself, several kilometers from the reactor, a petrol tanker caught fire as it was offloading fuel at a station. The tanker exploded, setting fire to a cooking gas depot next door along the busy Haatso-Atomic Road. Seven people were killed and at least 68 injured in the short time it took for the Atomic Fire Brigade to respond. A spectacular orange mushroom-shaped cloud loomed over the suburb, showing that despite occasional fears about the risks of siting a small low-power nuclear reactor in the area, poor regulation of petrol stations was a more pressing worry for the country. *Atomic Junction* is an African dream-story where scientists manage the risks and benefits of nuclear power in an ever-changing, chaotic postcolonial city.

Acknowledgments

My thanks go to the staff of the Ghana Atomic Energy Commission, especially former directors and senior leadership including Benjamin Nyarko, Edward Akaho, the late Francis Allotey, John H. Amuasi, John Fletcher, B.W. Garbrah, E.O. Darko, Virginia Appiah, and GAEC librarian Mary Abakah for their early and consistent support of my research. My sincere appreciation to all of their many colleagues in the medical physics, radiation protection, and nuclear engineering fields who agreed to participate in this study. I thank the residents of the towns of Kwabenya and Haatso, including elders and community leaders for their candid answers to my questions about the history of the area. All those who wished to be recorded by name are listed in the List of Persons Cited and Consulted.

In Accra, Eyram Amaglo became a research partner and friend, from her days as a recent graduate of Ghana's National Film and Television Institute to our shared experiences as working mothers. Together, we documented the Atomic Junction area in film and audio over a decade. We also worked with Cassandra Appiah, Michael Acquah, Mr. Afari, and Kofi Opoku.

The staff of the Ghana Public Records and Archives Administration (PRAAD) made this project possible through their endless support locating and scanning documents for me. I especially thank search room head Bright Botwe for his close attention to my research over many years and director Felix Ampong for his warm enthusiasm and hospitality since 2002. My gratitude also goes to Killian Onai, formerly of PRAAD, who continued to support me in his capacity as archivist at the University of Ghana, Legon.

The National Science Foundation's Office for Science, Technology, and Society generously supported this research through grants #0958104 and #1457784. I thank director Frederick Kronz for his flexibility as I had to adjust my plans and request extensions during two pregnancies. As a result, I was able to send many students at the University of

California, Berkeley and the University of Texas at Austin to conduct archival research in my stead, edit video footage, and write up interview transcripts. I thank Rhiannon Dowling Fredricks and Katherine Eady for research in Russian archives, Diana Gergel and Yuxi Wang for research in Chinese archives, Ogechukwu Ezekwem Williams for research in the British Public Record Office, and Chase Arnold for his trips to archives in the United Kingdom and the International Atomic Energy Agency in Vienna. For literature reviews, newspaper searches, and transcripts I thank Jon Cole, William Moines, Pablo Palomino, and Daniel Jean-Jacques. I really benefited from insightful conversations with Reginold Royston and Artemis Anastasiadou as we edited the "Atomic Junction" documentary film, a companion to this book available at www.atomicjunction.com. My thanks to Cathryn Carson and Diana Wear at Berkeley for assistance preparing and implementing the original proposal. At Austin, I thank Randy Diehl and Marc Musick in the Dean's office of the College of Liberal Arts for their support.

I thank my departmental chairs at the University of Texas at Austin, Jackie Jones and Alan Tully, for their immense inspiration and confidence in me. I especially benefited from the opportunity to workshop written chapters during 2017–2018 at the Institute for Historical Studies led by Miriam Bodian and Seth Garfield and the Humanities Institute Faculty Seminar run by Polly Strong. My gratitude to all my colleagues and visiting fellows at UT who offered many useful suggestions on these occasions, including my faculty mentors Toyin Falola and Bruce Hunt, as well as Rob Abzug, Phillip Barrish, Daina Berry, Benjamin Brower, Erika Bsumek, Titas Chakraborty, Indrani Chatterjee, Caroline Faria, Peniel Joseph, Madeline Hsu, Neil Kamil, Iris Ma, Alberto García Maldonado, Alberto Martínez, Tracie Matysik, Julie Minich, Sharmila Rudrappa, Lisa Thompson, Yael Schacher, Keri Stephens, Charters Wynn, and many others. I would like to give special thanks to members of my writing group Lina del Castillo, Brent Crosson, Ashley Farmer, Joshua Frens-String, Megan Raby, and Sam Vong. I never imagined that I would find a group of colleagues equally invested in thinking about science and society in Africa, the Caribbean, and the Americas.

A pivotal moment came for me as I attended a Symposium for African Writers at UT in December 2014 organized in part through the efforts of Aaron Bady. The symposium helped me link my own thinking on African science history to the robust field of African science fiction, and to see a parallel universe of African women science fiction writers. I thank participants Taiye Selasi, Maaza Mengiste, Sofia Samatar, Nnedi Okorafor, and Laila Lalami for their inspiration and conversation.

I really valued the early feedback on my work from Emmanuel Akyeampong, Peter Galison, Hugh Gusterson, and Itty Abraham. My earliest inspiration for research on nationalism and science came from independent study with physicist and theorist Abha Sur beginning in 1996 and I thank her for my first invitation to present at the History of Science Society in 1999. I first thought through the ideas of scientific citizenship and the spread of science in a panel I organized on the impact of George Basalla at the History of Science Society meeting in November 2008 with Kenji Ito, Buhm Soon Park, and Gabriela Soto Laveaga. My thanks to Peter Bloom and Stephen Miescher for the opportunity to continue thinking about access to science in Ghana during the Revisiting Modernization conference they held at the University of Ghana, Legon in July 2009, with valuable comments from Yao Graham.

Hugh Gusterson and Allison Macfarlane invited me to present on a panel rethinking nuclear energy after the Fukushima meltdown at the 2011 meeting of the Society for the Social Study of Science, where I first drafted my chapter on Atomic Lands. Miwao Matsumoto offered a cogent and cynical perspective on Ghana's nuclear ambitions that greatly shaped my thinking on the parameters of risk. Peter Galison and Robb Moss inspired me to situate Ghana's experience within the context of nuclear wastelands and provided ongoing conversation and suggestions since I worked as a graduate research assistant helping to put together their course "Filming Science" at Harvard.

I have workshopped versions of the "Atomic Junction" documentary in a number of venues including meetings of the Society for the Social Study of Science and African Studies Association. I especially thank Barbara Cooper at Rutgers and Adam Branch at Cambridge University along with their students and colleagues for the opportunity to present my work on Atomic Junction.

My friends and colleagues in the Ghana Studies Association, including successive presidents Nana Akua Anyidoho, Ben Talton, and Dennis Laumann, provided wonderful camaraderie and support over the years. I especially thank them for the last-minute opportunity to present during the Ghana Studies Association Tri-Annual meeting at

Cape Coast University in 2016 where I first screened a version of the film "Atomic Junction" in Ghana and received great suggestions.

I benefited from early conversations with Gabriel Hecht when she presented her work on nuclearity at Stanford, Michael Gordin when he spoke about the Russian language and science at Berkeley, and Julie Livingstone when she described cancer therapy in Botswana at the University of California, San Francisco Medical School. My thanks also go to Robyn d'Avignon for the invitation to present my chapter on physics from the Soviets during the Africa-Soviet Union Workshop she organized at the Jordan Center for the Advanced Study of Russia in 2017 and to Alden Young, Nana Osei-Opare, Asif Siddiqi, Kristin Roth-Ey, Pedro Monaville, and others for their helpful comments.

I acknowledge that an earlier version of Chapter 6 appeared in 2016 as "'Atomic Lands': Understanding Land Disputes near Ghana's Nuclear Reactor," *African Affairs* 115, no. 460 (2016): 443–465, published by Oxford University Press and my concept of "Scientific Equity" and several paragraphs in the introduction first appeared in 2013 as "Scientific Equity: Experiments in Laboratory Education in Ghana," *Isis: A Journal of the History of Science Society* 104, no. 4 (2013): 713–741, published by the University of Chicago Press. I thank Justin Dowling for permission to reprint the lyrics from *Redemption Song* by Bob Marley for the epigraph on page v (courtesy of Fifty Six Hope Road Music Limited/Primary Wave/Blue Mountain).

My gratitude goes to my editor at Cambridge, Maria Marsh, and her team, including Abigail Walkington, Cassi Roberts, Lisa Carter, and Atifa Jiwa, for their support of *Atomic Junction*. Audra Wolfe of the Outside Reader provided useful insights on Cold War history as I drafted the manuscript. I wish to make special mention of Allan M. Brandt, Emmanuel Akyeampong, Anne Charity Hudley, Waldo Martin, Tyler Stovall, and Liz Watkins for their ongoing support of my research and career. For their crowdsourced feedback on this book, I thank my virtual support network of colleagues and friends including Asiedu Acquah, Jean Allman, Lloyd Amoah, Adams Bodomo, Tammy Brown, Jenna Burrell, Sara Byala, Jimena Canales, Stephen Casper, Chipo Dendre, Kim Yi Dionne, Barrington Edwards, Christine Folch, Lara Freidenfelds, Jeremy Greene, Nancy Jacobs, Kenji Ito, Jennifer Hart, Nick King, Wen-Hua Kuo, Mohacsi Gergely, Benjamin Lawrance, Deborah Levine, Jennifer Mack, Alondra Nelson, Augustus Osseo-Asare, Marina Peterson, Anne Pollock, Jon Roberts,

Naaborle and Naaborko Sackeyfio, Naunihal Singh, Christen Smith, Charis Thompson, and Meriel Tulante.

I thank the many caregivers for my children including leadership of the University of Texas Child Development Center, Tracy Dyess, Sylvia Martindale, Rhoda Taylor, as well as lead teachers Nasreen Bhatti, Vanesa Fulcher, Ana Lerma, Cindy Pinto, Jadwiga Proga, Sonia Robles. At the University of California, Berkeley Clark Kerr Center I thank Fanny Corne, Rosa Gomez, Ngoc Tram Dong, Elise Magno, and Janet Esposito. Without their daily concern for our family this book would have been impossible.

For their incredible love and support during my many trips to Accra and forays into Ghana's nuclear futures I thank my family, especially my parents Fran and Kwadwo Osseo-Asare, and my parents-in-law Elizabeth Ohene and George Ofosu-Amaah. My cousin Henrietta, who built her home not too far from Atomic Junction, always offered a grounded view of life in Accra. My husband's cousin Duanyo Doh provided unique perspectives as an employee of Areva, France's nuclear power company, one summer when we converged in Accra. My brother DK, who lived in Ghana during much of my research, provided countless ideas. My sister Masi always reminded me that Cold War politics and nuclear energy are kind of cool and pushed me onward. I treasure my husband Koranteng who even drove the winding mountain road to Los Alamos as an obvious research-related component of our honeymoon in New Mexico in 2005 and fed, clothed, and kept our two kids going as the project unfurled further and further afield. I dedicate this book to Kumiwah and Danso.

Abbreviations

DRC	Democratic Republic of the Congo
GAEC	Ghana Atomic Energy Commission
GHARR-1	Ghana Research Reactor Number One
IAEA	International Atomic Energy Agency
SNAS	School of Nuclear and Allied Sciences
UK	United Kingdom
UCGC	University College of the Gold Coast
US	United States of America
USSR	Union of Soviet Socialist Republics

1 | *Introduction: "No Country has Monopoly of Ability"*[1]

One Saturday in November 1964, Ghanaian physicists and political leaders assembled on a hill in the village of Kwabenya near the University of Ghana to lay the foundation stone of a building designed to house a nuclear research reactor. They invited the country's first president, Kwame Nkrumah, to dedicate the reactor site. With high hopes, the crowd listened to his speech for the day: "Let me say that in the age of science and technology, in this age of atomic revolution, neither Ghana nor Africa can afford to lag behind other nations, or to ignore the scientific developments of our time."[2] Ghanaians lived in a period when other countries such as the United States and Soviet Union were directing nuclear programs; why not Ghana? From their site in Kwabenya, Ghanaian elites were reassured to hear Nkrumah explain that, "We make our start from the great body of scientific and technological attainment which is the common heritage of mankind. Beginning so loftily as we do, there is no reason for us to be timid in joining the forward march of knowledge."[3] With Nkrumah, they visualized how the reactor would form the center of a "Science City for Ghana," from which they would guide research teams seeking innovative solutions to industrial questions in the new nation.

Leading the Kwame Nkrumah Nuclear Research Institute project, the engineer Robert Patrick Baffour worked tirelessly to bring the president's plans to fruition. Baffour was a stocky, energetic patriot who some say Nkrumah was grooming to be the next leader of the country. Baffour ran the Kwame Nkrumah University of Science and Technology, traveling at the behest of Nkrumah to the Soviet Union to negotiate a reactor for Ghana in 1961.[4] Baffour hoped that the Soviet research reactor would launch an era of unprecedented scientific achievement in the country, though he apparently advised Nkrumah against installing a power reactor and his Soviet contacts agreed. He planned out a series of experiments that the nuclear institute would be able to facilitate. He was devastated when the coup d'état in 1966

1

that ousted Nkrumah prompted Soviet consultants to abscond with the reactor blueprints and halt the shipment of fuel rods. On the eve of his removal as head of the Ghana Atomic Energy Commission (GAEC), Baffour confirmed that his team was on the cusp of realizing Nkrumah's vision, "the mechanism and construction of this reactor is peculiar to the Soviet Union and only an expert familiar with the construction and erection of this unit can undertake the task of erecting the one already acquired and waiting to be installed at Kwabenya."[5] In 1966, just as Ghanaian scientists were poised to start staging nuclear experiments, politics intervened and the Kwame Nkrumah Nuclear Institute stalled.

Baffour's disappointment was understandable given the heady atmosphere in Ghana in those days when Nkrumah's prestige projects could operate without any budgetary oversight, and dreams had no costs (Figure 1.1). After Ghana became the first African country to push aside colonial occupiers, Baffour witnessed a brief period when the nation could fantasize that it was a fully independent republic eligible for any new innovation, able to assert its authority on the world stage and negotiate as an equal with other countries. Baffour, known for his commitment to consensus-building in politics, served as president of the International Atomic Energy Commission's (IAEA) sixth conference in 1962. Believing that all nations were eligible for a seat at the table, and that Ghana's planned reactor was her inalienable right, he led the series of internal elections that brought Iran, Italy, Mexico, Brazil, and Indonesia onto the board of the IAEA.[6] As the Cold War buffeted countries on a sea of mistrust and unease, that September in Vienna, Baffour reminded delegates that, "Underneath, all were brothers of a single nation, a single people and a single creation. He earnestly hoped that the cordial spirit in which the General Conference had met would be an omen for the future, and that politics would be laid aside for the good of mankind."[7] Baffour represented a positive outlook for international cooperation in atomic energy where Africans could take leadership positions.

This book considers the afterlives of Baffour and Nkrumah's vision through a historical analysis of one of the first national nuclear reactor programs in postcolonial Africa.[8] While Nkrumah provided some early momentum and encouraged Baffour, he played a somewhat muted role in the overall story of Ghana's nuclear program after 1966. Rather, this book centers on how Ghanaian researchers took

Figure 1.1 "Atomic Power Programme Moves Ahead: Nuclear Reactor for Ghana." Adjacent photo: Kwame Nkrumah congratulates soldiers of the Airborne Training School at the Military Academy, Teshie, Accra. Editorial begins, "The nation looks ahead: Two years ago on July 1, the last relics of our colonial past were removed from Ghana's free land. Our Republic was born"
(*Source*: *The Ghanaian Times*, June 30, 1962)

leadership positions in nuclear affairs both at home and abroad over the next five decades. The initial push to install a nuclear reactor in Ghana occurred at a pivotal moment when members of the independence generation demanded to be stakeholders in scientific work and championed full rights to technological innovations. Their calls for scientific equity provide a new framework for understanding how Ghanaian scientists and political leaders sought full membership in science for all citizens not just in the 1960s, but into the twenty-first century. The Nkrumah generation of scientists benefited from this push toward scientific enfranchisement over the course of their careers. They continued to seek equal access to nuclear technology throughout the Cold War in their efforts to establish an independent scientific regime. While the details are specific to Ghana, the challenges these scientists faced, and their strategies for circumventing them, are common to many emerging nations. Over half-a-century, these scientists made nuclear physics their own, becoming key players at the International Atomic Energy Agency, the Ghana Atomic Energy Commission, and other nuclear bodies in African countries. From their outpost in Kwabenya, they trained subsequent generations of African nuclear scientists.

Their quest for equal access to nuclear power in Ghana and beyond frame the chapters in the book. Ghanaians participated in a contest for atomic power in Africa during the Cold War, from their response to the atom bomb tests that France conducted in the Algerian desert that sent radioactive fallout to Ghana; to trips students made to learn physics in the Soviet Union; to the appropriation of land from Ghanaian farmers for independent Africa's first reactor; to the eventual transfer of a low-power reactor from China to Ghana. Over time, Ghanaians shifted their relationship with nuclear power from the signal of national autonomy and modernity to a sign of interdependency within an international community of outside agencies and governments. Thus, nuclear independence was hard-fought and incomplete for the scientists. Further, the experiences of select employees of the Ghana Atomic Energy Commission contrast sharply with those of community members in the Kwabenya environs who have not fully reaped the benefits of nuclear technology. It is along the Haatso-Atomic road that we gather traces of their stories, and map out the promise and perils of nuclear technology in an African suburb.

On this bustling road to nuclear power, the Ghana Atomic Energy Commission campus has nonetheless emerged as a major gathering place for African scientists interested in furthering their nuclear programs, including researchers from as far away as Tanzania and Zimbabwe. While Ghana's current 30kW Miniature Neutron Source Reactor is relatively small, scientists there use it to train hundreds of students in nuclear physics. The hope is that this next generation of nuclear physicists will help maintain much larger reactors, perhaps with enough capacity to generate power, that Ghana and other countries hope to install within the next decade. This study examines the historical context of these grand ambitions and considers possible nuclear futures not only in Ghana but throughout Africa.

Scientific Equity: African Independence and the Atom

After World War II, emerging from a century of colonial rule, new countries in Africa and Asia sought equal access to scientific goods for all their citizens, or what I conceptualize as "scientific equity."[9] They were no longer content to serve as vassals of colonial powers, restricted by inferior training in medicine, science, and engineering. They built modern hospitals, laboratories, hydroelectric dams, and even nuclear reactors. In this sense, independent scientists, like Baffour in Ghana, wanted to be able to fully participate in scientific life. They sought shares in what was increasingly a highly regarded, valuable system of testing and creating new knowledge on plants, fluids, metals, and the universe through scientific research. For them, full access and participation in world science meant the well-being of their citizens and the success of their nations. Particularly, access to nuclear physics became a test case for a nation's level of full participation in scientific endeavors.

The concept of "scientific equity" captures this desire of scientific and medical workers, and their advocates, to gain equivalent training, and to participate fully in international discussions of scientific research. It is a term that only recently has been gaining currency in discussions of the preparedness of African countries for the impact of changes in the global climate.[10] Here, I use scientific equity retrospectively to capture a mood of fair and just participation of Africans in scientific endeavors since the 1960s. It is a concept that would work broadly throughout the Global South, where scientists, engineers, doctors, and nurses continue the fight for access to global science, as knowledge "producers" rather than dependent "consumers."[11] In a call to action for the improvement of medical publishing in Brazil, journal editors stated, "In trying to avoid reproducing the asymmetrical power relations we experience internationally … we have taken some initiatives that we believe move us towards greater scientific equity."[12] These initiatives included publishing in Portuguese, Spanish, as well as English, plus "capacity building to achieve common and quality-based standards for nursing journals in Brazil, Latin America, and Ibero-America."[13]

Scientific equity began in the primary and secondary schools in newly independent nations. Through ambitious national programs, young students learned basic scientific and mathematical concepts grafted onto lingering colonial curriculums that emphasized vocational skills like carpentry and welding. For instance, in Ghana, Nkrumah implemented no-fee compulsory education to encourage families to send their children to school beginning in 1961. Nkrumah had attended the innovative government school Achimota in the Gold Coast Colony and then continued his undergraduate and graduate studies at Lincoln College and the University of Pennsylvania in the United States. When Nkrumah returned to the Gold Coast and worked to usher in independence, improving education and adult literacy became a primary goal to redress colonial wrongs. In particular, Nkrumah's socialist CPP government was committed to the full popularization of science among everyday people. Nkrumah demanded that officials, "reach out to the mass of the people who have not had the opportunities of formal education. We must use every means mass communication – the press, the radio, television and films – to carry science to the whole population – the people."[14] Some of these students went on to be farmers, or factory workers, while new universities like the Kwame Nkrumah University of Science and Technology and Cape Coast University allowed more to pursue tertiary training in science.

The desire for broad science learning in Ghana stemmed from the prevailing principles of social justice and equity that Nkrumah embraced in his agenda for African socialism as the leader of the first independent country on the continent south of the Sahara. The cult of science ushered in during the Nkrumah era can be read as part of this radical call for equality and equity, which culminated in the request for a nuclear reactor. Nkrumah traded on a new moral equivalence between Africans, Europeans, Americans, or Asians where there was "no monopoly of ability," and any country could be expected to have mechanized agriculture, robust factories, and the capacity to sponsor nuclear research. Scientific equity implies a level playing field in terms of actual intellectual capabilities and intelligence between people living in different countries. Nkrumah emerged as a charismatic independence leader not just for Ghana, but for all of Africa as he supported anticolonial movements from Algeria, to Guinea, to the Congo and worked to establish a United States of Africa with himself as president. Thus, the initial push to install a nuclear reactor in Ghana occurred at a critical moment when members of the independence generation demanded to be stakeholders in scientific work and championed full rights to technological innovations for all citizens. While Nkrumah did not live to see it realized himself, his ambitious goals provided the energy and vision to fuel them for many years to come.

Ghanaians embraced this vision for African nationalism linked to access to science and ultimately atoms. Recognizant of the colonial structures that emphasized rudimentary and vocational skills, truncating opportunities for those with black skin, they welcomed Nkrumah's scholarships and furthered their studies far beyond what had been possible just a few years before.[15] They strongly believed that people of African descent have a right to scientific training at the highest levels and can be expected to succeed as well as anyone else. These nationalist scientists were eager to gain access to atomic theory and nuclear physics, to mine the vast gold deposits in the country themselves. In the process, the emerging Ghanaian scientists were happy to have strange bed fellows, including the controversial British physicist Allan May, who joined the University of Ghana in the early 1960s as a lecturer after spending over half-a-decade in jail for sharing nuclear secrets with the Soviet Union. Ghanaian academics listened when, in his inaugural lecture at Legon, May emphasized that "a lively and wholehearted grasp of the atomic nature of matter" would allow students to exploit Ghana's vast mineral wealth.[16] According to May, a staunch communist, atoms were merely the building blocks of the world, which anyone should be able to manipulate and control, including people living in Africa.

The passion for science and atomic theory spread across the globe by the 1960s. Ghanaians were not alone in their sense that access to atoms would strengthen independent African countries. The Senegalese scholar and political activist Chiek Anta Diop pursued a course in nuclear physics while at the University of Paris in the late 1950s and translated Einstein's theory of relativity into Wolof. In 1960, he founded a radiocarbon laboratory at the Institut Fondamental d'Afrique Noire/ Fundamental Institute of Black Africa at the University of Dakar.[17] Tanzania's first president Julius Nyerere stressed that African scientists might be better situated to handle the military and energy potential of nuclear fission than their white counterparts. In a speech on nuclear imperialism, which he called "The Second Scramble," Nyerere noted that Western nuclear scientists were actually the ones who were backward and out of step with the times (as opposed to Africans attempting to industrialize): "one of the troubles in the modern world is that nuclear power is being handled by people who were born in the Nineteenth Century and educated in the Nineteenth Century; people with a Victorian turn of mind, who have been overtaken by the achievements of science and by modern ideas about human society."[18] More egregiously, white South Africans sought to create a nuclear bomb with US and Israeli assistance. In the context of white-minority rule under apartheid (1948–1992), how could they be trusted not to expose all of Africa to radioactive particles?[19]

For black African nations, being shut out of nuclear science meant infantalization within an imperialist world order that misjudged their potential and saw their emerging nuclear capabilities as a threat. As Indian historian Itty Abraham has argued for the case of Indian nationalists, atomic expertise represented not only "a means of over-coming neo-colonial domination," but also "a sign of masculinity and intellectual prowess to scientists."[20] In advocating that African countries in the early 1980s forgo signing nuclear non-proliferation treaties, the Kenyan political scientist Ali Mazuri stressed that Nigeria in particular should take the lead in an African nuclear renaissance. "Going nuclear," he wrote, "would be a new initiation, an important rite de passage, a recovery of adulthood. No longer will the great powers be permitted to say that such and such a weapon is not for Africans and children under 16."[21] New nations, extricating them-selves from colonial occupations, used nuclear technology to bolster their sense of independence, both scientifically and politically. In the span of several decades, African countries transitioned from a more pacifist stance, decrying nuclear weapons, to one in which they might be a necessary evil. African nuclear desires are a further example of what US sociologist Alondra Nelson terms "African diasporic technophilia."[22]

Thus, this book examines how Africans sought a stake in modern science and all that it might offer. It considers how scientists in Ghana pursued recognition and equality on the world stage through nuclear power. Fundamentally, this book suggests ways that nuclear science became "more real" outside of Europe. Much as you might find Catholicism to be more cherished in Rio de Janeiro or Lagos than in Rome, adherents to the faith of nuclear technology proliferated out-side traditional centers of nuclear expertise (creating new anxieties in Washington, Paris, London, and Moscow).[23] On the supply side, some Africans of course were laborers mining uranium for growing global demand, as historian Gabriel Hecht unearths in her compelling study of the extraction of uranium, for the benefit of the West.[24] On the demand side, however, black African scientists pursued nuclear reactions themselves.

In subsequent years, the expense and complexity of the nuclear enterprise defied national scientific autonomy. Securing a nuclear age for Africa demanded dependence on external support for training and equipment, and supervision within international regulatory authorities, like the International Atomic Energy Agency (IAEA). Given the high costs, representatives of different countries, for instance, Soviet experts or British consultants had the power to bar or clear Ghana's access to nuclear physics and associated equipment. These moments of gatekeeping shaped Ghana's access to nuclear goods. At these critical points, Ghanaian scientists were keenly aware of how their course compared with that of scientists in other African countries including Egypt, Libya, South Africa, Senegal, and the Democratic Republic of the Congo. Ghanaian experiences intertwine in this book with stories from other African states seeking nuclear power. Further, not all in Ghana's nuclear neighborhood benefited from the proximity of a reactor. The goal of science for all was only a partial reality in the years after independence.

Manpower: Energy and its Producers

Kwame Nkrumah's quest for global recognition and wealth centered on access to energy. Development and rapid industrialization required access to electrical power. Ghana joined the World Power Conference in 1959, an organization dedicated to finding ways to balance access to "sources of heat and power … nationally and internationally." The following year, Ghana became a member state to the International Atomic Energy Agency. Ghana expected to open a nuclear power plant with Soviet support, although Baffour and others tempered Nkrumah's plans. As this book details, even the smaller swimming pool research reactor to be constructed at Kwabenya was not fully realized during Nkrumah's tenure as leader of independent Ghana (1957–1966) and the citizens of Ghana were hardly part of a world power in the sense of having access to nuclear weapons. But during the early years after independence, Ghana's leadership stressed the need to increase several forms of power in the coming years, including hydropower, atomic power, and the crux of it all, "manpower."

In addition to the nuclear reactor project, Nkrumah authorized the damming of the Volta River in 1964 to create the largest human-made lake in West Africa and establish the necessary conditions for Ghana's hydroelectric power plant. He built on British colonial plans to use hydroelectricity to produce aluminum after the discovery of bauxite deposits in the Gold Coast. In the end, Nkrumah awarded the contract to US and Canadian companies.[25] The dam displaced communities, flooded ancient forests, and introduced new diseases and ecologies, along with providing significant gains in electricity for Ghana and neighboring countries. While this book considers the legacy of Nkrumah's nuclear visions, it takes cues from related investigations on the Volta dam that place Ghana's infrastructure schemes in ecological, historical, and ethnographic context.[26]

Large projects like the nuclear reactor and hydroelectric dam were part of ambitious development plans in the 1950s and 1960s as new nations set their sights high after World War II. Nkrumah's government formulated elaborate and frequent "Development Plans," which the more progressive Colonial Governor Gordon Guggisberg had initiated from the 1920s. In 1957, Ghana introduced its "Consolidation Development Plan," followed by the "Second Development Plan" in 1958.[27] Government officials took inspiration from rapid industrialization efforts, particularly in the Soviet Union after Nkrumah's visit there in 1961. With the "Seven Year Plan for National Reconstruction" in 1964, government presented the most ambitious plan for industrialization of the country to date.[28] The plan called for the implementation of mechanized agriculture and a twofold increase in production. The government moved further toward centralized planning with state control of construction projects, cocoa marketing, universities, and all major industries.

The development plans put manpower front and center. Government was certain that, "Science personnel will be required in ever-increasing numbers in industry and agriculture as well as for teaching in the secondary schools."[29] Manpower – an educated citizenry – was necessary to produce the electricity and distribute it and run the new industries and mechanized agriculture. Manpower would allow for a cadre of elite scientists to run the planned hydroelectric and nuclear power reactors Nkrumah felt would amplify the industrial ambitions of the new nation, perhaps even propelling them to space someday.

Nkrumah sought to balance access to scientific information, including training in physics to allow for better access to electrical power, which directly meant financial and political gains for the new nation. In the lead-up to independence, Nkrumah sent scouts to the United Kingdom to meet with Ghanaian students and identify their courses of study. The degree programs of students were discussed at the highest levels with individuals slated for jobs in the electricity department and beyond.[30] For instance, it was learnt that only one student was in the UK on private scholarship studying electrical engineering.[31] After independence, officials created projections for new infrastructure to improve not only electrical power, but also "manpower" in a series of development plans.[32] Development plans provided projections on actual numbers of students required in areas of engineering and science subjects. University faculty in Ghana provided updates on whether or not targets might be met, including how many graduates might be expected to go into primary and secondary education to spawn more young scientists.

Despite the shortcomings of Nkrumah's regime as it became more totalitarian and the economy floundered, improvements in access to science education have remained one of the key positive outcomes of his policies. The Ministry of Education in Ghana created elaborate schemes to improve manpower in keeping with the official development plans. Scientists frequently recall how they gained training in biology or physics during this period, which set them on a path to a research career at one of the universities or scientific institutions founded after independence. As Daniel Kwesi Asare, a senior research scientist at the Department of Plant and Soil Science in the Biotechnology and Nuclear Agriculture Research Institute at the Ghana Atomic Energy Commission, expressed to me: "Nkrumah was not a scientist, but he was so fascinated with science that he wanted to modernize the whole country through science and technology."[33] Similarly, the biologist Letitia Obeng recalled, "Early in his struggle for the independence of the Gold Coast, [Nkrumah's] strong belief in the potential of the sciences for the development of his country had been a central factor in his vision … Students were given special incentives to study science."[34] After the reactor import scheme stalled when Nkrumah lost political power, Soviet-trained Ghanaian scientists continued their studies to the PhD level in hopes of learning to manufacture nuclear reactors themselves.

Looking at development schemes through the lens of manpower and human capacity-building among Ghanaian scientists re-centers the story of post-independence in the lived experiences of real people in the decades since independence. Newspapers from the 1950s and 1960s are full of hopeful images of the new Ghana Airways planes, gold refinery at Tarkwa, cars, tractors, and other pieces of equipment. Histories of the aftermath of Nkrumah's regime often highlight a landscape of decay and failure. A technology-centered story foregrounds the challenges of importing equipment, a struggle to "catch up," with African scientists destined to be "global shadows."[35] Such an approach engages in endless handwringing about the technological underachievements of African scientists that falls just short of questioning their *intellectual* capacity.[36]

But hidden below the empty reactor building is a resilient and vibrant community of researchers. This dynamic world only comes out through careful scrutiny of their vast publications, and conversations and interactions with the proud individuals who survived iterations of military coups and relocations for training and work. Many of the physicists I spoke with for this project were highly religious, emerging as church reverends while working to continue Ghana's nuclear prospects. As Reverend Professor Samuel Akoto-Bamford explained, "the world is made up of the physical and the non-physical."[37] This study pays close attention to the intangible aspects of scientific survival, which in some cases brought scientists deep into the spiritual realm. The chapters that follow examine the history and legacy of Nkrumah's manpower plans, particularly around efforts to train mainly men in nuclear physics, through the lives of those who took on his call to scientific equity and access to energy. Through their stories we learn that, in fact, the decaying reactor buildings were an artful strategy to sustain occupation on a nuclear frontier.

This book joins a growing body of literature on the careers of African scientists that takes a social and cultural approach to understand the construction of scientific enterprise.[38] The book builds on the growing canon of self-published memoirs and histories written by African scientists, including those of the radiography lecturer Lawrence Arthur, and the medical physicist John Humphrey Amuasi, who published a comprehensive history of the Ghana Atomic Energy Commission to commemorate the fortieth anniversary.[39] My study centers on the reminiscences of individuals involved in the manpower and nuclear power schemes, including educationist Sam Bortei-Doku, Ghana's first female radiologist Salome Francois, and the Soviet-trained physicists

Benjamin Woarabe Garbrah and John Justice Fletcher. Additionally, this book shows linkages between the experiences of Ghanaian scientists with physicists in other African countries building upon work on the history of nuclear power in Libya, Egypt, and South Africa, the only place on the continent to successfully install reactors large enough to generate electrical power. While it is the first social historical examination of nuclear physicists in West Africa, it bears resemblance to earlier analyses of the quest for atomic reactors and even weapons in such post-independence settings as India and Pakistan.[40]

As Nkrumah stressed, "No Country has Monopoly of Ability" in the realm of nuclear physics. He explained that Ghanaians "witnessed the valuable contributions which science and scientific research have made in the rapid development of the modern world" and had "no intention of lagging behind." Nkrumah promoted scientific investigations and was confident "that the genius of our people shall contribute to man's mastery of the universe."[41] Through a lot of hard work and determination, Ghanaians were able to establish themselves as a leading force in Africa for nuclear physics using their minds, despite challenges building and importing equipment and concerted efforts of other countries including the United Kingdom to stymie their efforts to create an independent African nuclear program.[42]

Manpower and scientific equity stand as an alternative viewpoint to narratives of failure or incomplete mimicry.[43] Postcolonial actors did look to Europe, Asia, and North America to fashion science for their countries to claim their equivalent humanity. But this interest in scientific norms was not mere imitation, inferior duplication, or even hybridity.[44] Rather, African scientists fought tooth and nail for access in the face of dismissive attitudes of their teachers and policy-makers abroad. They met global standards and helped to shape policies on nuclear science going forward.[45]

The Empowered and the Disempowered: Mobility in the Nuclear Neighborhood

Atomic Junction is a place and a state of mind – a crossroads where different ethnic groups have mixed for centuries and a geographic site where nuclear energy remains a possibility for Ghana's future. This book also interrogates the experiences of people living and working near the chaotic interchange outside Ghana's capital city Accra to show uneven access to science. The stories of entrepreneurs, local chiefs, and community members who live and travel along the Atomic-Haatso road provide a counter balance to the experiences of the physicists who settled among them. *Atomic Junction* incorporates historical, ethnographic, and geographic information to consider the mundane aspects of nuclear and radioactive residues in a Ghanaian suburb.

Atomic Junction is a space where nationalist scientists designed Africa's high-technology future, or afrofuture, earlier than many might assume, and continue to aspire to technological heights, including at the new Ghana Space and Technology Institute situated opposite the reactor complex.[46] Ghana's atomic crossroads have long led to actual high-technology, not merely an Afro fantasy. Yet while some elite scientists managed to chart a path to scientific equity and nuclear access over time, their neighbors nearby did have trouble accessing pipe-borne water and other basic necessities and their stories are part of the social stratification behind Ghana's nuclear power. Thus, Ghana's technological hub coexists with scientific, political, and economic disenfranchisement. Here, we witness again a long-standing rift between those with lab coats and those without in an African setting.[47]

For nearby residents, the scientists were complicit in the theft of their territory along the Haatso-Atomic Road. The expropriation of land in the Kwabenya area in the 1960s introduced a new way for land to be valued, as an empty buffer zone near a reactor at the exclusion of those who had lived there before. This government property, known popularly in Ghana as "Atomic Lands," as in land belonging to the Commission, extended areas around the world that hold or may someday hold radioactive matter.[48] The scientists who moved to this "Science City" created an example of what US historian Kate Brown termed a "Plutopia" in her examination of the American and Soviet *Akademgorodok* (Academic City).[49] Originally an isolated enclave in the midst of a few farming communities an hour from the capital Accra, the Kwabenya research campus set aside staff housing on neat streets like "Proton Avenue" and "Gamma Lane" (see Figure 1.2).

Increasingly, roads are the sites of extensive research in African studies, given increased attention to infrastructure and the breathtaking growth of urban areas. Sidewalk and roadway activity provide an important view into what Ghanaian theorist Ato Quayson coins the "African cosmopolis" in his cultural excavation of the Oxford

Figure 1.2 Gamma Avenue, Kwabenya
(*Source*: author photo)

Street district in Accra. Further, as Zimbabwean science scholar Clapperton Mavhunga emphasizes, roads, transportation, and energy come together in Africa as social spaces for "human engineered-mobilities."[50] The creation of an atomic road in Ghana allows for an important twist on African street studies, given the potential for radioactive exposure in the open fields alongside it.[51]

This atomic dream space has a longer history of contested claims. The book examines ongoing land conflicts in the Kwabenya area, emphasizing the porous nature of what US sociologist Joe Masco first termed a "nuclear borderland" in his study of the Los Alamos laboratories where the United States developed the bomb. From the Haatso-Atomic Road, the book traces lines of local networks (including the Kwabenya and Haatso kingdoms and Commission settlement), national connectivity (through radiation monitoring and radioactive waste disposal), and global linkages (through the migration of scientists and visits of International Atomic Energy Agency officials). While Ghana does not have uranium deposits, the creation of Atomic Lands does allow us to consider the extent to which ordinary people on the continent came to experience what Hecht terms "nuclearity."[52] Stories gleaned from conversations, archival reports, and site visits over more than a decade emphasize the lived connections between local, regional, and global affairs and the relative degrees of mobility different members of the community experienced. The communities along the Haatso-Atomic

Road sacrificed land for the government project and brought gravel to fill in the road itself, believing that the reactor – while a dangerous newcomer – would provide some benefit to the nation as a whole. Their reminiscences allow us to assess Nkrumah's "Science City" over time from the perspective of those involved in remaking the neighborhoods along the Haatso-Atomic Road.

In visiting the Atomic Junction area, I was struck by how an African nuclear future has been simmering for decades, with limited international attention. I wanted to start a more robust conversation about the benefits and disadvantages of siting nuclear technology in African settings. The atomic revolution is often seen as Janus-faced – atomic energy for good (electricity, medicine, research) and atomic energy for bad (weapons of mass destruction). But both sides produce radioactive matter of varying half-lives that can impact generations as it sits under the earth, or immediately as it touches the skin, the water. From the time the French introduced nuclear bombs outside, in the Sahara Desert, to the more recent period when Ghanaians have brought nuclear reactors inside the country, Ghanaians have monitored radiation exposure. Part of the process of the creation of an Atomic African landscape involves the half-lives of radioactivity.

Outline of the Book

This quest for equal access to nuclear power in Ghana after independence frames the chapters in the book. I use "nuclear power" to represent both a systematic plan to generate atomic energy as well as an avenue to political power in the Kwabenya environs, national arena, and global affairs. Ghanaians experienced nuclear power differently over time and across different classes and communities. Under the glare of nuclear imperialism, fallout from the French bomb tests led Ghanaians to better understand atomic matter and participate in nuclear research even as they were largely seen as outsiders to nuclear power in terms of international prowess. Once Nkrumah's government opted to set up a national nuclear program, not everyone benefited in the same way, complicating the initial push for scientific equity for all citizens in the socialist postcolony. Top physicists garnered travel opportunities, staff housing, and laboratories, leading to their positive relationship to nuclear power. In contrast, outside the gates, disenfranchised farmers who lost land for the Ghana Atomic Energy Commission resented Ghanaians wielding nuclear power. In the long battle for a low-power research reactor and now a nuclear power plant capable of producing electricity, the highly respected Ghanaian scientists nonetheless became dependent on the International Atomic Energy Agency for equipment, training, and even jobs.

The next chapter locates Ghana's quest for nuclear power within the context of the French bomb tests in the Sahara that sent radioactive materials across West Africa. The prospect of French nuclear weapons extended the terror of Western atomic bomb activity from Nagasaki and Hiroshima, and the South Pacific test fields to the African continent at Reggane in the Algerian Desert. Once fallout from the French detonations reached Ghanaian towns, the outrage from Nkrumah's government and his international supporters was tremendous. The French bombs helped to mobilize interest in fallout monitoring on the future grounds of the Ghana Atomic Energy Commission. As a direct result, Ghana joined the International Atomic Energy Agency (IAEA) and worked to eliminate bomb testing across Africa through the United Nations.

Chapter 3 considers the afterlife of Nkrumah's vision of scientific equity through the careers of Ghanaian scientists who trained in the Soviet Union to gain access to nuclear power. This chapter relies heavily on reminiscences of Ghana's first generation of nuclear physicists, detailing their trials learning physics in Russia, the rejection of their Soviet training in Ghana after the overthrow of Nkrumah, and their ongoing efforts to secure further training and employment abroad, whether in Gaddafi's Libya, or at the IAEA in Vienna. It highlights important research they conducted into nuclear physics over the years and the training they provided to subsequent waves of physicists.

Chapter 4 goes behind the gates to show how Ghanaian scientists tapped resources from different countries in their quest for a nuclear reactor, from the United Kingdom and the Soviet Union, to Canada, the United Arab Republic, India, and China. It begins with Nkrumah's urge for scientific equity, showing how scientists did not give up their dream of nuclear after the heady days of independence once international concerns for more "appropriate" technology for Africans stymied their efforts.

Chapter 5 details how during the long battle to secure a nuclear reactor, Ghanaian physicists applied their skills in arenas outside of atomic energy per se, under the watchful eye of the IAEA. They created research programs pertinent to Ghana, including the study of minerals and plants. Further, the Commission sustained one of its additional roles as outlined in the initial 1963 Act 204 that had established it: monitoring radiation at the nation's X-ray facilities. This role arguably became the Commission's main purpose over the years. Monitoring risks of ionizing radiation allowed staff at the Commission to use their skills in the interest of the Ghanaian public. At the same time, dependence on the IAEA tempered the goal of national autonomy through nuclear power.

Chapter 6 moves outside the gates of the Ghana Atomic Energy Commission to consider how people living in the Kwabenya environs experienced nuclear power. While many nearby residents believe the Ghana Atomic Energy Commission campus has hosted a reactor since around 1966, this was a misconception that scientists tacitly allowed to commandeer more land in a popular part of a growing city. I consider how everyday Ghanaians relate their experience with Atomic Lands (i.e., Commission property) to the advent of nuclear spaces around the world where the potential for radioactivity excludes populations.

An epilogue considers Ghana's nuclear futures within the landscape of African nuclear ambitions. Ghanaian scientists used the promise of nuclear power to take land and resources from other citizens for the national scientific good. Within Ghana, they held themselves up as the purveyors of nuclear authority, despite ongoing reliance on the support of greater nuclear powers to continue their research programs. The story of Ghana's ongoing battle for access to atomic goods opens up questions about the safety of nuclear reactors, sustainable energy, and the management of atomic landscapes across Africa – questions that continue to engage us all.

2 | *Nuclear Winds: Particles without Boundaries*

"Radio-active winds know no international frontiers."

–Kwame Nkrumah[1]

On February 13, 1960, unusually strong winds swept across the Sahara Desert. The currents touched down on an ancient oasis at Reggane where traders on camels had long traveled along a road that ran between the Malian city of Gao on the Niger River and the Algerian town of Béchar just south of the border with Morocco.[2] These gusts of air picked up invisible particles emanating from an atomic bomb the French Government had detonated in Reggane that day. The winds carried the smoky wisps of nuclear spectacle to towns and farms as far away as Ghana and Nigeria. "Death Dust," Ghana's propaganda paper declared it.[3] It would lead to disease and fatalities. Nuclear winds were blowing into Africa, unsettling newly independent governments and colonial occupations.

When nuclear devices explode above the ground, they release substantial amounts of radioactive dust. Since the French bomb was a secret prototype, the kind and quantity of dangerous particles it could produce was not public knowledge. Nor could the direction of winds in early February be fully predicted. Despite assurances from scientists working for Charles de Gaulle's government about the relative safety of their device, the confluence of unexpectedly strong winds and a substantial debris field meant that radioactive materials floated much farther than the French had anticipated. For their part, scientists working in other African colonies and emerging nations, especially those within the British field of influence, worked diligently to document the extent of damage. With the support of politicians, activists, and diplomats, they turned international opinion against the French.

In Ghana, premier Kwame Nkrumah's government was initially reluctant to announce publicly that measurable amounts of nuclear fallout had reached the country. At a cabinet meeting two days after the bomb test, on February 15, Nkrumah and his closest advisors met with

19

scientists from the University of Ghana to review preliminary reports of mixed fission products at twenty-two monitoring stations in Ghana. He thanked the physicists for the investigations they conducted out of a makeshift monitoring station at Kwabenya near the University of Ghana, now the guesthouse for Ghana Atomic Energy Agency. The premier was alarmed to learn from them that the levels of radioactive particles, especially strontium-90, were much higher than what the French models had predicted. He asked the army, meteorological department, and agricultural officers to continue to cooperate to measure fallout across the country in the coming days. Nkrumah also asked two senior physicists at the University of Ghana and the chief meteorological officer to call a meeting with the French Ambassador to Ghana to register their concerns. Those briefed on the radiation levels worried that continued French nuclear testing could produce enough cumulative fallout to create health problems in affected areas. Without alarming the public, Nkrumah's office hoped to quietly set the groundwork to pressure France to abandon any further detonations.

Nkrumah's hesitation to approve a public press release on radioactive fallout was a product of his own successful campaign to raise awareness of France's nuclear program in Algeria in the months prior. He whipped Ghana's citizens into a frenzy about the proposed "atomic bombing" of Algeria, staged mass protests, and invited peace activists from the Sahara Protest Team into the country. Perhaps he had been overly confident that these actions could convince France to stop the bombing, with the activists ready to travel overland from Ghana to Reggane, the bomb site, to sit with the Algerians. In the end, once Ghanaian newspapers leaked the story on February 25, Nkrumah's media office decided it would be politically expedient to widely publicize the extent of the fallout to help delegitimize French colonialism.

The three bombs that France detonated in 1960 had a more extreme impact, of course, on the Algerians living and working near the "test" sites. They nonetheless produced a definite ripple effect in places like Ghana where the "Death Dust" raised the specter of an African nuclear apocalypse. It is unclear up to today how many Algerians fell sick from radioactive materials or were even killed during the tests; Ghanaian newspapers published photographs of the purported victims. For Nkrumah and others in independence movements, France's relentless aggression in Algeria even to the point of dropping an atomic bomb showed how a new form of colonization, or what they called "nuclear imperialism," was a credible threat to African autonomy and required a fierce resistance.[4] And indeed, by the end of the year, France was to lose all of its West African colonies.[5] Thoroughly disgusted with the detonations, Ghanaian diplomats further lobbied the United Nations for an "atom-free" Africa where both nuclear tests and foreign military bases would not be welcome. This was not to say that Asian and African countries did not seek access to the atom themselves and a stake in nuclear science, as we shall see in the next chapters.

"Another Hiroshima in Africa"[6]: Nuclear Imperialism and Ghana's Outrage Before the Tests

Ghanaian anxieties about nuclear dust circulating from the Sahara reflected very negative associations with atomic weapons. Ghanaians well remembered the ashy bodies fallen at Hiroshima and Nagasaki. Colonial subjects across Africa listened to radio broadcasts and pored over newspaper articles describing the burning of "practically all living things, human and animal" when the United States dropped the first atomic bombs during World War II. Nationalist newspapers in the Gold Coast colony carried dramatic stories about the atomic bombings in Japan in August 1945. "One Atom Bomb Smashes Four Square Miles of Hiroshima" was the lead headline for the *Gold Coast Independent* on August 11, three days after the event.[7] The editors of the newspaper were stunned when a second bomb was released by the United States onto Japan later that month: "The Atomic Bomb Entirely Sweeps Another City into River."[8] They reprinted statements from Tokyo Radio describing how after the Hiroshima bombing, "those outdoors burned to death while those indoors were killed by indescribable pressure and heat."[9] With these dusty bodies on their mind, Ghanaians were unwilling to applaud any news of atomic bombs on the African continent.

In the intervening fifteen years since the United States released atomic weapons in Japan, people in West Africa continued to monitor the rise of atomic bomb making and the dawn of the "Cold War," which superpowers stockpiled weapons to gain political clout. In Anglophone areas, families closely followed British Broadcasting Corporation news reports on the state of the nuclear race.[10] When the United Kingdom entered the nuclear club in October 1952, the *Daily Graphic* noted that Britain had joined the United States and the Soviet Union as a country with "atom-bomb know-how" and would most likely see an increase in "her international bargaining power."[11] West Africans, like South Asians, North Africans, and others with less global influence in the mid-twentieth century, watched closely as wealthy countries channeled resources into the quest for the atom bomb. They saw how access to nuclear weapons impacted a small island country like the United Kingdom, furthering its military power and increasing its standing in the hierarchy of nations.

But for those without bombs, nuclear imperialism represented a new iteration of colonial occupations with lasting environmental and health consequences. French nuclear testing in Algeria meant that a small European nation had both the audacity and capacity to spew radioactive fallout across West Africa. The French were not the first nation to conduct atmospheric tests, where military researchers exploded bombs above ground despite the potential for air currents to pick up radioactive debris. France was to join three other countries involved in atomic bomb detonations for research purposes: the United States, Soviet Union, and the United Kingdom. After the initial tests leading up to the first atomic bombs dropped on Japan, the United States began atmospheric tests in 1946 in the Marshall Islands, followed by the Soviet Union in 1949 with detonations in Kazakhstan. In the intervening years, nuclear nations opted to site bomb tests in islands off of Australia, the USSR, the United States, and Kiribati. The United States conducted controversial tests in the South Pacific in the Bikini Islands during 1954.

At a meeting of twenty-nine Asian and African countries in Bandung, Indonesia in 1955, the threat of nuclear war and dangers of atomic testing captivated delegates. In particular, the Indian Prime Minister Jawaharlal Nehru brokered conversations on regional security including the end of nuclear bomb testing. In the next few years, Nehru led the way for proposals for a "total ban on atomic weapons."[12] It was a time when Asian and African nations were constructing new alliances, including military agreements, as British and French colonial influence was in question.

But in West Africa, French power was still intact by late 1959 and early 1960. France was the first country to propose releasing atomic bombs on the African continent.[13] French officials also chose to do so at a time when other nuclear powers were in the throes of developing a nuclear test ban treaty and had temporarily suspended further tests.

A major risk of early testing was unexpected winds.[14] In the Bikini Island tests, winds had carried debris across inhabited atolls, and injured Japanese fishermen, killing one. By Pauling's estimation these tests distributed fallout over 7,000 square miles. Adamafio, Nkrumah's political colleague, extrapolated from this data to explain, "a bomb of similar strength exploded in the Sahara would have disastrous consequences for the people of Morocco, Algeria, Sudan, Mauritania, Guinea, Mali, Ghana and others."[15] French scientists stressed that the planned explosion would be quite small, downplaying the risks of the first atomic explosions in Africa. They claimed, in fact, that the weapon would emit less than 0.001 percent of all the nuclear energy released to date from previous bomb tests.[16] In contrast, Ghanaian officials echoed less-conservative estimates made by physicists like Linus Pauling, who led an international scientific movement in favor of a test ban.

For anti-imperialists, the detonation of an atomic bomb extinguished whatever remaining legitimacy France had as a colonial occupier, especially in Algeria, which was already wracked with conflict as resistance fighters sought to remove French settlers. A newspaper for Nkrumah's Convention People's Party, the *Evening News*, printed photos to remind party faithful of the danger of nuclear radiation. Harkening back to the Japanese experience, one image of the distorted skin on a man's back showed "An Innocent Victim of Radio Active Fall-out after Hiroshima Blast."[17] Cartoons in the newspapers, drawn primarily by an artist known as Ghanatta, showed typical Ghanaian women, lying on the ground, or holding onto children, with missiles directed toward them.[18] Other political cartoonists and editors equated a bomb test with a journey into hell, with France urged on by the devil to destroy Africans (Figure 2.1).

With Nkrumah's government's strong urging, citizens took to the streets when stories circulated that France, in its bid to join the "nuclear club," had plans to bring atomic bombs to African soil. In a speech condemning the French nuclear tests in Reggane, Adamafio, then secretary of Nkrumah's political party, declared that they were an "attack upon the children of Africa ... and upon the sovereignty, dignity and personality of our people":

Every one of you can tell France what the answer is; it is NO! NO! to all nuclear imperialism in Africa; No! to the murder of women and children

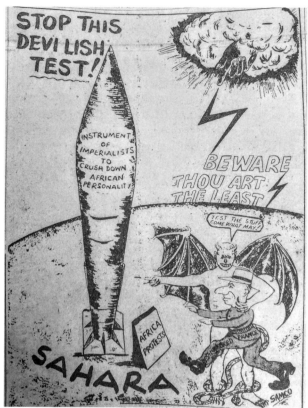

Figure 2.1 Political cartoon on eve of bomb tests by artist known as Samco in Nkrumah's propaganda newspaper: the devil advises France to push aside the protest team and detonate the bomb: "Stop this Devilish Test! Instrument of Imperialists to Crush Down African Personality! Beware Thou Art the Least. Test the Stuff Come what May!"
(*Source*: *Evening News*, February 13, 1960, p. 4)

through radio-active fallout. It is NO to the Cold War which provoked these evil tests. It is NO to the destruction of mankind with which these weapons threaten us.[19]

After recalling the imposition of slavery, forced labor, and resource extraction on African communities in years past, Adamafio went on to explain that, "At last the African people can work out their own destiny, and they will not allow the power of foreign money or foreign bombs to deter them."

If France, or any other country for that matter, establishes the tradition of using Africa as a laboratory for obnoxious experiments, too dangerous to be carried out in her own territory, the African people will be under a constant threat of blackmail … *All* our strength must be put into the fight against nuclear madness in Africa … Tomorrow we shall march to the French Embassy.[20]

For Adamafio and others disgusted with colonial occupations, the Reggane tests represented the worst in a long series of France's repressive policies in Africa. Ghanaian disdain for French colonialism related to a protracted war between Algerian resistance fighters and the colonial occupiers. The conflict in Algeria was one of the most violent anticolonial struggles on the continent, on par with the British war with the Mau Mau in Kenya several years later.[21] After French officials ignored Ghanaian requests to abandon the bomb tests in July 1959, Nkrumah sent Ghanaian fighters to assist and recognized the "provisional Algerian government."[22] In response, France withdrew its ambassador from Ghana.

Nkrumah attempted to use the atomic test to galvanize the opinions of independent African leaders against the French. The protest efforts against the Reggane test were part of his attempt to recognize a common African condition and promote unity.[23] On December 31, 1957, he married Fathia Rizk, an Egyptian woman, in a symbolic gesture designed to solidify ties between Africans south and north of the Sahara Desert. At the time of the French tests, Ghana was one of the few independent African countries; others included Egypt, Morocco, Tunisia, Libya, Sudan, Ethiopia, Liberia, and Guinea. In coming years, Nkrumah attempted to set up a "United States of Africa" with himself at the helm, a project that ultimately failed.[24]

In a pledge of pan-African unity, the leadership of Egypt sided with Nkrumah and issued similar statements condemning France's nuclear imperialism. Egypt's Al-Shab stated on Cairo radio:

There is no longer any doubt that the African continent is facing the most colossal peril in its history – a peril that threatens its present and future. France is insisting on conducting its A-bomb test in the Algerian Sahara. The threat of these tests is cast over the entire African continent. The explanation for these tests in the heart of Africa can only be genocide of the Africans. This explanation seems indisputable. The matter is thus one of life or death as far as the Africans are concerned.[25]

Al-Shab went on to state that the threat of the French experiments "requires the consolidation of all Africans to deter this threat by every possible means. Ghana has taken an excellent step in this regard which must be supported and backed with similar measures by all African States and Peoples."[26]

At the beginning of 1960, France's other West African colonies, which included Mali, Upper Volta, and Côte d'Ivoire, remained intact. The issues of nuclear testing and independence became intertwined as Africans formulated plans at regional gatherings like the Congress of the African Confederation of Free Trade Unions. During a meeting in Abidjan, 123 delegates – including notably those representing Côte d'Ivoire, Senegal, and Mauritania – voted for "two resolutions, demanding an end to the Algerian war and no nuclear tests in the Sahara."[27] Côte d'Ivoire was not expected to go against colonial masters France. But in the face of French nuclear experimentation, francophone Africans became more bold; by August 7, 1960, Félix Houphouët-Boigny declared Côte d'Ivoire independent. By the end of 1960, France had lost all of its African colonies, except Algeria (which gained independence in 1962).

A few African leaders sided with the French, embracing the so-called "nuclear madness" as a means to an end. For instance, Philibert Tsirinana, who was then prime minister of the Madagascar Republic, an autonomous state within the French Community, expressed the belief that a viable French atomic bomb would provide safety and security for all francophone Africans. In its reporting on the story, the *Manchester Guardian* noted, "as a reply to the protests of Ghana or any other independent African state against the forthcoming explosion in the South of the Algerian Sahara, it is at least very neat. The bomb belongs, it would seem, to Senegal and Gabon as much as to France."[28] Through their positioning in relation to the bomb, African governments showed their relative dependency on colonial authorities that still had a great deal of control in 1959, especially in francophone Africa.

But in Ghana, where British authority had been firmly removed, the specter of radioactive dust drifting from the bomb site in Algeria to Ghana mobilized national opinion leaders. Nkrumah's Convention

People's Party sponsored daily "noisy but peaceful" protests outside of the French Embassy in Accra.[29] As far as Ghana's newly established Council for Nuclear Disarmament was concerned, France "joined the nuclear club and contracted out of the club of decency and human rights."[30] This Ghana Council for Nuclear Disarmament worked closely with opponents in other African countries including Nigeria and Basutoland and sympathizers in the United Kingdom and France to fashion a "Saharan Protest Team." The team took up a nonviolent approach in the tradition of Mahatma Gandhi in their bid to gain worldwide attention.[31] It included the British religious leader Michael Scott and pan-Africanist Bayard Rustin. According to exhaustive research by historian Jean Allman, "at least ten Ghanaians (C. Ablorh, B.M. Akita, K.M. Arkhurst, George Asante, K.A. Dornu, K. Frimpong-Manso, F.A. Koteye, P.G. Marshall, George Odoe, and R. Orleans-Lindsay); a Nigerian student, H. Arinze; [and] Ntsu Mokhekle, president of the Basutoland National Congress" joined in the convoy up to the border with Burkina Faso.[32] A Ghanaian member of the Sahara Protest Team, K. Frimpong-Manso, pleaded for young people to protect "Mother Africa … from yet another deadly blow from Imperialist France. We should not allow another Hiroshima in Africa."[33]

In November 1959, foreign anti-nuclear activists began arriving in Ghana to the excitement of the nation. Michael Randle and Francis Hoyland of the Direct Action Committee Against Nuclear War came to Accra first. A woman rounded out the activists; British officials reporting on the events in letters to colleagues in London noted the addition of a "French girl," Esther Peter, and described those assembling "as a harmless starry-eyed group."[34] A number of American political activists of African descent were vehemently opposed to the French tests, including Bill Sutherland and Bayard Rustin, who also joined the Saharan Protest Team.[35] Refused visas to enter French territory, the activists found that the French Embassy in Accra "[were] not taking them too seriously."[36] In December 1959, Ghana provided funding and transport for activists to travel from Accra to Reggane. The team hoped to enter the test site and convince Algerian personnel not to cooperate with French authorities. At the northern border between Ghana and the French colony of Upper Volta, however, the team was met by French military police. Nor were French officials deterred when a French activist went on a dramatic hunger strike, with the gaunt man pictured reading a Ghanaian newspaper from his bed in Nkrumah's party mouthpiece *The Evening News*.[37] The week of the first bomb, a delegation from Japan, standing in solidarity with Ghanaian officials, arrived in the capital to publicly decry the French plans.

Thus, the bomb tests emerged as a polarizing force, not only in African colonies and countries but also around the world. The proposed bombs in the Sahara led to fierce debates, even in places that tacitly supported the detonations. In the British House of Lords, the foreign secretary came under scrutiny for his decision not to urge France to reconsider the bomb site, as well as for his claim that it was the United Kingdom's position "that we do not think that this test will do any physical damage to anybody."[38]

European countries could not ignore the concerns of African leaders who strategically mobilized Asian and Latin American leaders to join their cause. In April 1958, Ghana hosted an inaugural conference of the first independent African states. The assembled nations revisited many of the concerns reviewed during the non-aligned meeting of African and Asian countries at Bandung in Indonesia, including the rights of people in Palestine, and the ongoing war in Algeria against French occupation. A major outcome of the Accra conference was "an appeal to the great powers to stop the production and testing of nuclear weapons."[39] Then, in 1959 at the United Nations, Ghana joined the Afro-Asiatic block in the presentation of a resolution urging France not to explode any atomic bombs on the African continent. Ghana voted with Guinea, Morocco, Libya, Liberia, Ethiopia, and Tunisia for the resolution, along with emerging states like India and Iran. Communist countries like Cuba, Ukraine, and the Soviet Union, where leader Nikita Khrushchev had been promoting a test ban, also voted with the Africa, Asian, and Middle Eastern countries.[40] In contrast, Ghana noted the rejection of this resolution by her former occupier, the United Kingdom, alongside the United States, Portugal, Belgium, Spain, Israel, and other nations, including the white-led Union of South Africa. While the resolution ultimately passed, France was not deterred.

"The Death Dust Swinging Round Africa": Measuring Radiation During the Tests

In 1960, France detonated three nuclear weapons in the Tanezrouft desert within the Sahara. Overall, between the start of testing in 1960 and its end in 1963, France conducted four atmospheric and thirteen underground tests in Algeria. With each atmospheric test, Ghana's meteorological experts, physicists, military personnel, and agricultural officers became more coordinated in their efforts to monitor radioactive particles across the country. The process of countering nuclear imperialism allowed Ghanaian experts to hone their skills and tap into the reservoir of nuclear power themselves. They showed that information on nuclear technologies could be shared democratically around the world, with African sites at the edge of debris fields as likely as bomb-making nations to make contributions to nuclear science.

French scientists and government officials took a paternalist approach in their initial discussions of the proposed bomb tests. As international debate grew, the French Government assured the Ghanaian Government that the radioactive fallout from the tests would be negligible and pose no risk to people living in Ghana. By January 25, 1960, the French Embassy in Ghana circulated a memorandum on the "Sahara Test" laden with charts and diagrams. In the brief, French officials emphasized that "Paris and Accra are at an equal distance" from the bomb site of Reggane (1,450 miles).[41] The memo described how the United States had detonated more than forty bombs in the Nevada Desert only 250 miles from the city of Los Angeles. In contrast, France planned to unleash bombs of a similar magnitude with the nearest town being 500 miles away. Responding to concerns that seasonal Harmattan winds (which blow Saharan sand across the tropical rainforest belt from November to February) might take up radioactive particles, the memo said that "systematic studies" indicated no chance that wind could move debris more than 600 miles southward, northward, or westward. In conclusion, it argued, "the inhabitants of Los Angeles or San Francisco, of Cmsk or Novosibirsk have been more exposed – yet without any risk – than will be those of any African village or town."[42]

Very little information is publicly available for what actually happened during the French bomb tests in the Sahara in the early 1960s. The French did not make public statistics on the number of people exposed in the village at Reggane, nor did they offer follow-up studies on the rates of thyroid or bone marrow cancers in later years, as was the case in the United States, where large portions of the data related to bomb testing were eventually released (in part in response to lawsuits).[43] In the fifty years since, Algerian researchers have continued to seek additional information about the effects of the bomb tests.

After the nuclear meltdown of the Chernobyl reactor in 1986, the Algerian Center for Radioprotection and Security worked with the Laboratory of the Environment to disaggregate measurable amounts of fallout in the country related to Chernobyl, other global events, and the French tests in the colonial period.[44] By 2008, a follow-up study made with the assistance of the International Atomic Energy Agency recognized that people at Reggane had indeed been ill-affected by both the atmospheric bomb tests, and at least one of the underground tests, which was "poorly contained."[45]

Confidential reports from research teams in Ghana, Nigeria, Sierra Leone, and Guinea provide critical data points about what really happened during these controversial tests. And the *political* fallout that France endured may have forever shaped efforts to create a nuclear-weapons-free zone in Africa, and halt additional atmospheric tests on the continent. Had France, or Britain, had the bomb earlier, it is conceivable that the "laboratory" of African empire, as historian Helen Tilley has emphasized, could have provided a ripe terrain for further nuclear weapons testing.[46] But, working for a newly independent regime, scientists in Ghana were well poised to produce independent investigations on the range of radioactive particles.

As the French tests loomed, anti-nuclear activists in Ghana emphasized their deadly effects. But how would Ghana determine the actual levels of radiation particles in the weeks after the first Reggane test? As early as June 1959, V. Wassiamal at the Ghanaian Ministry of External Affairs sought assistance from the handful of physicists in the country to aid in monitoring of radioactivity. Wassiamal had been approached by the newly founded World Radioactivity Warning Centre in Geneva to participate in systematic collection of samples during the first four months of 1960.[47]

Early efforts to monitor radioactive dust in Ghana led physicists at the University of Ghana, Legon to the establish a semi-permanent monitoring station near the village of Kwabenya, in a building now home to the Ghana Atomic Energy Commission guesthouse. At this point, the University of Ghana was affiliated with the University of London. The faculty included some African lecturers from the ranks of elite Ghanaians who had attended missionary and government boarding schools during the colonial period. A small department of physics also depended on teachers from England. Two of them, Raymond Wright and Alan Howard Ward, led a group of Ghanaian research assistants to document the level of nuclear fallout before and after the French tests. Wright served as a professor in the physics department at the University of Ghana, Legon, and Ward worked at the radioisotopes unit there.

These scientists understood the scientific potential of documenting radioactive fallout from the French bombs. Ghana had received very little fallout from previous tests elsewhere in the world, and the country had very little background radiation from naturally occurring radioactive materials such as thorium or uranium that were absent from Ghana.[48] This was a highly unusual confluence of events that made Ghana an ideal location to monitor subsequent testing in West Africa. Thus, Ghanaian scientists ironically had optimal conditions to study the extent of any fallout and were interested in the tests from a scientific perspective. Researchers in the university's physics department were deeply familiar with these radioisotopes, having used them for research since 1951. The physics lecturers increasingly held responsibility for medical and agricultural applications of radioisotopes in the colony. By 1958, the physics department set up a University Radioisotope Unit with the assistance of Ward, to which the Ghanaian Ministry of Defense turned to for assistance in studying radiation from the French bomb tests.[49]

To ascertain the levels of radiation in Ghana before and after the explosion, the scientists in Ghana decided to sample substances that might retain and transmit fallout to humans and livestock, water, soil, dust, crops, and milk.[50] It was on the outskirts of the hilly Legon campus, near Kwabenya, that Wright and Ward, accompanied by a meteorologist, Walker, conducted initial measurements and analyses. All were British but worked for the Ghanaian Government. In early 1959, they publicly stated that nuclear fallout would have a detrimental effect on the health of Ghanaians. They found themselves under pressure from the British Government to shift their expert opinions. While Wright's standing as an excellent physicist did not come under close scrutiny, Walker's grooming led British officials to doubt his credibility, "applying the maxim that good wine need no bush, it may be relevant to observe that he has a large handlebar moustache."[51]

As the crisis grew, British officials also questioned the credentials of Ward and Wright. One visiting scientist noted, "it was necessary to explain fall-out measurements and effects in detail" to the team.[52] Ward had actually participated in some of the earliest research on the lasting effects of strontium-90, the major byproduct of plutonium bombs. He and a team working at the Korle Bu Hospital in what was then the Gold Coast found that thirteen monkeys injected with a solution of strontium-90 all died within two months. They conducted autopsies on the monkeys and found significant distribution of strontium-90 within bone tissue.[53] Since the chemical strontium is similar to calcium, the body can easily absorb it. By the 1950s, researchers around the world were concerned about the lasting effects of strontium-90 on bone marrow (Figure 2.2). They began to study how the chemical prompted bone cancer like osteogenic sarcoma, and sometimes blood cancers when animals and humans were exposed to large quantities.[54]

The French code name for the first bomb was Blue Gerbil (*Gerboise Bleu*), an experimental "animal" released into the air from a tower probably about 300 feet high.[55] This atomic "gerbil" traveled from France, where it was manufactured, to the Saharan Military Test Center at Reggane. The bomb transformed an ancient oasis and watering spot for travelers into a forbidden territory, still abandoned today. It became one of several locations on earth, beginning with Alamogordo, New Mexico, that were remade into what historian Jerry Jessee, in his study of radiation ecologies and atmospheric testing, terms "radioactive deserts."[56]

When the fallout from the first French test, conducted on February 13, 1960, was higher than officials in Ghana had expected, they actually tried to contain the information Wright and Ward had collected. At the aforementioned cabinet meeting on February 15, Nkrumah met with his closest advisors to review Ward and Wright's initial radioactivity readings. Heavy winds had blown more radioactive dust down from the Sahara Desert than the French had predicted. By now, this had become a common mishap in nuclear testing. Models for wind and air circulation were imperfect at the time.[57] In the United States, Congress was holding hearings on radioactive winds; a nuclear testing station there was facing lawsuits.[58] It is plausible that Ward and Wright advised Nkrumah to be cautious until they could verify their figures and confer with a Canadian consultant, John Marr.

Wright and Ward continued their measurements at twenty-two monitoring stations. The physicists coordinated with Ghanaian military personnel, weathermen, and agricultural station staff in Ghanaian towns and farms, implementing careful plans put in place before the detonation:

Figure 2.2 A "strontium-90" cartoon
(*Source*: *Ghana Evening News*, February 10, 1960, p. 4)

Air-borne dust is collected by filtration under forced flow, using the method developed by the Radiation Protection Division of the Canadian Department of Health and Welfare; an air pump is fitted with a glass-fibre filter paper and with the average loading of dust has a capacity of about 720 m.³ a day. Each pump and filter is in a Stevenson screen, that at Tamale being 3 ft. above ground-level, that at Accra being on a flat roof 21 ft. above ground-level. Deposited dust was swept up daily from the measured area of flat concrete roof, 21 ft. above ground-level at both Tamale and Accra; during peak periods the same area was swept each day until any remaining activity was negligible.[59]

As expected, "the contamination reaching Ghana was dust-borne."[60] Three days after the bomb test, they found a substantial increase in levels of radiation in towns in Northern Ghana. By February 17, significant fallout had reached the capital city and other towns in Southern Ghana. They calculated the "Dose due to Bomb" in northern Ghana to be 90 TKunits, 30 in "Mid-Ghana," and 15 in southern Ghana, compared to a "maximum permissible dose" of 400,000 TKunits, as recommended by the ICRP.[61] While Paris and Accra might have been equidistant from Reggane, Accra was more likely to receive any fallout given southerly wind patterns at this time of year.

Nkrumah was keen to make sure that the initial readings and analysis at the University of Ghana were accurate. His government requested that British and Nigerian researchers travel to Ghana to corroborate the findings. Ghana also invited Canadian monitors to the country to do their own independent assessment. With the findings confirmed, Ghana shared its data with the World Radioactivity Warning Centre in Geneva as well as the United Nations' Scientific Committee on the Effects of Atomic Radiation.[62] The nation also fielded requests from government scientists in Morocco. Presumably, colonial subjects in Mali and Burkina Faso (then the French colony of Upper Volta) were also wary and benefited from Ghana's interest, though I only have indirect evidence of monitoring of animal products from Burkina Faso. As officials in the Ghanaian Ministry of Defense put it in a note to Nkrumah, "The more publicity we have, indicating that there has been a rise in radio-active contamination of the air in Ghana as the result of the French explosion, the better it would be for us."[63]

Despite successfully drawing international attention to the rise in radioactivity in Ghana, Ghanaian officials and scientists could not stop France from detonating additional bombs later that year. Nkrumah's government eventually released rather alarmist press statements, expressing that "there was a phenomenal rise in the quantum of radiation" recorded in parts of Ghana, including "fantastic limits (i.e. 128) for Tamale."[64] They sided with the Canadian Government, which supported an end to all bomb testing and feared the French explosions would have enduring impacts on Ghana's environment. Ghanaians particularly studied Canadian predictions that even in the event of an end to all bomb testing:

the problem of ionizing radiation will still exist. There will continue for several years to be fall-out of radioactive particles already in the atmosphere. There will also be long-term effects from the movement of radioactive isotopes through food chains. Even more important, there will continue to be for a long time genetic and biological effects from radiation, both man-made and natural, on the health of human populations.[65]

After the second and third tests on April 1 and 13, however, the levels of radiation were not as high as during the first test. Still, the researchers had detected enough, particularly in cows' milk and beef from cattle raised in Burkina Faso, to worry the agricultural department. Radioactive particles could be hosted in animals and cultivated foodstuffs. Even if the radioactive livestock and food originated out of Ghana, herdsmen brought flocks across borders, and farmers in neighboring countries sold their produce in Ghana. Radiation levels in Ghanaian cocoa crops, a primary export during the early Nkrumah years, were, thankfully, negligible.

By the fourth atmospheric test in January of 1961, all departments involved in the testing were well coordinated and prepared for efficient sampling. They shipped soil, milk, beans, and other items to laboratories at Legon. The Ministry of Defense provided funds to the Ministry of Food and Agriculture to arrange for renewed collection of foodstuffs and leaves. The Ministry of Food and Agriculture then sent them on to Ward and his colleagues at the Radioisotope Unit in the physics department at the University College.[66] Well in advance of the fourth announced test in the Sahara, Ghana Airways reserved a large bed in its cargo hold to quickly transport samples on December 30, as well as January 3 and 10.[67]

European, American, and African scientists monitoring fallout across West Africa showed that, as Nkrumah had noted as early as 1958 at a meeting of independent African leaders, "Radio-active winds know no international frontiers."[68] Reports from British colonies including Nigeria, Sierra Leone, and Guinea showed the extent of the debris field, especially after the first test, when unexpected winds widened the fallout area. While I did not locate reports from francophone settings, scientists like Ward expressed interest in taking measurements in the newly independent country of Mali. Ward felt that since their northern neighbor was geographically closer to the bomb site in the Sahara, the levels of fallout "might easily reach what is accepted as a dangerous level."[69]

Ample evidence from Nigeria suggests that this hypothesis was definitely plausible. In Nigeria, confidential reports detailed surprisingly high levels of strontium-90 during the detonations. Still a British colony, Nigeria set up a joint British-Nigerian scientific committee to monitor fallout. Once the French announced their test plans, a group of Nigerian scientists and government ministers traveled to the United Kingdom to discuss their concerns. Nigerian scientists were the first to raise what would become a significant worry – what impact would the bombs have on "regular commercial flights from London to Lagos?" These flights traveled within 1,000 miles of the site; even at a height of 20,000–30,000 feet, they would not escape "the cloud."[70] After the Nigerian visit to Harwell, the center of the British Atomic Energy Research Establishment, a Nigerian physicist, B.E.C. Agbu at the University College of Ibadan, worked with the Director of Nigerian Meteorological Services, J.R. Clackson, and the Senior Specialist in Radiology in Nigeria, Dr. O.D. Macnamara, to set up six monitoring stations in October 1959. They selected the northern towns of Maiduguri, Kano, Sokoto, and Kaduna, and the southern cities of Port Harcourt and Lagos.

On the day of the bomb, a representative from the United Kingdom Atomic Energy Authority, J.A.T. Dawson, traveled by plane from London to Lagos. He overheard an air steward talking nervously about the bomb, and learned from her that there was a radiation monitoring device installed on the plane itself. Dawson spoke to the captain about his interest in reading the meter en route. Just as they were about to fly over the Nigerian town of Kano, cruising at an altitude of 22,000 feet, the captain called him excitedly into the cockpit. "The instrument had recorded suddenly 3 milliroentgen per hour at 0420 hours at position 15°30' N, 09°00' E … It was evident that the track of at least a portion of the weapon debris was very different from that which had been expected and that the chance of measurable fall-out activity appearing in Nigeria was not then so very remote."[71]

The official report from Nigeria on the first bomb test was completed just as France conducted a third test – this one a surprise – on April 13.[72] Nkrumah received his copy from the Nigerian Federal Prime Minister Abubakar Belewa on the morning of April 14, as scientists in both Nigeria and Ghana began studying fallout from yet another bomb test.[73] The joint United Kingdom-Nigerian Scientific Committee found that, as in Ghana, the level of radiation in Nigerian towns after the first detonation was higher than the French had predicted. Also as had been the case in Ghana, ministers in Nigeria were initially reluctant to publicize the findings. The UK-Nigerian scientific team noted that a combination of factors, including a larger bomb than had been anticipated, and specific meteorological patterns allowed radiation to reach Nigeria.

Some of the highest levels were recorded in northern Nigeria. After one test alone, the level of radiation was as high as 25 percent of the annual maximum. In particular, the fallout at the station at Maiduguri in northern Nigeria was much higher than expected, given the unusual wind pattern, which swept the fallout further south of Algeria than the French had predicted.[74] Samples of fission products collected on sticky paper and air filters registered the highest levels of radiation on February 14 for Maiduguri and February 15 for the other five stations. By February 26, the samples had only negligible levels of radiation. The UK-Nigerian team compared the level of strontium-90 now spread on Nigerian soil to that found at British monitoring stations in 1959 after previous tests around the world. Nigeria's load was about one-third of what had been found in the UK, suggesting Nigerians were overall at less risk than their British counterparts from atmospheric tests, but in the absence of prior data it is unclear how much of the measured radiation was from the French test or earlier detonations.

The British also supported radiation measurements in Sierra Leone and Gambia, both still British colonies in 1960. Collectors at two stations in Sierra Leone (Bo and Freetown) registered the highest levels of fallout on February 19, though the scientists blamed people in the area who "re-stirred" the "active material" when they walked across the sample sites several days later.[75] Overall, the strontium-90 spread across land in Sierra Leone was at most 10 percent of that found across the UK by the end of 1959.

The names of the many individuals who assisted at the sample stations across West Africa are difficult to trace. Countless questions remain in the search for the ubiquitous assistants of scientific labor and the targets of scientific experimentation. For instance, who were the students at the University of Ghana sent to the field to monitor fallout (Figure 2.3)?[76] Did they fear for their safety? What of the local populations who "re-stirred" fallout when their paths criss-crossed piles of debris?[77] Who were the many people who undoubtedly inhaled radioactive sand as it swept down from Reggane to towns thousands of miles away? Airport managers at Nigeria's northern Kano facility sought "the necessary equipment and people to undertake the job"

Figure 2.3 Original caption: "A student of the Physics Department of the University of Ghana, measuring radioactive fallout from an atomic bomb test"
(*Source*: "Focus on Ghana Atomic Reactor Project: Nuclear Research in Ghana," *The Ghanaian Times*, November 14, 1966, p. 8)

of examining aircraft for contamination after the bomb tests.[78] Who had the unenviable task of cleaning the plane that flew so close to the bomb en route to Nigeria when it landed?

Despite France's official stance that it would carry on with further atmospheric tests, a French scientist named Dr. Dando agreed to discuss concerns of scientists. In Accra, Dando met briefly with the UK specialist Dawson, who had flown on the plane across the Sahara on the morning of the first test. After attending the detonation at Reggane, Dando was "concerned with the fall-out predictions." Indeed, despite efforts to limit information on the radiation readings, the Ghanaian public demanded answers.

"We Refuse to Allow Anyone to Throw Dust in Our Eyes"[79]: Diplomatic Responses

Over the course of 1960, people living south of the French bomb tests increasingly made calls to "keep Africa atom free."[80] From street protests, to diplomatic responses, to wider calls at the level of the United Nations, Ghanaians as well as Nigerians, Sudanese, Guineans, and others were eager to cast aside colonial abuses and assert the equality of Africans. In particular, the United Nations became a forum for representatives of newly independent nations to air their grievances about nuclear imperialism in Africa. By the end of 1960, Ghanaian efforts to eliminate atomic weapon testing and remove foreign bases from the continent showed that at the same time that European countries like France and the United Kingdom sought to increase their global dominance through membership in the nuclear club, they were also losing power in Africa. From July 1, 1960, Kwame Nkrumah served as president of the newly established Republic of Ghana, without oversight of the crown. The circulation of atomic winds, whether or not they were hazardous, created what anthropologist Tim Choy terms a "political atmosphere."[81]

Popular concerns over the death dust could immediately be felt in large towns and cities south of Reggane. African leaders capitalized on the discontent to increase their own authority. When France went ahead with the first set of tests in February 1960, there was outrage in the streets of Ghana, and Nkrumah had to call in the army and police.[82] Ghanaians threatened to loot French-owned shops and businesses until Nkrumah took "a grip on the situation" and convinced his public to remain calm.[83] Ghanaians were already embroiled in agitation to stop the French occupation in Algeria. Immediately after the first detonation, Nkrumah expressed "the horror and the disappointment" of Ghanaians in particular and Africans more generally that France went forward with "exploding a nuclear device on African soil in defiance of the conscience of mankind."[84] Nkrumah's government immediately froze the assets of French companies.[85]

British officials were not keen to have lost control of the former colony and were wary of Nkrumah's motives. Reporting to the British

High Commission in Accra, one official observed, "Dr. Nkrumah's attitude is, I fear, disingenuous. He is far less concerned with the health of West Africans than he is with seizing political leadership in West Africa and with making things as difficult as he can for the French."[86] Indeed, Nkrumah's propaganda newspaper made much of each bomb test in a period when the Ghanaian leader sought tighter control over politics, eventually culminating in a campaign in 1964 to establish a single-party state for which he expected to serve as president for life.[87] Nkrumah's ubiquitous silhouette and admonition that "The Party is Supreme" hovered over stories on the bomb tests and his campaign (Figure 2.4).

For their part, the Nigerian elite were irritated that they were not yet independent from Britain, and therefore unable to fully express their distaste for France's activities. P.C. Agbu's newspaper, the *West African Pilot*, expressed this frustration two days after the first test: "From now on we regard France as the greatest enemy of Africa and Africans. Nigeria is not yet independent. If we had the necessary power we could have put France in her right place just as Germany did when she overran the feeble France in less than twenty-four hours."[88]

Leaders of other emerging African countries also criticized France's decision to move forward with the tests. In Khartoum, Sudanese officials staged a meeting with the French ambassador to express their "utmost concern" that the first atomic bomb test in Africa had been executed.[89] In Guinea, which declared independence from France in 1958, the radio stations broadcast nationalist statements condemning the first bomb detonation in February. The government in Guinea felt that the bomb test was designed to "intimidate the African nationalist movement."[90] In particular, Guinea was concerned that the bomb meant that France had no intention of leaving North Africa, or granting independence to other West African colonies. As a new country already trying to control natural resources within its jurisdiction, Guinea was especially wary that shortly before the bomb tests, France used its authority as an occupying nation to give oil concessions to countries complicit in their Algerian war, including Italy and West Germany.[91]

When news spread that French engineers planned a second bomb test, Nkrumah invited African countries that had attained independence, political organizations in areas still under colonial occupations, and a number of African American activists to a meeting on "Positive Action for Peace and Security in Africa" at the Pan-African Anti-Bomb

Figure 2.4 Headlines on evening of first French test: "Nkrumah Must Remain President for Life" and "France is Finished: Bomb Exploded!" (*Source: Evening News*, February 13, 1960, p. 1)

Conference.[92] Nkrumah welcomed delegates to Accra on April 7, just as France completed a second test. Discussion at the meeting focused on the fact that the measured fallout from the first test was significantly higher than the French had predicted.[93] According to historian Jean Allman, "At the start of the conference, the Sahara Protest Team, echoing the connections between the anti-nuclear struggle and African liberation, presented its manifesto to the delegates, calling not only for an end to nuclear tests and nuclear arms, but for a thousand volunteers for a renewed Sahara protest movement."[94] The overland protest efforts did not grow, however, with Nkrumah seeking other routes to a solution.

Hoping to draw international attention, Nkrumah recalled the Ghana Ambassador to France in April, after the second test. The ambassador attempted to soften this action by emphasizing that his departure "was a decision of principle which did not amount to breaking off diplomatic relations."[95] The assets of French companies in Ghana remained frozen. Soon, West African antipathy toward the French expanded to include other imperial powers. The United Kingdom High Commission in Accra was especially concerned as the situation escalated, since many of the French-owned businesses in Ghana actually sold British goods.[96] For whites in West Africa, the situation became increasingly tense, regardless of nationality. In Morocco, British subjects feared for their safety as resentment against the French grew and the Moroccan Government and the king lost control over public order.[97]

While the United States was wary of France's growing nuclear program, US government officials and even non-politicians were reluctant to side with Nkrumah.[98] When Billy Graham, a prominent white American religious leader, visited Accra several weeks before the first detonation, Ghanaians peppered him with questions on his view of the "French Atom Test." But he was reluctant to say much, stating "no comment, that's political. We are in a political year in the United States and I want to make as few statements as possible on political questions."[99] This was a disappointment to Ghanaians in the highly Christianized south of the country, and Nkrumah's editors put a racial cast to Graham's statements. Indeed, African Americans joined the Saharan Protest Team, and W.E.B. Dubois, who settled in Ghana with his wife Shirley after independence, would speak at Nkrumah's "World without the Bomb" conference two years later.[100]

In London, the tests shifted British policy slightly away from France, largely due to appeals from a rising legion of African leadership in Ghana and Nigeria.[101] As early as September 1959, a pressure group of Nigerian Ministers had traveled to the UK to meet with British scientists to discuss the dangerous path France was on. The delegation felt that it was worth it for the United Nations to hold a session to discuss this grievous attack on Africans. Instead, the Nigerian ministers received assurances from British experts that fallout from the bomb tests would be negligible, and they were outraged when the first bomb detonation occurred.[102] The British Colonial Governor in Lagos was keen to stave off concerns from Nigerian ministers over levels of potential fallout in Lagos from successive tests. After the first test, the British admitted that there had "been more fall-out in Ghana and Nigeria than [the French] ever thought possible."[103]

On the eve of France's second test, anxious British officials faced "an awkward dilemma."[104] "This is a serious affair … [W]e do ourselves irreparable harm with Nigerian public opinion if we appear to be blocking the special session of the United Nations to discuss the French atomic tests."[105] Indeed, the British hoped to quietly lobby Iceland, Sweden, and several neutral countries in Latin America to vote against France in the United Nations. British officials took a rather paternalistic tone, not wishing to instruct France on their nuclear program. They claimed, "our desire is to help them as much as we can in overcoming the political embarrassments which they are likely to suffer."[106]

Before signatures could be collected for the special session to go forward, however, French leadership stunned everyone with a second and third test in rapid succession.[107] At the last minute, when France recommended that no one fly across the Sahara Desert beginning at 4:45 am on March 31, everyone knew that another test was imminent.[108] After releasing yet another bomb the next day, French officials circulated a memorandum through the French mission at the United Nations that implied that previous detonations were sufficient and that there would be no need for further plutonium bomb tests in the Sahara.[109] But French scientists continued to conduct additional tests anyway.

Pressure from a growing pool of African leaders made things complicated for British officials seeking to look like they still had control of the situation. Meeting with Nkrumah on April 4, the British official A.W. Snelling lied, telling him that the British had tried to persuade France not to detonate a second device. In reality, British officials, like Ghanaian politicians, had been caught unawares. In a secret report, Snelling wrote, "I believed that only by so doing could I take the anti-British heat out of his attitude on the bomb, and I think I have succeeded in doing so."[110] The situation was very delicate for Snelling, since his superiors had told him not to give the impression that any "approach to [the] French was made at Ghanaian instigation."[111] For his part, Snelling asked his superiors whether it was in "the interest of the United Kingdom to be on the losing side on the bomb," which he equated with supporting France.[112] A British official in Nigeria was instructed to tell Prime Minister Abubakar a similar fib.[113] Tensions escalated to the point that the French president, Charles de Gaulle, made a visit to London in the days after the second test, but it is clear that the British did not demand that the French stop all bombings, as they implied in their conversations with Ghanaian and Nigerian independence leaders.[114]

In the wake of the surprise bomb tests in April, Nigerians were hopeful that they might break off diplomatic ties with France. By May, however, Lagos reinstated relations with France, having been assured that no further tests would occur. Nigerian officials had come under pressure from those in Chad and Niger/Dahomey who used Nigerian ports to bring French equipment into their landlocked countries.[115] In October 1960, Nigeria declared itself independent of British colonial rule. When the fourth test came in January 1961, Abubakar was at liberty to immediately sever commercial and diplomatic ties with France.[116] At the time, Nigerian Federal Minister of Information T.O. S. Benson declared "that Africans refused to accept nuclear tests on African soil, whether in the Sahara or elsewhere and no matter whether they were French, British or American tests." He further suggested, "If they [the atom tests] are so inoffensive why not carry them out in your mountains or on one of your European islands?"[117]

Once Nigeria was also independent, it joined Ghana in calls for a nuclear-weapon-free zone in Africa. In November 1960, Ghana once again turned to the United Nations to help stop France's nuclear imperialism. Ghanaian officials drafted a proposed resolution for consideration at the United Nations for a nuclear-free and military-base-free Africa. This proposed resolution would have eliminated further nuclear weapons testing in the Saharan Desert or elsewhere, and banned foreign military bases, such as the United Kingdom's stations in Nigeria. This was a period when, each month, new African countries announced their independence from colonial supervisors. Nkrumah's government wanted to use the United Nations to establish transparency in this period of immense transition. If a country on the African continent wished to join the UN, it would have to reveal any treaties with former colonial occupiers regarding collaboration for military bases.

The ratcheting up of the Cold War happened at the very moment that emerging atomic powers like France and the United Kingdom were actually waning in influence in Africa. Nkrumah's government capitalized on these two historical trends, Africa's rise and Europe's simultaneous rise and decline. For the drafters of the proposed UN resolution, the threat of nuclear war was at the time a very real possibility. From 1958 to 1961, a ban on testing was observed by other nuclear powers and France's actions were especially egregious.[118] Nkrumah's government saw the French tests as a real opportunity for "small nations" to push members of the nuclear club to reduce their atomic weapons: "Fall-out is no respecter of frontiers and a declaration of neutrality cannot save the people of any African State from nuclear poisoning, once atomic war is introduced into the African continent. A military alliance with any atomic power is therefore, in the view of the Government of Ghana, a threat to the security of Africa and world peace."[119] This was a time when the leaders of the Soviet Union and the United States were working toward a nuclear test ban treaty, and French testing called into question the feasibility of such efforts, with efforts toward a ban collapsing by 1961.

Beyond a ban on testing, officials in the United Kingdom were extremely concerned about Nkrumah's proposal to limit military bases in Africa. In Lagos and New York, they worked behind the scenes to get Nigerian diplomats to reduce their support for the resolution. They were concerned that the resolution would drastically limit British efforts to station military bases in Commonwealth nations and/or former colonies. Her Majesty's Government needed these bases as sites from which to launch nuclear warheads, whether into the Soviet Union or elsewhere. In addition to bases at Simonstown in South Africa and Freetown in Sierra Leone, the United Kingdom had defense agreements with both Nigeria and Sierra Leone. It also held "staging and over-flying rights in the Central African Federation and in Nigeria."[120]

For their part, the United States had bases in Libya and Morocco where the Americans might wish to house nuclear armaments in future.[121] Thus, Africa was pivotal not only for nuclear testing, but also for the housing and possible launching of viable nuclear weapons for members of the nuclear club.[122] Ultimately, because they hoped to keep Ghana and Nigeria within the friendly embrace of the Commonwealth to maintain some influence, British officials abstained from any vote on the proposal rather than oppose Commonwealth nations.[123] Similarly, the French were concerned about losing out on possible military bases, but again, throwing their weight against newly independent African nations would show the reaches of nuclear imperialism and perhaps lead new governments to choose socialism and Soviet influence over Western friendship.[124]

Nkrumah's proposal was novel in that it was the first time that an African country took the lead at the international level against nuclear weapons. In contrast to previous proposals for nuclear-free zones emanating from the Soviet Union, an African-led initiative at that particular moment of heady independence politics served to disrupt West-Soviet bickering with a third way.[125] The governments of Ethiopia, Guinea, Mali, and Morocco joined Ghana in presenting a first draft resolution to the UN on December 1, 1960 that would ban bomb tests and "bases of any kind or launching sites intended" for nuclear warheads to establish what they initially termed "a denuclearised neutral zone."[126] Behind the scenes, threats must have worked to produce dramatic revisions, because the next version allowed foreign military bases as long as they were not designed "for use in testing, storing or transporting" nuclear armaments. This revised version, submitted on December 5, 1960, had the added support of Nigeria, the United Arab Republic, and Sudan.[127]

This grand proposal to implement a nuclear-weapon-free zone across the African continent, which eventually passed at the United Nations General Assembly the following year, was one of the earliest attempts to forestall nuclear war through limitations on regional bomb testing.[128] Prior efforts had included a proposal from Poland introduced in 1958 to limit testing in Central Europe, on the fault line of the West-East nuclear divide.[129] And the efforts of Nkrumah dovetailed Nehru's lobbying since the Bandung conference, providing an African narrative of nuclear activism. In the coming decade, many parts of the world, from South Asia to South America, sought strategies to limit nuclear weapon testing on their soil and nearby waters. While the resolution for a nuclear-weapon-free zone in Africa was not fully implemented, given challenges in coordinating policies across the emerging African countries, it marked the entry of the Ghanaian Government into international discussions on global nuclear affairs.

After the four atmospheric tests in Algeria, as well as some underground explosions, French scientists opted to stop testing nuclear weapons in the Sahara by 1963. However, French officials did not sign the Partial Test Ban Treaty banning atmospheric and oceanic testing that year with the United States, the Soviet Union, and the United Kingdom. French scientists merely moved further nuclear experiments to the less controversial Muroroa atoll in French Polynesia, where they continued experimenting with bombs until 1996. Over more than thirty years, French nuclear physicists detonated at least 198 bombs in Algeria and Polynesia. Without the protests of Nkrumah and others, a larger proportion might have been deployed on the African continent.[130]

Conclusion: Particles without Boundaries

In the 1960s, Ghana witnessed the aftermath of the bomb tests in Algeria. The series of tests outraged Ghanaians at the political level. Radiation was an external threat, with radioactive material produced through European colonial power. Ghanaian leaders, especially Nkrumah and his associates, denounced what they called France's "nuclear imperialism" and sought diplomatic strategies to limit further testing on the continent. Radioactive winds swept down from the Sahara, destabilizing French authority in its colonies, and inspiring confidence in newly independent countries.

The circulation of strontium-90 and other particles across international boundaries demanded scrutiny from scientists based in West Africa. With world attention on the ramifications of the bomb, and competing members of the nuclear club keen to gain any insights on the size and design of the bomb, Ghana's burgeoning class of physicists gained access to research techniques and assistance from visiting consultants. An ironic side effect of the bomb tests was that it led scientists in Ghana to seek more knowledge on nuclear technologies themselves. Fundamentally, scientists and politicians in Ghana recast nuclear technology as something that would not, and could not, be the sole purview of imperial aggressors. While seeking to rid the continent of "the atom," they paved the way for greater levels of expertise on radioactive matter and its myriad applications in civilian life. Thus, Ghanaian newspapers decried French tests, but on the same page exclaimed "Ghana to get Atom for Peace." As we shall see, scientists and politicians in Ghana joined their counterparts in Egypt, China, India, Libya, Pakistan, Iran, and Iraq who were all courting different sponsors for access to information on nuclear technologies and would make strides toward setting up reactors and bombs within the next decade.[131]

These experiences monitoring radioactive fallout were pivotal to the Ghanaian Government's decision to join the International Atomic

Energy Agency on September 28, 1960. Ward and his colleagues in Ghana wrote proposals for admission, based on their desire to gain access to further training in nuclear physics and equipment through financial support from the International Atomic Energy Agency. After the United Nations set up the International Atomic Energy Agency in Vienna, Austria in 1957, newly independent countries like Ghana saw membership in the agency as a sign of their increased standing internationally and initially as a sign of national autonomy. The earliest members of the International Atomic Energy Agency included major world powers like the Soviet Union, the United States, the United Kingdom, and France, as well as postcolonial states like India and Pakistan.[132] Senegal was the first country south of the Sahara to join, in 1960.

As the Agency grew, it implicitly adopted tiers of membership based on the size of a nation's economy that determined the level of annual contributions to costs.[133] It also established a board of governors, to which Ghana soon aspired. In 1961, when two additional seats reserved for African countries came into play, Tunisia and Ghana first served as observers. They were removed, however, in favor of Morocco and Congo-Leopoldville (now the Republic of Congo) given "political pressure on the non-aligned countries."[134] Ghana first served on the board in 1965. Through engagement with the International Atomic Energy Agency, Ghanaian scientists gradually made radiation part of national life, indigenizing it and gaining local expertise.

The early monitoring station at Kwabenya became a hub of Ghana's nuclear future. Ghanaians transformed the threat of radiation into a platform for equal access to nuclear information and the political and electrical power that would bring. The African nuclear age had begun.

3 | Scientific Equity: Physics from the Soviets

"I am uncertain whether Ghanaians should 'learn their atomics in English.' The language of atomic energy seems to be fairly international and countries such [as] India do not seem to mind drawing from Western and Soviet sources impartially."

–H.B. Shepards[1]

In 1964, the Ghana Bureau of Languages published a series of short books on scientific topics in Ghanaian languages. The slim volume *Atom* in Fante, an Akan language spoken in southern Ghana, explained that atoms cannot be seen, though they are everywhere. Additional scientific titles issued in Twi, Fante, Ga, Ewe, and other languages addressed topics covered in the national science education scheme: space, color and light, weights and measures, magnets, and electricity. The easy-to-understand color paperbacks presented scientific concepts thought to be critical to industrializing the young nation (Figure 3.1). The *Atom* book began, "This is an atomic scientist. He does his job on the atomic science in a scientific laboratory. All things are made from atoms. Water we drink, air that we breathe, all the things that we see."[2] The *Atom* book further described nuclear fission, the makeup of the atom with its combination of protons and neutrons, and the ways that radioactive nuclides can provide a lens into the body through X-rays. Black bodies manipulated atoms to provide power and well-being.

By the mid-1960s, information on the scientific possibilities of atoms was within reach of more and more people, including those living in West Africa. From reports of the atom bombs that the United States deployed over Japan at the end of World War II, to protests over France's bomb tests in the Sahara, frequent use had transformed "atom" into a common everyday word. In the West African nation of Ghana, interest in atomic things was growing. As President Nkrumah sought a world without bombs, he increasingly linked the term atom to peaceful applications in engineering. For a new nation hoping to

49

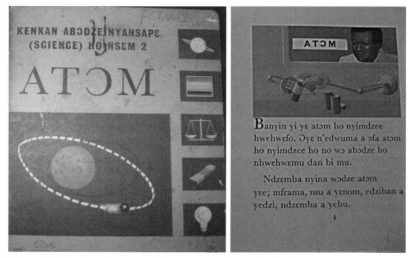

Figure 3.1 Ghana Bureau of Languages science book: *Atom*
(*Source*: Padmore Library, Accra)

industrialize quickly, atoms represented the potential for boundless energy and prosperity. Thus, atoms came to populate small colorful paperbacks for school children.

But were there nuclear physicists in Ghana? During the French bomb tests in the Sahara, the country relied on visiting physicists from abroad for assistance in monitoring fallout. Beyond merely monitoring activities, Ghanaian scientists wanted to understand how to split atoms to increase electrical power resources for the country. By the 1960s, two of the three universities in the country, the University of Ghana, Legon and the Kwame Nkrumah University of Science and Technology, initiated plans to begin degree courses in nuclear physics. The idea was that the graduates of these programs would be available to staff a proposed Ghana Atomic Energy facility. In order to train new students, the Ghanaians with tertiary training in science needed to learn the latest in nuclear physics themselves. Nkrumah tasked Robert Baffour, the engineer in charge of the Kwame Nkrumah University of Science and Technology, with heading an initiative to establish a nuclear program in the country. Since the country did not have facilities to break apart atoms, officials sought equipment – and, importantly, information – from other countries. Specifically, Nkrumah instructed Baffour to work with the Soviet Union to expand access to nuclear science for Ghanaians. This chapter considers the creation of a cadre of Ghanaian nuclear physicists through this initiative, while the next chapter considers their long journey to a reactor.

In this early moment, Nkrumah preferred if Ghanaian students did not pursue nuclear training in the United Kingdom or France; nor did he cooperate with the United States for nuclear training and a reactor, and even Canada's peaceful nuclear program was out. The Soviet Union welcomed Nkrumah's delegations, invited Nkrumah himself to visit, and even sent its leader, Nikita Khrushchev, to Accra. Ironically, Ghanaian scientists learned the physics behind nuclear reactors in Russian at just the moment that, as historian Michael Gordin has argued, English was replacing French, German, Chinese, and Russian as the primary language for international scientific publishing.[3] The Ghanaian case shows how people in a postcolonial setting experienced a linguistic cold war through battles over the language of science. The students who traveled to the Soviet Union grafted on an additional language as they expanded their scientific training, only to find that Russian language skills had limited value over the course of their careers.

This chapter traces the experiences of this nationalist generation of scientists through extensive oral history interviews conducted with leading scientists in 2006, 2008, and 2014–2016, as well as through archival documents from the Ghana Public Records and Archives Administration Department, Archives of the University of Ghana, Legon, the Russian State Archive of the Economy, and the State Archive of the Russian Federation. These records make clear that Ghanaian scientists patched together information on nuclear physics and reactors from multiple sources. Nascent socialism in Ghana by the 1960s led nationalist scientists, already fluent in English, Ga, Twi, Ewe, and other Ghanaian languages, to commence courses in nuclear physics in Russian. However, they saw nuclear knowledge as interchangeable and moved on to courses in English, French, or German as the opportunity to study in other countries arose in the period after the Nkrumah reactor scheme collapsed in 1966.

In subsequent years, Ghana's nuclear scientists did not give up the dream of nuclear power. When they learned nuclear physics, they demonstrated that Africans could gain entry to all scientific arenas. These intrepid individuals emerged as leading experts who taught generations of college students in Ghana, ran programs for students from other African countries, and served in leadership positions for the International Atomic Energy Agency. Ghanaians were some of the first Africans south of the Sahara to train in nuclear physics at a high level, a key legacy of the nationalist move to give Africans access to knowledge of atoms. Their lives after Nkrumah became an experiment in scientific equity.

"Science to the Masses": Expanding Access to Science in Ghana at Independence

Modern science training in Ghana began in English during the British colonial period but was reserved for elite students. In the Gold Coast Colony, laboratory-based instruction in science subjects existed in top boarding schools like Mfantsipim, a Wesleyan boy's secondary school in Cape Coast founded in the 1870s, or Achimota College, a government secondary school and junior college founded in the 1920s.[4] For the vast majority of young people in the Gold Coast, however, science instruction lay out of reach. The omission of scientific subjects was a systematic ploy of British officials to produce colonial subjects with limited skills in keeping with racialist ideas of "Bantu" education.[5] Under colonial occupations, rudimentary instruction at mission and government schools emphasized religious studies supplemented with such practical skills as cooking, sewing, bricklaying, and carpentry. The underdevelopment of science education remained a bitter legacy of British colonialism.

One of first president Kwame Nkrumah's earliest projects was to "bring science to the masses." Nkrumah sought to make Ghanaians stakeholders in scientific study to increase what his administration commonly termed "manpower" in their extensive plans for national development. Manpower meant that everyday citizens would gain the basic science education necessary to upgrade agriculture and manufacturing to global industry standards. It also would allow for a cadre of elite engineers to run the planned hydroelectric and nuclear power reactors that Nkrumah felt would amplify the industrial ambitions of the new nation. Toward this end, Nkrumah worked with the growing number of Ghanaian science educators along with foreign consultants to popularize science and integrate a system of satellite school laboratories into vocational schools. Nkrumah's interest coincided with efforts to popularize science within schools globally, including the Entebbe mathematics initiative for African countries, which the United States sponsored.[6]

Nkrumah asserted that "in all things scientific and technological, Ghanaians are on the run," and this enthusiasm permeated his speeches.[7] Announcing a new science museum in Ghana (still under construction to this day), he hoped the museum would "arouse and increase the interest of Ghanaians, young and old alike, in science and scientific techniques."[8] While opening a British exhibition of science at the Central Library in Accra that same week in June 1962, Nkrumah condemned world powers for using scientific knowledge for ill will. He "assure[d] every scientist working in Ghana or who wishes to come to work here that he will never be required to work for any purpose other than for the progress and benefit of mankind."[9]

Sam Bortei-Doku, who served under Nkrumah as a director of the national science centers initiative from 1962 to 1964, recalled his own introduction to science and his desire to extend access to scientific knowledge to a larger number of individuals. He trained as a secondary school teacher and went on to Achimota School and the University of Ghana where he earned degrees in science and education (granted through special arrangement at the time through University College of London). He then taught chemistry to students at Achimota in the 1950s. But he was aware that outside of the top schools, science subjects were unavailable to the majority of citizens who would not attend secondary school:

Science was not taught in the elementary schools [primary and middle]. We had subjects like nature studies, which was largely botany, well, the study of plants and animals. But, in an elementary form. And then, hygiene, they teach a little bit of health science. That was all. But, experimental science, yeah, this was the bit, experimental science was not taught.[10]

Further, trained science teachers in the country even after independence tended to be expatriate. Ironically, white teachers, many of them from the UK, comprised the majority of the newly established Ghana Science Teachers Association.

Bortei-Doku recalled how Kwame Nkrumah rallied young Ghanaian science instructors like himself to extend access to science.

[In June 1962] Dr. Nkrumah organized what he called the World Without Bombs conference in Ghana. And [professors] from all over the world came to Ghana for the conference. And [after that] Nkrumah spoke to Parliament and he made the announcement about his desire to introduce, or to see science taught in the schools.[11]

Bortei-Doku explained how the World Without Bombs conference brought together an international consortium of experts committed to denuclearization, with Nkrumah and Baffour seen as able negotiators.[12] He witnessed how 120 delegates assembled in Accra for the conference, including representatives from many African, Asian, and Latin American countries, to encourage nuclear powers to divert their military budgets to relieve poverty in emerging nations.[13] Bortei-Doku and others learned through ample coverage how Nkrumah reminded attendees of the dangers of nuclear tests, which the French had been inflicting on African people over the previous two years, calling not only for "the banning of atomic tests" but also "the destruction of all weapons of mass slaughter and reduction of conventional armament." They witnessed a revolutionary environment where Nkrumah likened socialist and capitalist bomb-holders to slave-holders in previous centuries that held slaves while maintaining different religious and ideological standpoints. Ghanaian educators learned that Nkrumah viewed himself as a type of abolitionist who needed to promote "a new doctrine of hope" that would allow for "the abolition of the threat of nuclear conflict and the ending of the cold war."[14]

In the wake of this conference, Nkrumah tasked the University of Ghana, where Bortei-Doku was then working as a lecturer in science education, to establish a pilot program of science centers, which Bortei-Doku headed. The scheme set up science centers in four main cities in the south of the country, Accra, Cape Coast, Sekondi, and Kumasi. Essentially, the science centers were freestanding laboratories where students from nearby schools could visit for weekly instruction and experimentation. There, students would leave their courses in bricklaying, metalwork, and carpentry (the primary target of the initiative was male students, despite Bortei-Doku's suggestions to broaden the scheme to include young women), for an hour or two in a real laboratory.[15]

"Energy" comprised one of the main course streams taught at the new pilot science centers in Ghana. The focus was on the sun as the ultimate source of energy, with students instructed to consider questions like, "All machines use up energy when they do work. Where does all this energy come from? Is the supply of energy likely to become exhausted?"[16] Ghanaian officials were glad to obtain support from any country or institution that expressed interest. To that end, they eagerly accepted wall charts, films, books, and visual aids sent in from companies like Procter and Gamble, British Iron and Steel Federation, and Ford Motor Company.[17] The Ghana Bureau of Languages also produced paperback books in several languages on topics related to the curriculum, including the one on the atom (Figure 3.1). Other books in the series included overviews of space, colors, weights, magnets, and electricity. Ironically, they were printed in London.

It was a time of optimism as Nkrumah hoped to transform discussions on nuclear proliferation into avenues for scientific access for young people. Educators like Bortei-Doku gained opportunities beyond teaching in one school to head national schemes through the University of Ghana, and then the Ministry of Education. In 1963, Bortei-Doku even traveled to Canada to earn a doctoral degree. In other cases, young people keen to learn more about science moved to the Soviet Union, with Russian increasingly seen as a viable language for educating African scientists. From the perspective of those active in expanding access to technology after independence, scientific information emerged as a good for Ghanaians to acquire and innovate, regardless of the language of the supplier.

Scientists working in Ghana, including the British scientist R.W.H. Wright who headed the Physics Department at the University of Ghana, Legon and worked to monitor radioactive fallout from the French bomb tests, applauded these efforts to increase access to science. He noted that widening science instruction to the elementary level would "hasten Ghana's advance towards a modern scientific and technological State""[18] Indeed, once Wright left Ghana, he moved to Jamaica, where he was involved in efforts to increase access to physics in a way that would make sense to people of African descent. Similarly, his British colleague Ward moved to teach physics at the University of Zambia, where he authored books on science for African school children.[19]

Speaking "Afro-Russian": Soviet Support for an African Renaissance

In the independence moment, Ghanaians wanted to be seen as equals on the world stage of scientific achievement, alongside the Americans and the Soviets. Nkrumah's government sought to extend access to scientific training, viewing it as a right for all people and "common heritage of mankind." Ghanaian students were eager to learn scientific theories at home and abroad, regardless of the language required. However, increasingly, government newspaper stories depicted the Soviets as benevolent partners in this project to expand scientific equity, in contrast to the British and French colonizers who truncated access or even deployed weapons on Africans. A massive propaganda effort stimulated the trips many students would take to the Soviet Union and Communist bloc for further training.

In 1962, a children's columnist for *The Ghanaian Times*, "Auntie Mansa," explained, "Dear Children, This is truly the science age. Men have gone into space and circled round the orbit."[20] She encouraged young people in Accra to go to the youth center of Nkrumah's Young Pioneers to view a replica of the Friendship 7 spaceship in which the US astronaut John Glenn had recently taken on three orbits around the earth (still housed at the Ghana Museum of Science). Next to Auntie Mansa's letter, the newspaper published an image of a recent school musical performed in the Soviet Union with young people dressed as "a Mexican, Negro … and [American] Indian" holding hands with a child dressed as a "Russian (Space Pilot)." The caption for the photograph noted that this image was meant to "appeal to the peoples of all races for peace and friendship." This call for friendship and equality with the Soviets shaped efforts to upgrade science education and access.

By the 1960s, Russian was the second-most used language in scientific publishing, after English. Until its decline as a language for scientific communication in the 1970s, there was a brief period when it seemed Russian might be the second-best choice for people interested in learning scientific topics.[21] African linguists participated in systematic efforts in the Soviet Union to define scientific vocabularies in African languages. Hausa experts worked with Dmitry Olderogge to produce a Hausa-Russian dictionary with "20,000 words, including the most widely used scientific and technical terms."[22] Hausa, extensively spoken across West Africa with an estimated 20 million speakers at that time, could have arguably become a vehicle for expanding interest in Soviet culture as well as technical know-how. Similarly, at Leningrad University, Asafa Gabra-Mariam of Ethiopia worked with Soviet colleagues to produce an Amharic-Russian dictionary. Simultaneously, Nigerians were keen to learn Russian.[23]

African leaders appreciated efforts in the Soviet Union to combat the atrocities of Western imperialism and treat them as equals. When the French were testing their bombs in the Sahara, Nkrumah noted that Moscow Radio broadcasts to colonies and countries on the continent had condemned nuclear imperialism. Moscow Radio was appalled when "The black mushroom of death rose over Africa" in February 1960.[24] Nkrumah welcomed the idea that it would be possible to sit in harmony with a major world power like the Soviet Union, after years of disrespect under British rule. As the Soviet Representative to the United Nations Vasily Solodovnikov described it in 1964, "The USSR, which maintains diplomatic relations with the majority of independent African countries, is developing economic and commercial relations with them on the basis of equality."[25] The position of the Soviets was that this equal relationship was "possible only with socialist countries, where the socio-economic order does not seek to exploit, either within their own countries, or on the world market."[26] Nkrumah thus emphasized Ghana's socialist leanings and its people's willingness to learn Russian to promote the country's bid for scientific equity and a nuclear program.

Nkrumah's CPP party emphasized the rising importance of the Russian language in government news articles. Atukwei John Okai, then a young propaganda writer for Nkrumah who sought to spend more time on his poetry if possible, was rewarded with a scholarship to study youth organizing in Moscow. Donning kente, the colorful woven fabric reclaimed at independence, Okai took to the dais with participants in a Tashkent Afro-Asian writers conference. Before a large audience, the young writer Okai passionately read out anti-imperialist words in English, translated readily into Russian. Okai joined other African writers in the early moments of their career eager to get an international stage, including the soon-to-be renowned filmmaker and writer Ousmane Sembene of Senegal and Ablokai Usman of Mali.[27] Okai emerged as an expert in Slavic literature, earning graduate degrees in Moscow and London, and went on to become one of Ghana's leading academics and poets.

Media reports in Ghana even went so far as to suggest that Russian culture was African at its heart. During celebrations of the life of Aleksander Pushkin, 125 years after his death in a duel with his brother-in-law, Ghanaians studied photographs of grand monuments to "the Great Afro-Russian poet" in the government's *The Ghanaian Times*. They learned that Pushkin was "a world-renowned Russian poet of African ancestry who was very proud of his ancestors." Indeed, across the USSR could be found monuments to this great man, with Soviet school children annually commemorating the day of his birth. "His works have been translated into many languages and staged in many famous theatres."[28]

Granted, the introduction of Russian as a possible language for scientific and cultural engagement complicated an already-complex linguistic terrain in Ghana. English continued to be the primary language of governance after independence from British rule in 1957. Multilingualism in more than one indigenous Ghanaian language was also common. Many people could converse in Asante Twi, and the related Akan languages of Akuapem Twi and Fante. Twi gained prominence during the rise of the Asante Kingdom from the mid-1600s to the 1800s, a period during which the language was adopted in towns and tributary villages across much of what makes up Ghana and parts of eastern Côte d'Ivoire today. Another major lingua franca in the sub-region was Hausa. Either Twi or Hausa might have made sense as a second national language. In addition, people across Ghana spoke more than 120 other languages including Ewe, Ga, Nzema, Kasem, Gonja, Dagbani, Dangme, and Dagaare. But, since Nkrumah did not want to "fan the embers of tribalism," English provided a vehicle for communication that did not favor a particular ethnic group.[29] In the same way, Russian could be used to unite a diverse population, and Ghanaians were relatively proficient in language acquisition.

Ghanaians were thus well primed and linguistically equipped to take advantage of educational opportunities in the Soviet bloc. In 1960, the Soviet Union announced the establishment of the Friendship of Nations University in Moscow, to aid "the countries of Asia, Africa and Latin America in training their own specialists – engineers, agricultural workers, doctors, teachers, economists etc."[30] The university was later renamed the Patrice Lumumba University after the Congolese nationalist leader who promoted African control of natural resources, including uranium, before his assassination. Indeed, with these gestures, Soviet leaders appeared to be true supporters of efforts to uproot imperialism in African countries.

It was in this moment that Ghanaians interested in learning physics found themselves traveling to the Soviet Union for training. They hoped to increase opportunities for students back home when they returned. Ironically, in order to become proficient in nuclear science themselves, some Ghanaians had to study scientific topics in Russian. In particular, Ghanaian scientists who sought to introduce the benefits of boundless electricity created through nuclear reactions were desperate for access to information and equipment. Ghanaians who studied physics in the USSR participated in a Soviet program to extend socialism, science, and the Russian language to the newly independent countries on the African continent.

"To Know More about Atomic Physics": Ghanaian Sojourns in the Soviet Union

Economic incentives complemented the push for Russian language studies. Ghanaians began to study in the Soviet Union and other communist countries through formal agreements meant to facilitate scientific and technical exchanges and promote trade.[31] In 1960, E. Ayeh-Kumi signed the first Agreement for Economic and Technical Co-operation with the Soviet Union on behalf of the Republic of Ghana. Ghanaians brought the rich resources of the West African nation to the bargaining table. Ghanaians agreed to export agricultural commodities like cocoa, coffee, cola nuts, fruits, and rubber, as well as animal skins. For their part, the Soviets brought technical aid, including education and equipment necessary for mineral processing and prospecting.[32] The Soviets also provided a loan of 160 million roubles (Ghana £15 million). A.J. Dowuona-Hammond, Ghana's Minister of Education, signed a further Agreement on Cultural Co-operation between the Soviet Union and Ghana in Accra, which included training in higher education, provision of scientific consultants, and distribution of books.[33] As part of this later agreement, a protocol outlined the specific number of Soviet scientists, physicians, artists, and footballers to travel to Ghana, and the numbers of Ghanaian researchers and teachers to travel to the Soviet Union.[34] The Ghanaians arranged for Ghanaian students to have technical training in Moscow and other Soviet towns, while the Soviet Union would lend money and skilled workers to help Ghana exploit its mineral resources.

Through these agreements, Ghanaians trained at a number of institutions in the Soviet Union, including the Moscow Energetic Institute at Kurchatov. They gained access to information and training unavailable in Ghana while representatives of Nkrumah's government essentially bartered access to key resources including gold and manganese to the host country. Physics programs at Ghanaian universities remained small in the early 1960s, still emerging from their origins as outgrowths of laboratory work associated with elite boarding schools. The University College of Ghana, now the University of Ghana, Legon, developed a physics program from the workshop at nearby

Achimota Secondary School during the 1940s and early 1950s. During the late colonial period, around 1953, researchers there started using radioisotopes to study the absorption of fertilizers and insecticides in cocoa plants. By the 1960s, the University of Ghana physics department involved several senior staff from the UK and housed a Health Physics and Radioisotopes Unit. A report on activities there in 1961 listed the key activities as monitoring X-rays, measuring radioactive fallout, and examining the potential for radioactivity in food. Several hours north of the coast, the Kumasi College of Technology, later Kwame Nkrumah University of Science and Technology, also included training on radioisotopes for pharmacy students.[35] However, faculty at both Kumasi and Legon were not able to offer extensive courses on nuclear physics adequate to prepare staff for employment at the proposed nuclear reactor.

By January 1964, A.H. Ward, one of the two British physicists on staff at the University of Ghana who helped with radiation monitoring after the French bomb tests, expressed some concerns about the feasibility of finding enough Ghanaian physicists to run a nuclear reactor program. At that point, there were exactly thirteen students expected to graduate with bachelor's degrees in physics from the University of Ghana in June. Their future occupations were already the subject of speculation at the highest levels, with Ward suggesting it was prudent to only assign three to work at the research reactor, with two earmarked to continue for graduate studies at Legon, and the rest assigned to science and math instruction in primary and secondary schools. As described above, expanding scientific education in schools remained a key priority of the manpower component in the government's successive development plans.

Nkrumah's key scientific advisors, including Baffour, had set their sights on the proposed IRT 2000 research reactor to be imported from the Soviets by 1964 (described in Chapter 4). This reactor would require at least "30 top-level scientists and engineers."[36] Factoring in the needs of the National Research Council, Ward, the head of the Radioisotopes and Health Physics Unit at Legon, estimated that Ghana needed roughly sixty "top-level Ghanaian scientists."[37] Nkrumah felt that Ward was not fully supportive of his work with Russian contacts, so by 1965 he had him replaced by Alan Nunn May, a British dissident who had shared nuclear secrets with the Soviets during World War II and spent time in prison. As a visiting Professor in the Physics Department at the University of Ghana, Legon, May received a special appointment from Nkrumah, with a particularly high salary of £3,000 per month. May welcomed speakers like the Russian astronomer D. Shchegolev from the Pulkovo Observatory in Leningrad, who spoke in the Physics Department at Legon on February 15, 1966, three weeks ahead of the coup d'état that ousted Nkrumah.[38]

To increase manpower, Ward had sought Canadian assistance to train students in nuclear physics. However, as Nkrumah and his delegate Baffour made strides with the Soviet Union, the physicists at Legon were initially forced to abandon their plans and cooperate with the Soviet scheme. Baffour pushed scientists at the university to delay efforts to bring in Canadian equipment for a proposed Radio Isotope and Health Physics lab, and to perhaps cancel scholarships for students slated to train in Canada. He was afraid connections with Canada would "embarrass" his Special Atomic Energy Committee, which also hoped to bring in a cyclotron, reactor, and other expensive pieces of equipment for the planned Kwame Nkrumah Nuclear Research Institute through Soviet channels.[39] Initially, Baffour conducted the groundwork "under very secret cover," making it difficult for the physicists in Ghana to know precisely what the Soviets planned to provide.[40] In this atmosphere, it was possible that university faculty working on parallel initiatives would garner duplicates of the same kinds of equipment from both Canada and the Soviet Union. Ironically, once Nkrumah left office, Canada was one of the only countries willing to continue supporting Ghana in its efforts to improve access to radioisotopes training, with training courses staged in Accra.

Ward's proposals for the Canada training scheme list the names of a number of emerging Ghanaian scientists who may have been on the cusp of receiving a scholarship or had already received one to travel to North America. Baffour requested this list of names; not surprisingly, some of the same individuals were then sent to the Soviet Union. After all, there were not that many Ghanaians with tertiary training in physics who might be up to the task. One of the names that appeared on both lists was Lawrence Twum-Danso, discussed below. The Ghanaian Government covered the cost of roundtrip airfare, accommodations, and food for the students, while the Soviet side provided instruction free of charge. Ghana's ambassador in Moscow, John Elliot, orchestrated the visits of Ghanaian officials and constantly pressured Goskomitet, the Soviet State Department, to broker better terms for the Ghanaian side.[41]

It is unclear if the renowned Ghanaian physicist Francis Allotey and eventual head of the Ghana Atomic Energy Commission might have been included in these initial plans, or if Ward and others at Legon were aware of his interest in physics. The son of a general merchant and bookseller on the coast, Allotey was among the first generation of scientists to benefit from a series of schools Nkrumah set up in Ghana at independence. After completing secondary school at the new Ghana National College in Cape Coast, he traveled to the United Kingdom where he studied at South Bank University and Imperial College. He then taught math in Ghana at the Kwame Nkrumah University of Science and Technology from 1960 to 1962. Just as the Soviet scheme was falling into place, he had the opportunity to do his doctoral studies in mathematical physics at Princeton. He wrote a letter to Baffour, who was then Vice-Chancellor of Kwame Nkrumah University of Science and Technology, explaining that his professor at Imperial College had successfully recommended him for a scholarship at Princeton and requesting three years' leave to complete the PhD. Why Baffour did not send him to the Soviet Union after their personal meeting to discuss the scholarship is unclear, though Allotey did stress to Baffour that his hero Albert Einstein had once taught at Princeton and perhaps this trumped Nkrumah's designs.[42] It is plausible that some of Allotey's relative success might be linked to the networks he established in the United Kingdom and the United States, and his good fortune to have to write theses in English, unlike his peers sent to the Soviet Union. His research into condensed matter physics began with his investigations at Princeton on electron-hole scattering.[43] He went on to be Pro Vice-Chancellor of the Kwame Nkrumah University of Science and Technology, head of the Council for Scientific and Industrial Research, as well as head of GAEC on several occasions.[44] Similarly, the Ghanaian physicist Kwaku Aning, who took up key leadership positions at both the IAEA and GAEC, also began graduate work at Princeton in the late 1960s before completing his PhD at Columbia.

For those sent off to the Soviet Union, J.E.O. Lindsay and K.A. Kufuor established the pod of Ghanaian scientists in March 1962. Lindsay was "attached to the Ghana Embassy in Moscow and accorded diplomatic status" in his capacity as liaison officer between Ghana and Moscow on the reactor project.[45] While in Moscow, he wrote his PhD in nuclear science, "Ghana's Programme in the field of the Peaceful Uses of Atomic Energy," presented to the Kurchatov Institute of Atomic Energy, Moscow in 1964. Kufuor also studied at Kurchatov, where he conducted chemical research. According to John Amuasi, other scientists who trained in Moscow between 1962 and 1966 with government sponsorship included Dr. L. Twum-Danso, Dr. S.K. Amasa, Mr. A.A. Baidoo, Mr. J.P.H. Brown, Dr. A.K. Ahafia, Dr. B.W. Garbrah, Dr. Owusu-Bempah, Professor E.K. Agyei, Dr. Ampomah, Mr. Adwedaa, Dr. Lutterodt, Mr. Sekyim-Kwandoh, Mr. A. Osei-Boateng, Professor J.E.O. Lindsay, and Professor F.K. Kufuor.

The initial group of Ghanaians included not only scientists but also technical staff associated with the proposed reactor unit. James Bailey, an electrician, mentioned that he responded to an advertisement in the *Daily Graphic* in 1961 to go train in Moscow for the reactor project at the Moscow Power Engineering Institute.[46] Other Ghanaian technicians who trained with Bailey included the blacksmith A.E. Snyper, the electrician F.E. Aidoo, and Dowuona-Hyde. Apparently these individuals did not receive specific training in electricity and mechanics, but rather joined the other Ghanaians for lectures in physics and other scientific topics.[47]

It is debatable whether the Soviet Union ever intended to provide Ghana with access to a nuclear power reactor large enough to generate electricity, or whether or not they really expected Ghanaian scientists to run even the small research reactor they eventually conceded. But from the perspective of Ghanaian students, traveling to the Soviet Union was definitely a bonafide chance for them to gain information on nuclear physics. Isaac Newton Acquah recalled that he grew up in the time of the atomic bomb. From the 1940s, he was fascinated by nuclear technology.

Actually, I grew up when we [i.e., scientists] were doing testing of nuclear bombs. I remember quite well. And, when we asked our science teachers, they tried to explain it to us. They made me to understand that it was something very, very tiny. And, at the same time what I heard about was discussion of Hiroshima, Nagasaki, small bomb but a big destruction. So, I was so enticed by it, [that I became] interested to know more about atomic physics.[48]

When he learned of Nkrumah's plans to build a reactor, Acquah jumped at the opportunity to go to the Soviet Union to study physics. For Acquah, as for many of the other Ghanaian scientists, one of the biggest hurdles for accessing information on nuclear physics was learning Russian. In his case, he undertook one year of training in the language first, with the second half of the program devoted to mathematical and scientific words. He studied in the Soviet Union from 1961 to 1970, returning only to find that the reactor program had been suspended.

Benjamin Woarabae Garbrah was in the first class to attend the University College of the Gold Coast (UCGC), which later became the University of Ghana, Legon. Initially, Garbrah hoped to study mathematics at UCGC, but when the primary maths lecturer W.W. Sawyer left the country and the remaining one was uninspiring at best, he opted to study physics. In conversations with me, Garbrah expressed he was "more or less the first to study physics, to get a degree," in Ghana. He funded his coursework through a teaching scholarship and was forced to teach upon completion of his studies in physics. "At that stage that was more or less the limit. The colonial government was really focused on teaching. They didn't even imagine that" someday a person like Garbrah would go on to do research in nuclear physics. As the first Ghanaian physics teacher, Garbrah was to educate emerging elites such as the engineer Joseph de Graft-Johnson, Ghana's first Vice President (1979–1981).

Garbrah took a circuitous route to pursue his dream to learn more in the physics field, accepting various positions to grant him further access to information. As one of the highest-trained scientists in Ghana by the mid-1950s, Garbrah was later tapped through the colonial government's Africanization program to work as a factory inspector. Through this role, he traveled to Europe for the first time, to England in 1954 for a short course in factory guidelines. However, he felt factory management was not truly his calling, and he jumped at the opportunity after independence to further his physics education in the Soviet Union in 1962.[49]

He arrived in Moscow in September 1962 with a group of Ghanaian students to study physics in Russian for a nineteen-month program. After an initial three-month training program tailored to his subject of interest, he dived into coursework.

AOA: So you had to learn Russian? So you can read the Russian characters and all that. You can read the letters? You learned how to read Russian in three months?

GARBRAH: Oh yes! That's what I'm saying. They had a very effective way of teaching it. And it was done in such a way that you could follow. And after that, for maybe three months or so, you would attend classes and there would be an interpreter as well, and then after some time the interpreter would be gone. But it was good. It's a difficult language but I liked it.[50]

Garbrah bonded with the others who lived together in a converted hotel, preparing all of their own meals and studying scientific concepts far from family and loved ones. All of the Ghanaians were males in their thirties or older who were intent on studying the necessary information they would need to lead Ghana's nuclear program.

Cohorts of Ghanaians traveled for courses in scientific topics in 1963, 1964, and 1965.[51] Garbrah found that after the first year, when a second batch of students came from Ghana, the Russian instructors repeated all of the lectures from the previous cycle despite requests from the first group for advanced coursework. Frustrated that he could not learn further concepts in physics, Garbrah started to sit in on the chemistry lectures, transitioning into studies in radiochemistry.

Some scientists had a penchant for learning languages and served as interpreters in future years. Lawrence Twum-Danso traveled to the Soviet Union with the initial group sponsored through government support. His colleague, Garbrah recalled, "Twum-Danso was very good at learning languages. He was very good at Russian." In later years when health concerns limited Twum-Danso's ability to speak, he greeted me in Russian and recalled his time at the Moscow Power Engineering Institute in the 1960s. He remained an honored guest at events of the Ghana Atomic Energy Commission, receiving an award in recognition of his contributions to nuclear research at the anniversary celebrations in 2015.

This early period of Africans training in the Soviet Union was not all a bed of roses. African students experienced acute racism alongside challenges learning Russian. William Anti-Taylor, a Ghanaian student who traveled to study at the Friendship University, explained how he was enticed with the offer of a large monthly stipend of 90 roubles, three times what the average Soviet student received: "For many Africans, including myself, the Soviet offer was irresistible, especially when it was made with an assurance that the USSR, the land of the giant rockets, the sputniks and so many other technical and scientific achievements, was a democracy that knew no racial distinctions."[52] Once there, he found himself subject to constant racial profiling and discrimination as well as oppressive instruction in Marxism. He eventually gave up his scholarship and moved to the UK.

Ghanaian popular news reports and memoirs from the period suggest that it was the perceived sexual prowess of black students that precipitated the most egregious incidents, including murders of students from Ghana and other African countries.[53] In 1963, Ghanaian students studying in the Soviet Union marched on the Ghanaian Embassy in Moscow to protest the mysterious death of Ghanaian medical student Edmund Assare-Addo, who they believed to have been murdered for expressing affections toward a Russian woman.[54] In addition, they wanted to be given their stipends in pounds, rather than roubles which they came to view as an unstable currency.[55] It is not clear if any of the nuclear physics students participated in the watershed protest, since they were training at a different university and lived in separate quarters.

The sequestering of Ghanaian physics students in a hotel could also be read, then, as a policy of segregation. However, when it came to keeping the men in the Ghana Atomic Energy training program away from Soviet women, it seems that placing them in a hotel may have backfired. Ghanaian students who trained in nuclear physics through government support remember it as a fairly luxurious experience, and that the quality of their accommodations surpassed that of their peers. Essentially, they were put up in a small hotel, with a room modified into a kitchen where they cooked for themselves. In contrast, their Soviet peers shared rooms in campus buildings. According to interviewees, their apparent prosperity in the hotel served to attract suitors. Young Soviet women saw them as wealthy African princes, which led to romantic relationships. Some of these turned to long-term relationships, with a few even surviving the move back to Accra.

Whilst Garbrah and Twum-Danso received essentially a diplomatic treatment, staying in hotel-caliber accommodations, and others found camaraderie with fellow African students at the Friendship University, others like John Justice Fletcher were posted to universities outside of Moscow where they had to integrate more fully with Soviet campus culture. A pillar of the Ghana Atomic Energy program, the affable Fletcher went to Minsk. He was an avid guitar player who made friends easily, performing on weekends and in his rooms. A gregarious and outgoing man to this day, he enjoyed his time in Minsk. His awareness of differences in skin color, and perhaps the ways that he was treated, mapped onto his research project, where he examined how light and radiation presented on black skin as opposed to white skin. He studied all the way to his PhD, returning after Nkrumah was overthrown:

My topics for the masters, for example, I did something about finding the blood vessels, you know the skin? You have white skin almost, mine is black and to detect – to do something with the veins here – you have to take into account the optical properties of the skin itself and we did something like that and I did plethysmography and all that for my PhD.[56]

Fletcher had a peripatetic career in Ghana. He returned as Garbrah sought to reinvigorate the Ghana Atomic Energy Commission and rose fast within the organization, moving to a top position by the late 1970s. But, after the successive coup d'états in 1979 and 1981, and efforts to import the TRIGA reactor through US support faltered (Chapter 4), he moved to Nigeria, where he taught. Later, he traveled to Libya with his family to supervise radiation services at the Health Physics and Radiation Protection Center at the Libya Nuclear Research Institute in Tajura set up by Muammar Gaddafi.

Technical Assistance: Soviet Scientists in Ghana

Even prior to the training of Ghanaians in the Soviet Union, Soviet scientists and their Ghanaian counterparts developed collaborations at Ghanaian research institutes. After Ghana became independent from Britain, Soviet researchers sought to affiliate with the University College of Ghana.[57] For instance, as early as 1958, I.I. Potekhin, deputy director of the Institute of Ethnography at the Academy of Science in Moscow, traveled to Accra to conduct research on a book about Ghanaian history. The following year, a Soviet graduate student named Pyotr (Peter) Ivanovich Kupriyanov stayed at the University College of Ghana's Akuafo Hall whilst visiting on a UNESCO grant to research "the mode of life and history of African people."[58] Kupriyanov specialized in the sociology of agriculture and complemented his investigations in Ghana with a comparative study in Liberia.[59] Soviet researchers benefited greatly from such hospitality. Kupriyanov became an expert on peasants and agriculture in African countries, later serving as a scientific attaché in Ghana, Liberia, Somalia, and Nigeria for the Soviet Embassy. He went on to become a leading figure at the Institute for African Studies of the Russian Academy of Sciences. The Soviet Academy of Sciences was appreciative of support for such researchers and offered to cover costs for a researcher from the University of Ghana to come to Moscow.[60]

Starting in 1960, government officials began to arrange formal agreements for exchanges of scientists between the two countries.[61] In 1962, leadership at the three main universities in Ghana conferred on whether or not they might require Soviet expertise. In what areas did they require support and what might a visiting Soviet academic provide? The University College of the Cape Coast, established in 1962 through UNESCO support primarily as a teaching training school with focus on science education, declined the offer. The Ghana Academy of Science sought the support of biologists to help with work identifying insects and combatting parasite-borne diseases. The University of Science and Technology looked for assistance with instruction in several departments, including pharmacy and architecture.[62] These universities requested specialists in a number of fields, including pharmacy, parasitology, virology, and veterinary diseases. Ghanaians sought assistance with research on trypanosomiasis (sleeping sickness) in cattle, as well as helminths (worms) in farm animals. They were also hoping to get insights into "less familiar veterinary viruses including Lumpy Skin Disease and Bovine Enzootic Haematuris."[63]

As might be expected, Nkrumah's government was particularly delighted to host nuclear physicists (Figure 3.2). The first group of thirty-eight Soviet specialists arrived in Accra in September 1962, before the Ghanaians had completed their training in Moscow. Thus, Soviet scientists were the first to advise the Ghana Atomic Energy Committee on the construction of the reactor.[64] It is debatable, too, how much faith the Soviet experts had in Ghanaians and their projected acquisition of nuclear physics training. For comparison, when the Soviet Union worked with Cuba on the missile project there, they used Soviet experts, rather than local Cuban staff, to man their operations. Arguably, the Soviet Union may have conceived the training of Ghanaian scientists as a symbolic gesture and planned to run any reactor themselves. From accounts of those involved, the

Figure 3.2 J.E.O. Lindsay, Kwame Nkrumah, and R.P. Baffour (front row) with Soviet advisors for the Nuclear Project, c. 1964
(*Source*: Ghana Atomic Energy Commission)

Soviet team in Ghana divulged very little on the reactor design to local partners; provided most of the key documents in Russian; and left no copies of the blueprints behind.

Ghanaians, for their part, maintained close communication with Soviet scientists and policy-makers. After Ghana was the first African nation to join the IAEA in 1960, the country regularly sent delegations to meetings, where they took up leadership positions. In a report on Ghanaian participation in the 1961 IAEA General Assembly, Quansah and other delegates reported that Soviet and other Eastern Bloc participants were wary about the election of Swedish scientist Sigvard Eklund to be Director General after a four-year term by the American Sterling Cole. Emilanov, part of the Soviet team, claimed that "Eklund had once been prosecuted in his own country for having leaked out Atomic secrets of the Swedish Government to Western Powers, and he dramatically showed a letter that he had received that very day from Sweden, to substantiate his statement." Once Eklund successfully refuted these claims and was elected despite Ghana and several other countries abstaining, Emilanov reportedly conferred with the Ghanaian, "'Well Quansah, in electing Dr. Sigvard Eklund as Director General for the next 4 years the Western Powers have *killed* the Agency.'"[65]

"So I Went There": Further Travels of Russian-Trained Ghanaian Scientists

Upon his return to Ghana in 1964, Garbrah was given a position as the person responsible for Atomic Energy at the Ghana Academy of Sciences, though the reactor was not completed. While the nuclear program was dormant, Garbrah looked for avenues to provide other Ghanaians with training abroad. Disappointed with the pace of atomic energy development in Ghana, he opted to arrange his own scholarship through the International Atomic Energy Agency to study at the Scottish Research Reactor Center in East Kilbride near Glasgow from 1965 to 1967. "Because here there was a National Engineering Laboratory, where they do serious research in various areas: mechanical engineering, whatnot. And there was this reactor there under a research laboratory. So, and since it was a reactor I thought that would be the best place to continue. So I went there." Garbrah used the reactor to experiment with new methods to irradiate materials like boric acid and steel to determine the amount of boron and other minerals present.[66] He found ways to reduce the amount of time needed to keep samples in the reactor using improved shielding methods.

Although Garbrah outpaced his European classmates and completed his doctoral thesis on thermal neutron capture in two years, by the time he returned to Ghana, Nkrumah had been ousted in a coup and the reactor project was in shambles. And yet Garbrah and the others did not give up on their dream of bringing a nuclear reactor to Ghana (Figure 3.3).

There were more sociological problems than scientific, I think. As far as science was concerned, we tried to make do with what we had at that time. And it was also more or less training periods. And my idea was to train more and more people in the hope that the budget was revived. So the emphasis was more or less on training on the campus itself and also outside, and cooperating with the universities.[67]

Figure 3.3 Physics, culture, and religion: Very Reverend Professor Garbrah at home. Note the books on Ghanaian culture (Gye Nyame) alongside *The World of the Atom* and *The Ten Commandments*
(*Source*: author photo)

Ghanaians were extremely flexible in their willingness to travel far and wide, and to study in any language when it came to details on nuclear technology. Between 1962 and 1973, Ghanaian scientists accepted IAEA support for several-month short courses taught in places as far-flung as Finland, Greece, Israel, the US, and also the USSR. With the Ghana Atomic Energy Committee in a dormant period, they taught at the universities. For instance, G.F. Nsowah, who taught at the University of Science and Technology ("Kwame Nkrumah" was temporarily omitted from the name after the leader's downfall) took a one-month study tour to the Soviet Union to learn about using radiation for plant breeding. S.B. Asiedu of the Chemistry Department at the University of Ghana took a year off to learn more about maintaining and operating nuclear equipment in the UK in 1971. Similarly, J.R. Acquah, a faculty member at the University of Science and Technology, managed a nine month course on radiation in the UK.[160] Individuals who had been part of the initial training program that Baffour had set up in Moscow also took advantage of these supplemental courses. For instance, Twum-Danso did a three-month course on radioisotope applications for agriculture, medicine, and industry in the UK.[68]

Ghanaian scientists participated in shorter international conferences related to nuclear physics in addition to longer training courses. After Nkrumah lost power, the Soviet Union continued to court their participation in conferences there through partnerships with the IAEA. For instance, in 1968, J.A. Boateng at the Ministry of External Affairs asked the chairman of the Management Committee of the Ghana Atomic Energy Commission, then based in the Chemistry Department at Legon, to look for scientists interested in traveling to the Third Conference of Plasma Physics and Controlled Nuclear Fusion Research to be held in Novosibirsk in the Soviet Union.[69] Even though Ghanaian scientists had had to put the construction of the Kwame Nkrumah Nuclear Research Institute on hold, they could participate in events looking into possible ways to achieve "the controlled release of fusion energy."[70] Of course, up to now the production of electricity from fusion power stations has yet to be achieved. Yet, in the earliest moments of theorizing on fusion reactions, Ghanaians were keen to sit with their scientific peers and speculate on the latest technologies.

Given their high levels of training in nuclear physics, Acquah and Garbrah emerged as key liaisons between subsequent Ghanaian governments and Soviet scientists once the Soviet scheme collapsed and pieces for the reactor lay in storage in Ghana. The post-Nkrumah situation put Ghana in a very challenging position as the Soviet scientific team absconded with the blueprints for the reactor and key components. Once the new government decided to reactivate the program in 1974, Acquah was asked to go through all the boxes that were in storage to determine if anything from the original nuclear reactor could be salvageable ahead of a return visit of Russian experts. He described this as a "very, very big task" that ran from October 1974 to March 1975. The materials were in storage in a large room. And Acquah found that it "contained many, many things [for the reactor]. Everything was there. Of course, with the exception of fuel. I think fuel was the thing coming, but the fuel was then diverted back to Russia [after the 1966 coup]." But when the Russian experts arrived, they found that some of the key components were rusted and that it would take a lot of time and money to upgrade the facility.[71]

Given this disappointing news, between 1975 and 1980, Acquah went to Slovenia to do his PhD, where he researched extending the life of nuclear reactors. He learned the specifics of reactor construction and maintenance and gained entry to nuclear techniques unavailable in his home country. Ironically, this time when Acquah returned to Ghana in 1981, there had been another pivotal coup d'état. The political instability in Ghana coincided with the Three Mile Island meltdown in Pennsylvania in the United States, further hindering an ongoing effort to import a US-made reactor. Between 1985 and 2000, Acquah was invited to relocate to the IAEA in Vienna where he worked as an inspector, traveling to East Asian countries to monitor reactors to make sure that there was no proliferation of nuclear weapons. He gradually retired to Ghana, where he reconnected with GAEC scientists to train up the next generation.

An important legacy of the Soviet-era support for Ghanaian nuclear physics has been the highly trained nationalist scientists who have worked tirelessly to sustain Ghana's nuclear program. It has been these scientists who have taken up the charge to train new generations of physicists. In a sense, they have realized the afterlife of Nkrumah's dream. Their constant attention to Ghana's atomic future meant that once a reactor arrived, there were still scientists available to make use of it at long last. Benjamin Nyarko was one of the scientists who worked to install the GHARR-1. He recalled the enthusiasm at GAEC during the period: "we'd been learning about reactors in school, and all those things, but we'd never seen how the real reaction even takes place." Nyarko worked with the team to make sure that the reactor would be operational by the close of 1994. Once the reactor was in the country, the young scientists could not be stopped. Nyarko explained, "we were excited to work with the Chinese and get the thing done. And I quite remember in 1994, those of us who were with the reactor, we didn't go for Christmas, because we were still doing the installation. The reactor went critical in December, on December 17, 1994. And that was a great day in the life of some of the scientists who are here."[72] Similarly, Amuasi smiled and recalled how, "So, in '95 the Commission was in high spirits."

The advent of a reactor at GAEC gave the commission new energy, prompting a generation of scientists to consider staying in Ghana to conduct research there. The GHARR-1's advocates envisioned many uses for it, not only for scientists, but also for Ghana's industrial, agricultural, and medical sectors. At long last, Ghanaians could produce their own short-lived radioisotopes locally, an original objective of the Nkrumah-era reactor. One of the first projects for scientists at the Commission was to calibrate the reactor and investigate the ideal amount of time to run the reactor before a cooling-off period. With the reactor, Ghanaian scientists went on to study the absorption of radioactive particles in herbal medicines, archeological samples, mineral ores, and foodstuffs. Over the next two decades, the reactor allowed them to develop new kinds of experiments without the hassle of traveling abroad with samples of archeological finds, foodstuffs, or other items they planned to study. They also cooperated with the International Atomic Energy Agency's efforts to substitute in new types of enriched uranium that are virtually impossible to repurpose into material for bombs.

Even as they were fading from view, some of the earlier Ghanaian scientists sought to spark more generations of nuclear advocates. Victoria Appiah recalled that, by the early twenty-first century, the majority of nuclear physicists in Ghana were close to retirement.[73] She along with a cadre of other retired scientists came to start the School of Nuclear and Allied Sciences to teach the younger generation what they knew of nuclear physics. One of the leaders at the Ghana School for Nuclear and Allied Sciences (SNAS) was Fletcher, often visible on campus in a Ghana Nuclear Society polo shirt, chatting with students and faculty alike at the school's canteen. According to Fletcher, "I came back when they started the SNAS. I was heading the biggest, in terms of load. I taught almost all of the courses."[74] Similarly, Garbrah and Acquah joined the faculty there after their retirements. Their tireless efforts to conserve the strides made in learning nuclear physics fit within models of resharing knowledge of nuclear technology to maintain tacit knowledge across generations.[75]

A key legacy of the Soviet-trained scientists has been hundreds of publications with their many students. Alongside new generations of physicists, they worked on designing new casks for the country's research reactor.[76] In particular, the medical physics instruction was a high point. Fletcher's students and collaborators went on examine the radiation dosages among X-ray operators, television workers exposed to high radio frequencies, and children who underwent brain magnetic resonance imaging.[77]

Today, students at the School of Nuclear and Allied Sciences study in English, but their professors gleaned information on nuclear engineering, nuclear medicine, nuclear chemistry, nuclear physics, and related topics in several different languages and trained and worked around the world. In addition to Ghanaian students, the IAEA has partnered with the school to train students from across Africa, making Ghana's nuclear program a regional hub for information exchange with other anglophone African countries. This facilitates relations between African research institutions and atomic energy commissions, as many nuclear researchers have trained at Kwabenya. For instance, Mungubariki Nyaki from the Tanzania Atomic Energy Commission did a fellowship through IAEA support. He commented to me that, compared to his experience in Tanzania, he had observed a greater public understanding in Ghana of the role of nuclear science. "I have been here for 4 weeks in Ghana, but I understand that people are aware about the base applications of the nuclear science and radiation. They are aware. [Ghanaian scientists] have tried their best to foster public awareness."[78] He also felt that there were more female nuclear physicists in Ghana and was impressed with the quality of the science training in Ghana at the tertiary level.

Conclusions: Ghanaian Science in Russian

The early 1960s marked a transition for African countries, and the Soviet Union systematically worked to win converts to Russian scientific dominance. At this point, there was a linguistic war underway for the language of international science. Africans were eager to learn scientific concepts, like nuclear fission, and desperate enough to endure Russian language training along the way. This provided a terrain for the Soviet Union to expand Russian linguistic imperialism beyond the USSR and Soviet bloc. Russian emerged as yet another language in the extensive linguistic repertoire of young Ghanaian scientists. Non-African languages were therefore central to the fashioning of a new national identity in Ghana.

Questions of the language of science education in Ghana have resonance in more recent times. In 2016, the government of President John Mahama announced that all Ghanaian students would learn basic subjects in indigenous languages at the elementary-school level (a policy that did not see full fruition before his party lost the presidency in the next election). Six decades after independence, when English had clearly come to the fore in the "scientific babel," this was a surprising decision, but one that harkened back to the days of independence when Nkrumah's regime was casting about as to how best to express scientific concepts for mass adoption.[79]

The lasting legacy of the importation of Russian physics in Ghana can be seen in the nuclear reactor buildings that lingered on the landscape at Kwabenya. These hulking mementos of Nkrumah's fascination with science and the promise of nuclear riches tormented a generation who sacrificed everything to learn physics in Russian. In the shadow of the reactor buildings, a generation of Ghanaian scientists sought further training abroad and employment elsewhere as Ghana's economy floundered, whether in Gaddafi's Libya, or for the IAEA in Vienna. These Ghanaian scientists gleaned information on nuclear physics from different sources and shared information with subsequent generations of Ghanaian students as they gradually returned. Through sustained efforts, they made atomic work an African pursuit. Despite many setbacks, the Ghana Atomic Energy Commission, and later the Ghana School of Nuclear and Allied Sciences at Kwabenya, became a research hub where students from across Ghana and from other African countries traveled to learn how to become atomic scientists, in English.

4 | *Atomic Reactors: A Fission Facility for Ghana*

A ghostly shell of a building rises up from a hill on the outskirts of Accra. It dates to the years of Ghana's first president Kwame Nkrumah. The building is a great big cube with a flat roof, and a wall of windows without any panes. Behind it and slightly to the west are four stout concrete water tanks (Figures 4.1 and 4.2). This is the site where Ghana once planned to install a Soviet-made atomic reactor. In front of the old reactor building are the well-groomed grounds of the Ghana Atomic Energy Commission. Here, in the shadows of the abandoned reactor building, scientists fanned the embers of Nkrumah's smoldering nuclear power program, hoping to someday import a nuclear reactor into the small coastal African nation. Walking the paths between the laboratories, listening to scientists reminisce, and poring over years of abandoned reports and proposals, I gather stories behind the long quest for Ghana's first nuclear reactor.

The challenges of bringing a reactor to Kwabenya greatly shaped the experience of Ghanaian nuclear physicists who persevered through difficult circumstances. Even with a research reactor in place from 1994, they continued to lobby for larger reactors capable of generating power. Reflecting on his career at the Ghana Atomic Energy Commission (GAEC) over four decades, former director John Humphrey Amuasi recalled, "Nkrumah's dream was first of all to play with a research reactor and then later on to get a nuclear power reactor to supplement, or augment, the hydroelectric dam. This was his dream. Unfortunately, we did not give him [the] chance to complete this."[1] Nkrumah's vision of an African country with access to atomic power propelled those invested in Ghana's nuclear future, like Amuasi, forward. Taking their stories as a launch pad, we uncover a fuller view of the dimensions of Nkrumah's plans and some of the political, economic, and scientific reasons why they were thwarted for so many years.

In this chapter, I go inside the gates of the Ghana Atomic Energy Commission to understand why scientists spent five decades working

Figure 4.1 Original reactor building, Ghana Atomic Energy Commission
(*Source*: author photo)

Figure 4.2 Old water tanks, Ghana Atomic Energy Commission
(*Source*: author photo)

toward installing the GHARR-1. Each section focuses on the specific sets of "equipment" or reactor parts that Ghanaians hoped to import during each period, and the political landscape that shaped the ill-fated journeys of these proposed reactors. I have integrated oral testimonies of Commission scientists and their written perspectives on events, especially Amuasi's comprehensive fortieth-anniversary publication, with archival records gleaned from a number of sites, including the Commission Library, Ghana Public Records and Archives Administration Department, United Kingdom Public Record Office, Chinese Foreign Ministry Archives, International Atomic Energy Agency, and United States Department of State. This case study shows how Ghanaian scientists sustained Nkrumah's vision of scientific equity from their hill at Kwabenya, believing they could be stakeholders in nuclear technology in the face of domestic and international resistance.

"An Experimental Nuclear Reactor in the Gold Coast"[2]: Atomic Dreams Before Nkrumah

Despite the idea, commonly expressed at the Ghana Atomic Energy Commission today, that the dream of importing a reactor began with Nkrumah, my research suggests that physicists have been lobbying for a reactor close to Achimota for some time.[3] While the country was still under colonial rule, a British professor of physics at the University College of the Gold Coast, H.E. Huntley, provided the United Kingdom with the opportunity to supply fissile material for a small reactor he hoped to import to the small colony. As early as May 1956, Huntley expressed interest in purchasing a £100,000 swimming pool reactor from the British company Associated Electrical Industries, both to run experiments and to train young physicists.[4] Huntley argued that it would be good to introduce a reactor to the West African region as nuclear power reactors would undoubtedly become the norm and require experts to manage them. Huntley was actually competing with another physicist at the Kumasi College of Science and Technology who also hoped to get a reactor for a proposed engineering program at the rival school. The secretary of development for the Gold Coast colony also seemed to think that reactors were going to be commonly sited around the world, requesting that his colony "get a tentative place in the queue" for export of fissionable material.[5]

With independence in the eaves, the colonial authorities back in London regarded these requests with some concern, stating it would involve a "long process of discussions" and "no assurance can be given that fissile material will be made available."[6] The suppliers of the reactor claimed that they were overwhelmed with demand and could not take on new orders for at least a year. For their part, the United Kingdom Atomic Energy Authority said they would need to have a training center in place for a couple of years before allowing for the reactor to be imported into the Gold Coast.[7]

Huntley suggested the location near Achimota for its convenience, where it would be both near campus and a short drive from the airport to streamline the transport of uranium. Nkrumah had a connection to the area – he had graduated from Achimota Secondary School in 1930 – but Huntley only began to supervise activities at the workshop of the Achimota Engineering School in 1951 (later integrated into the Gold Coast College), so it is unlikely Ghana's first president overheard discussions on the reactor there.[8] It is, however, plausible that Nkrumah, with his leading role in governmental affairs as Prime Minister of the Colonial Government beginning in 1952, might have been obliquely aware of Huntley's proposal when it passed through government channels the year before independence.

The idea of an African colony housing a nuclear reactor was not so far-fetched. After all, the Belgian Congo colony had installed a US-made 50kW TRIGA Mark I nuclear reactor at the University of Lovanium, now the University of Kinshasa, shortly after the Gold Coast toyed with the idea of getting one. In this case, Congo was lucky enough to have ample natural deposits of uranium that could be processed to make fuel. The Belgians had supplied uranium from the Congo to the United States for use in the atomic bombs dropped in Japan. In return, the United States supported peaceful nuclear research in Belgium at the Nuclear Center in Mol and Interuniversity Institute of Nuclear Sciences after the war.[9] Luc Gillon, a priest and the head of the University of Lovanium in the Belgium Congo (now University of Kinshasa in the Democratic Republic of Congo) who trained as a nuclear physicist at Princeton, collected some extra small pieces of equipment for radioisotope research and Geiger counters from Belgium to use in the Congo. Gillon then learned about TRIGA reactors at an exposition in Geneva in 1956 and managed to import one to his university by January 1959. Initially, the US representative demonstrating how it might be used asked him why a missionary would want "to buy a reactor for pygmies" but Gillon lobbied physicists in Belgium for their support.[10]

While a small 50kW reactor of the sort installed in the Congo used far less uranium, and created less plutonium byproducts, than was used to create the bombs that destroyed Nagasaki and Hiroshima, the links between research reactors and bombs were stronger in the 1950s and 1960s than they are today. Small quantities of fissionable plutonium produced in research reactors could be hoarded and used to create an explosive device capable of releasing radioactive particles. To limit this possibility, nations with nuclear weapons, which at this point included the United States, the United Kingdom, and the Soviet Union, aimed to be the purveyors of both reactors and the necessary fuel.[11] For example, through the Atoms for Peace initiative, President Dwight Eisenhower's government in the United States supplied low-power research reactors and enriched uranium fuel to "friendly nations," beginning with a small reactor sent to Geneva, and later the one installed in Kinshasa, with plans to roll out many more.[12] Countries like the United States already had research reactors sited in small research units and on university campuses by the mid-1950s, including a small reactor at Pennsylvania State University where I grew up and where my Ghanaian father was an engineering professor. The first nuclear reactors for civilian use provided researchers with access to radioactive isotopes (or radioisotopes), unstable atoms often with short half-lives. A variety of radioisotopes, including carbon-14 and sulfur-35, were then employed in scientific investigations, especially to trace chemical processes in organisms. Institutions with research reactors supplied biologists and others with the radioactive elements, making ownership of a reactor a goal for small nations interested in expanding their radiation research capabilities.[13]

By the late 1950s, larger nuclear reactors held the promise of efficiently creating vast amounts of electricity without the use of coal.[14] The Soviet Union built the first reactor capable of generating sustained power in 1954 in Obninsk, a town south of Moscow. The 5,000kW reactor was the earliest of its kind to provide electricity for civilians for use in their homes.[15] The United States followed with its first commercial electric reactor in 1957, a 60,000kW plant installed at the Shippingport Atomic Power Station near the city of Pittsburgh.[16] To regulate emerging nuclear energy technologies globally, the United

Nations established the International Atomic Energy Agency in July of the same year. When Ghana became the first nation south of the Sahara to gain independence from a European colonial occupier on March 6, 1957, a nuclear reactor was one in a series of technological achievements that caught the imagination of nationalist leaders.[17] With Ghanaians free of imperial rule, why not release atoms for the use of Africans as well? This is in part what Kwame Nkrumah sought to do when he led calls for large nuclear reactors to power his new nation to an industrialized, futuristic utopia.

"This Significant Technological Achievement"[18]: Ghana Goes Pro-Atom

After Ghana's independence from Britain in 1957, Nkrumah renewed efforts to bring a reactor into the country. Ostensibly, Nkrumah's interest in nuclear research was solely for peaceful purposes. His public stance differed from that of Indian Prime Minister Jawaharlal Nehru, who had quickly built up a nuclear program after independence from Britain ten years prior, stressed the military applications of nuclear physics in government policy, and went on to exploit the Atoms for Peace initiative to get a research reactor to begin stockpiling plutonium byproducts for India's first bomb.[19] In contrast, Nkrumah strayed away from pronouncements about the potential for nuclear weaponry in Ghana. Atomic energy was part of his overall passion for science. Further, he situated nuclear access within a Left, socialist framework, as opposed to Right, conservative Indian politicians who claimed the atom.[20]

Nkrumah and his associates closely monitored the rise of nuclear technology in other African countries and colonies, coveting not only a reactor, but also uranium deposits. Individuals like Robert P. Baffour, the engineer and first president of the University of Science and Technology who also initially headed "The Ghana Atomic Energy Committee for the Peaceful Uses of Atomic Energy," had established communication with scientists in the United Arab Republic (UAR, now Egypt and Syria) by the early 1960s. He sent word from Kumasi to Nkrumah's office at Flagstaff House confirming that geologists in the UAR had identified deposits of valuable uranium. Baffour speculated on the implications for a planned radioisotopic research center in Cairo and the UAR's potential to "divert the use of the nuclear reactor they now possess to the manufacture of atomic weapons."[21] For while African countries at this point explored the uses of nuclear technology for peaceful purposes, the possibility of redeploying enriched uranium for weapon preparation always hovered over negotiations for equipment and fuel.

On the surface, it seems, Nkrumah was pro-atom, but anti-bomb. Publicly, Nkrumah situated Ghana as a broker of peace between world powers in an escalating contest for nuclear weapons. He continued to reproach the French for conducting tests in the Sahara Desert, working to establish a nuclear-weapons-free zone in Africa. Overall, he liked to depict himself as a world spokesperson on nuclear disarmament, making it his *cause célèbre*. As a writer for *The Ghanaian Times* declared, "Osagyefo Dr. Kwame Nkrumah has travelled from Africa to Europe and from Asia to America pleading for a world without the bomb."[22] At international gatherings, Nkrumah boldly stood in the middle of the nuclear weapons debate, speaking personally with both Americans and Soviet politicians in a bid to encourage disarmament. He first broached the subject with Soviet leader Nikita Khrushchev during their meeting in New York City in 1960 when Nkrumah delivered a speech to the United Nations condemning atomic weapons.[23] His efforts were not completely discounted; officials from the United States Department of State met with Nkrumah in Accra seeking his assistance in getting the Soviets to open up their nuclear warehouses to inspection.[24] It is unclear how much Nkrumah knew about the nuclear arsenals of different countries and to what extent he shared this information with various leaders, especially John F. Kennedy, with whom Nkrumah was friendly. Indeed, when Nkrumah asked Chairman Mao Zedong (Tse-tung) of China to support his bid to remove nuclear weapons from the world, Mao's advisors felt that Nkrumah might be acting as "a spy for the States to test whether China wanted to further develop nuclear weapons and become a powerful nuclear country."[25]

Indeed, we cannot rule out the interest of Ghanaian officials in someday obtaining access to nuclear technologies sufficient to manufacture a nuclear weapon. In a secret memo in early 1960, Joe Annan at the Ministry of Defence reported on his experience visiting the headquarters of the newly established International Atomic Energy Agency. Annan's correspondence provides one of the first written records of the Nkrumah administration's plans for nuclear research. In his correspondence he explicitly noted, "this Ministry's interest in the subject lies in the manufacture and use of atomic weapons." However, he emphasized that Ghana should identify a representative "to serve on any committee or other similar body that may be set up to deal with the peaceful uses of atomic energy."[26] Annan's letters appear to have been forwarded to Nkrumah, providing necessary advice to his regime on Ghana's nuclear potential. Both the renowned Chinese ambassador to Ghana Hua Huang and his advisors in Beijing during the period suspected that Nkrumah's aims to create peaceful uses for nuclear physics were merely a screen. The Chinese observers did not believe that there were any countries that would volunteer to give up nuclear technology and the option to develop bombs themselves, even Ghana.[27]

One of the earliest newspaper reports on Ghana's nuclear plans included the misleading explanation that a proposed "nuclear research institute ... will also be used for the study of peaceful uses of nuclear explosives for excavation, mining and recovery of gas and oil."[28] The report in *The Ghanaian Times* attributed this to B.W. Garbrah, the physicist sent to Moscow State University to study nuclear engineering. Garbrah made a presentation entitled "Atomic Energy Development in Ghana" on his return to the Kwame Nkrumah University of Science and Technology. The next day the newspaper printed a retraction after an "urgent correction" from the Ghana News Agency. They downplayed the role of nuclear explosives with a new explanation that while in his presentation to the Ghana Group of Professional Engineers Garbrah "traced the history of atomic energy and said the energy of the atom could and had been used to make atomic bombs but the Ghana Atomic Energy Commission had been charged by an Act of Parliament 'to promote only the peaceful uses of atomic energy.' He went on: 'So the destructive use of the atomic energy is ruled out straight-away.'" The correction noted that Garbrah said any efforts to use nuclear explosives in the mining sector was "rather in an early stage of development."[29] The early reporting belies the level of popular confusion on a subject in which only a few Ghanaian scientists were trained at this point. It is also the only reference I have found to the development of "peaceful explosives" under the guise of improving the mining sector. The mining and refining of gold ore within Ghana especially was a major component of Nkrumah's development plans to increase wealth for the nation with the construction of a modern gold refinery in the key mining town of Tarkwa.[30]

If Nkrumah's public position that "no matter what country holds them and no matter their size and nature, bombs are bad" was "as clear as crystal," he could not quite hide his awe of atomic weaponry in certain instances. In this sense, he represented the postcolonial ambivalence about the promise of nuclear science that historian Itty Abraham has demonstrated for India and other nations in the Cold War period.[31] Initially, in his relations with Chinese leaders on the topic of nuclear armaments, Nkrumah sought their support for a ban on bomb tests in Africa and the curtailment of nuclear weapons worldwide. However, when the People's Republic of China successfully exploded a nuclear device in October 1964, Nkrumah wrote a letter congratulating Mao Zedong on "this significant technological advancement by China" as "a positive indication of what the developing nations are capable of doing, given the necessary resources in men and material."[32] Nkrumah joined Indonesia and Mali among other emerging nations in publicly applauding the tests – a somewhat surprising stance given his activism against French testing just a few years earlier.[33] In his correspondence with Mao, Nkrumah did lament the proliferation of atomic weapons, even as he applauded the China's impressive "advancement." He further raised the flag of socialism, stating, "Now is the time to bring about harmony in the socialist camp" to prevent nuclear war and bolster "the liberation movement in Africa and Asia."[34] Similarly, the *Ghanaian Times* published a statement from the Chinese Communist Party expressing that "the test was a blow at the U.S. imperialist policy of nuclear monopoly and blackmail and a great encouragement to all peace-loving people."[35]

While claiming non-alignment, Nkrumah's cooperation with both Americans and Soviets, and increasingly Chinese trade officials and diplomats, confused Western observers and made them nervous. At stake were Ghana's rich resources and Nkrumah's influence on anticolonial movements in other parts of Africa with vast gold, manganese, diamond, and other mines. Nkrumah staunchly opposed capitalist and colonial forces and supported Patrice Lumumba, the first leader of independent Congo (Zaire) who was to be assassinated with Belgian, British, and American support for his efforts to implement African control of Belgian-held mines.[36] Meanwhile, Nkrumah gladly accepted private investment in Ghana's massive hydroelectric project through a relationship with the Kaiser Company of the United States, all at the same moment that CPP members publicly espoused the dangers of capitalism and private industry, working toward a socialist economy for Ghana.[37] At a ceremony to mark the final phase of construction of the Volta Dam, with the director of the Kaiser Engineers at his side, Nkrumah liberally poured out a stream of gin from a bottle, in a traditional gesture to call on the blessings of the gods through libations. A newspaper photo purported to show the gush of gin spilling on the ground as Nkrumah tipped it from his hand with a flourish in front of baffled white onlookers.[38] Exasperated with his embrace of both Soviet and American support, and perhaps also traditional and modern lifestyles, an American spy told Nkrumah that he and his supporters could not "have things both ways."[39]

Nkrumah joined Indian Prime Minister Jawaharlal Nehru and Egyptian President Gamal Nasser in a quest for what Kenyan political theorist Ali Mazuri would term, "not a neutrality in major debates, but the right of independent participation in international affairs."[40] The extent to which Nkrumah did believe it was possible to court both the Soviets and the Americans in his power plans, and the eventual demise of his regime, rests on the story of the failed Soviet nuclear reactor at the Kwame Nkrumah Nuclear Research Institute, and Western discomfort with an emergent African nuclear power.

"Our Friendship is Unbreakable!"[41]: Soviet Support for a Reactor

On November 19, 1960, Nkrumah met with members of Ghana's National Research Council at their fourth meeting. Nkrumah joined Member of Parliament Kojo Botsio; Minister Kofi Baako, responsible to the President for Research; R.P. Baffour, the engineer who headed the Kumasi University of Science and Technology, later named after Kwame Nkrumah; and several others. During this meeting, Nkrumah discussed the upcoming visit of the International Atomic Energy Agency fact-finding mission to Ghana, scheduled for February 1961, and appointed a Scientific Committee to consider the possibility of getting an atomic reactor for Ghana. According to meeting minutes, Nkrumah initially appointed F.E.V. Smith, Executive Secretary of the National Research Council, as Chair of the Committee, with other members, including Baffour and physicists Wright and Ward, along with Ghanaian scientists J.E.O. Lindsay and S.T. Quansah. Nkrumah felt that this core group, already engaged with plans for an expanded radioisotope unit and trusted confidants for him on radioactive fallout and monitoring, would be best suited to bring this dream to fruition. In particular, Nkrumah was to find that Baffour and Lindsay remained supportive of the scheme, even when it faltered after his overthrow.[42] The British researchers Smith, Wright, and Ward were to depart from Ghana, leaving Baffour, Lindsay, and Quansah, who replaced Smith as Executive Secretary of the National Research Council, to orchestrate the reactor project.

Government scientists and officials soon turned to the Union of Soviet Socialist Republics for assistance in realizing Nkrumah's elaborate engineering projects, including the reactor scheme. Nkrumah and Soviet leader Nikita Khrushchev emphasized that the burgeoning relationship between the two nations was one of mutual benefit built on friendship. "Ghano-Soviet Friendship," proclaimed the headlines in Accra after the first Ghana trade mission to Moscow in May 1960 (see Figure 4.3). Cultural gifts facilitated this trip; Kojo Botsio and his colleagues draped the Soviet head with a toga made from Asante kente, the iconic woven silk fabric in bright hues that the independence regime used to represent national heritage. *Pravda* similarly stated, "Our Friendship is Unbreakable!" when Nkrumah stood on the dais flanked by Soviet leaders during his July 1961 visit to Moscow, the flags of the two nations waving side by side on poles of equal footing.[43] When Khrushchev visited Accra on the invitation of Nkrumah in July 1962, he exclaimed, "the Soviet people, always with understanding and friendly sympathies, regard kindly the nation of Ghana, which occupies a worthy place in the avant-garde fight for the independence of all African nations from colonialism. Our intention is in the future to support and develop bonds of great friendship between nations, striving for freedom and independence in the bright future of man. The nation of Ghana can depend on the nations of the Soviet Union, as its unselfish, sincere and devoted friends."[44]

Newspapers in Ghana frequently ran stories with statements from Nikita Khrushchev, often with the same stock portrait, including his provocative statement at the Bandung meeting of non-aligned nations in 1955 as African countries surged toward independence that "the world must make one big coffin of colonialism."[45] Before the two leaders had even met, the *Evening News* stressed that Khrushchev had personally told the Ghanaian Ambassador to the Soviet Union, John Banks Elliot, that "the Soviet people ... have genuine sympathy for our

Figure 4.3 Soviet leader in kente in Moscow
(*Source*: *Ghana Evening News*, May 12, 1960)

aspirations and appreciate our difficulties. They are most friendly and
have love for everyone, especially people from Africa." Elliot explained
that, " 'We are fostering cordial relationship … within the framework
of our foreign policy of non-alignments and positive neutralism.' "[46]

From the perspective of Ghanaians, this level of respect was very
important to the fashioning of a postcolonial identity. By 1960,
Ghanaian officials signed a series of cultural and economic cooperation agreements with the Soviet Union, including a further agreement
with the USSR Committee for the Peaceful Uses of Atomic Energy.[47]
Initial press reports indicate that the Soviets planned to help with a
series of medium-capacity hydroelectric stations, although this did not
come to pass, with Nkrumah cooperating instead with private outfits
in the United States and Canada for the Volta River hydroelectric dam
project.[48] In January 1961, a scientific delegation left Accra to travel
to Moscow. Their mission, their *amanee*, was a nuclear reactor for
Ghana. Baffour, who now served as head of the Ghana Atomic Energy
Committee, led the delegation; Lindsay also took part. Baffour was
convinced that a series of top-level meetings in Moscow would get

him both the research and power reactors that Nkrumah had initially requested.[49]

On the eve of the International Atomic Energy Agency mission to Ghana, the delegation hoped to nail down the details of the atomic energy component of the exchange with the Soviets. While in Moscow, Baffour corresponded with Nkrumah through Ghana's ambassador to the Soviet Union. On February 22, Baffour received a message from Nkrumah to "do your best to have a preliminary Agreement of Intent signed before coming [home] on both the isotope reactor and the power reactor. I also want to reopen the question of the monitoring equipment for radioactive fall-out as part of this scheme."[50] Initially, in May 1961, it seemed that the Soviet Union had agreed to supply Ghana with an actual power reactor, along with the research one. It was to be modeled on similar reactors that the Soviets were then in the process of installing in a number of other countries, as I describe below.

The negotiations around a nuclear reactor corresponded to increasing ties between Ghana and the Soviet Union. But during this time, Nkrumah built relationships abroad beyond the Soviets. In August 1961, Ghana's Minister for Light and Heavy Industries, Krobo Edusei, led a trade delegation to Peking (Beijing), where he signed a Trade and Payments Agreement between Ghana and the People's Republic of China.[51] This was followed by the trip of Premier Zhou Enlai to Ghana. Even as Chinese and Soviet relations deteriorated in this period, Nkrumah continued his approach of seeking resources and inspiration from opposing parties. He increasingly styled himself as an independent communist leader, sometimes going by "Premier," hopeful that relations with the Soviet Union especially would allow him to pursue major development initiatives like a nuclear power program.

"Ghana Trying to Run Before it Had Learnt to Walk"[52]: British Scrutiny of Ghana's Nuclear Plans

When news of negotiations between Ghana and the Soviet Union on nuclear technology filtered to the United Kingdom, its former colonial occupier, officials were flabbergasted and confused. What were Ghanaians negotiating precisely with the Soviets? Which way would the endeavor go? It was several months, at least, before British spies obtained details of the agreement on a reactor.[53]

In the meantime, the British Foreign Office, Ministry of Science, and Board of Trade employees debated several tactics to avoid Soviet domination in an emerging field of nuclear physics in the "young African states."[54] First, they were disappointed that Canada had not agreed to supply Ghana with a reactor.[55] They were, however, keenly aware of the recent relationship between Canada and India, where Indian scientists used their imported reactor to create excess plutonium and eventually, as we know now, the development of the first atom bomb in South Asia.

While British officials did not explicitly mention the possibility of Nkrumah getting a bomb, their paternalist perspective toward Nkrumah was especially clear in discussions of the reactor proposal. If it was not enough that Ghanaians sought a seat on the governing board of the International Atomic Energy, they wanted power reactors, too![56] In a letter to the Commonwealth Relations Office, one official expressed that he felt Nkrumah's government was "trying to run before it had learnt to walk."[57] As far as another was concerned, "there are no scientists in Ghana."[58] Nkrumah was, of course, familiar with the staged theories of economic development and scientific growth, but he firmly espoused the belief that Ghanaians could catch up and become stakeholders in modern science.[59] In his view, "no nation had a monopoly on ability," so there was no reason why Ghanaians with proper training could not achieve what those in France or the United Kingdom could muster.[60] Nkrumah rejected the "racialist" view of Africans that colonists had once used to justify their occupation of the Gold Coast, and now used to restrict access to atomic reactors. As far as Nkrumah was concerned, Ghanaians could become nuclear physicists and they could manage their own fission reactions.

Quite reluctantly, British officials were forced to consider that the first of their African colonies to gain independence might quickly emerge as a nation with atomic energy capabilities, given Nkrumah's ardent quest for nuclear technology. The foreign office thought that an ideal solution would be for a British company to sell a reactor to Ghana. This way, the United Kingdom could avoid directly intervening in the affairs of the former colony, but could still retain some level of dependence and accountability. The reactor the officials had in mind was called a JASON reactor, created by Nuclear Engineering Ltd., owned by the Hawker Siddeley Nuclear Power Company. It is interesting to note that they did not even float the possibility of installing reactors large enough to generate electricity, as the Soviets had at the start of their negotiations with Nkrumah.

Siddeley was intent on tapping the underserved "Southern Hemisphere" market, where demand for nuclear reactors and isotopes was growing. Siddeley appreciated that scientists around the world were increasingly adopting nuclear technology; nuclear physics was not the sole purview of the United States, the United Kingdom, the Soviet Union, or France. The company had tracked the interest of more than 1000 individuals who had studied nuclear physics and experimented with British reactors through an initiative run by the United Kingdom Atomic Energy Authority and the Harwell Reactor School. Siddeley noted that these individuals were keen to continue their experiments, especially in the medical and agricultural sectors, but "a reactor on the spot is the only means of obtaining short-lived radioisotopes, which cannot be brought from Europe or North America, even by air, in time to be used effectively."

Unless a post-graduate student is provided with the means to continue and expand his work at home, he will inevitably wish to emigrate, instead of helping to build up in his own country the scientific traditions which her future must largely depend.[61]

Siddeley could sell to interested nations a JASON research reactor for research purposes, which included the ability to manufacture medical isotopes (Figure 4.4). The company estimated the costs for one of these reactors to be approximately £75,800. For additional fees, Siddeley could provide fuel plates containing enriched uranium-235. From correspondence, it seems that Siddeley may have put together a proposal for Ghana, but details on Nkrumah's response are not available.

The British officials additionally floated the concept of a training program for African nuclear physics in Ghana, which would be accessible to individuals from other emerging nations. This was a meager response to the Soviet Union's offer to actually train Ghanaians at a high level in Moscow at the Khrushchev Nuclear Institute (as I discuss in Chapter 3), but was affordable, and British officials hoped that it would stave off similar hopes for a reactor in Nigeria, which gained independence that year.

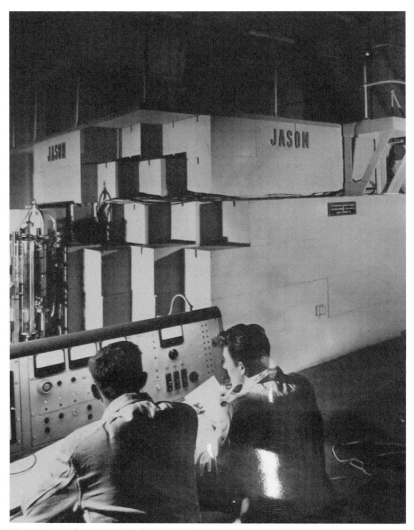

Figure 4.4 Photograph of JASON reactor
(*Source*: PRO DO 195/45 Ghana Desire for a Nuclear Reactor, January 1, 1960–
December 31, 1961)

Nuclear reactors and training programs were not cheap, and given other development needs on the table, as well as the potential of nuclear proliferation, wealthy nations mostly balked at supporting countries like Ghana in their bid for nuclear access. In previous years, the United States had provided partial funding for nuclear reactors through an Atoms for Peace program, but Ghana was at this point reluctant to pursue nuclear ambitions with the assistance of either the United States or the United Kingdom. Nkrumah flatly stated "that as a matter of policy" he would not request assistance from the United Kingdom or other Western countries given their "membership of the 'Bomb Club.'"[62] And even if the United Kingdom could come up with the estimated half-a-million pounds that might be necessary, they feared "the gift by us of a reactor to Ghana would probably provoke request for similar gifts from e.g. Nigeria."[63] Finances and politics combined to make the Soviet Union the best option for Ghana's nuclear program.

Building the Reactor: An Uncompleted Edifice

In April 1961, the first "Russian Atomic Scientists" visited Ghana for a one-week tour of the country to identify potential sites for the power reactor. It appears that at this point the plan was to have "one main monitoring station and a number of auxiliary stations."[64] The two scientists traveled to several areas to view possible geographic and geological settings, including Tamale in the north of Ghana, Kumasi in the Asante region (home to the College of Science and Technology, later called Kwame Nkrumah University of Science and Technology), and Ho in the Volta region, where construction of a massive hydroelectric dam was underway. At this juncture, the Soviet experts floated the possibility of establishing a main monitoring station a bit closer to the capital city Accra, in the highland town of Aburi.

Under Baffour's leadership, a Ghana Atomic Energy Committee began to meet every two weeks, keeping in close communication with a Professor Imilialoff, who led the Soviet side of the initiative.[65] Soviet officials gradually backed away from the initial plan to build power reactors in Ghana, perhaps because of expense or because the hydroelectric dam in the Volta region was poised to satisfy the country's energy needs. According to retrospective accounts, Baffour convinced

Nkrumah to downgrade his vision to a research reactor and abandon immediate plans for a power reactor on "technical grounds."[66]

By late 1961, Ghana and the USSR signed the Protocol Agreement to import a low-power atomic reactor to Kwabenya, Ghana. The proposed IRT-2000, a 2000kW swimming pool research reactor, was based on a prototype reactor initially built at the Kurchatov Institute of Atomic Energy in Moscow operational November 1957 with 1000kW of thermal power. It was described as "a heterogeneous thermal research reactor of the swimming pool type."[67] Other similar reactors were then operational in Minsk, Riga, Sverdlovsk, Tbilisi, and Tomskhe at a system of Institutes of the Soviet Academy of Sciences. These reactors were capable of producing isotopes used in radiation chemistry and biological experiments.[68] The proposed reactor would have been around a square meter in size, fixed inside an aluminum alloy tank set in the base of a pool of water.[69] Based on similar IRT reactors, the Ghanaian version would have required thin fuel rods composed of 10-percent enriched uranium-235 mixed with magnesium, no more than 1 cm in diameter and 50 cm long.[70]

Ghana's efforts to install a nuclear reactor coincided with similar developments elsewhere on the continent. Baffour went to the Soviets in 1961 with Nkrumah's request for a reactor. Egypt opened its first reactor, a 2000kW VVR Soviet-made reactor, in February 1961. Also that year, South Africa built a 20,000kW reactor, though it was not ready for use until 1965.[71] Still, the number of reactors in Africa was small when compared to the proliferation of research reactors on other continents during the late 1950s and early 1960s. For instance, in South America, Venezuela and Brazil installed research reactors of up to 10,000kW and 5,000kW, respectively. In South and Southeast Asia, India had two small reactors, including one with 1000kW of power, Pakistan had a 1000kW reactor, and Thailand, South Vietnam, the Philippines, and Indonesia were in the process of installing reactors around the same time.[72]

For a moment, it seemed as if Ghana would be in league with these emerging nuclear nations. In June 1962, Ghanaians learned in the state newspaper that there would indeed be a "Nuclear Reactor for Ghana." Downplaying the costs to the government, the news reports described the reactor as something of a gift, "given to Ghana by the Soviet Union." The story at the time was that the advent of a reactor "near Achimota" had the advantage of situating "Ghana in a leading position in West Africa."[73]

Nkrumah's government hastily secured properties in the Kwabenya and Haatso environs from royal households through eminent domain. Up to today, debates rage as to whether or not families were completely compensated (see Chapter 6). The government passed several acts to bolster the nuclear initiative, including Act 204, which established the Atomic Energy Commission.[74] To house the reactor and the research buildings, as well as provide accommodations for staff, Nkrumah's government awarded a contract to a Swiss-held company, A. Lang Ltd. After all, "the Swiss were said to be neutral and qualified" to handle the complex construction.[75]

In reality, the Kwame Nkrumah Nuclear Research Institute was extremely costly for the new nation. Baffour signed a contract with Lang on March 27, 1962. He did not follow standard procedures for gathering bids, negotiating solely with Lang for what was essentially one of Nkrumah's "prestige projects."[76] The Ghana Academy of Science had to devote nearly all of its available funding for the reactor in 1962–1963. In private correspondence, Ghana Academy members noted that Egypt's research reactor in Cairo was estimated to have a budget of at least £G3,000,000, remarking that "it seems much of the Ghana Academy financial provision will need to be re-allocated to the research reactor."[77]

With the impending arrival of Russian specialists to observe work on the reactor scheduled for April 1963, the government got caught up in a battle not to lose face. With Baffour on an international trip, E.K. Quartey, the assistant secretary at GAEC, scrambled to prepare for their arrival on several fronts; the Russian visitors would require transportation, housing, furnishings, and food. GAEC also needed at least £G30,000 to keep the Ghanaian students studying nuclear physics in Moscow housed and fed (Chapter 3). And above all, Quartey needed £G421,300 to sustain reactor construction when the contractor, Lang, threatened to stop work for lack of payment. Left on his own, Quartey disputed calculations with the Bank of Ghana that suggested the cost in roubles and equivalent in Ghanaian pounds might be less than GAEC's figures. Baffour sent pleading aerograms from Australia for Yanney-Wilson of the Ghana Academy of Sciences to "assist in getting funds available."[78]

On August 15, 1964, GAEC held a showy event to commemorate laying a foundation stone at the site of the Kwame Nkrumah Nuclear Research Institute in Kwabenya. The commission invited the president to comment on his pet project.[79] Nkrumah took this opportunity to celebrate the progress of science in the country, and to link Ghana's efforts to the march of science across the communist world; "Socialism without science is void," he declared. For Nkrumah, Ghana could get involved in nuclear science like any other country. "This Centre, when completed, will enable Ghana to participate in the developments now taking place in Atomic Science ... Indeed, we start with certain definitive advantages over many nations, which have preceded us in the scientific revolution ... [We] have not had to prove for ourselves that the atom can be split. We have not had to discover that steam can produce energy or that water power can be used to generate electricity. Indeed, we begin where many ended."[80]

Unfortunately, neither the Soviets nor the British would give a reactor to Nkrumah outright. The financial cost of reaching nuclear status was more than the country could bear once Western powers helped to remove Nkrumah from office. By 1966, when the reactor program stalled, GAEC had managed to bleed enough financing from several departments to nearly complete construction of the reactor building and cooling towers. Those closest to the project reflected in later years that they never actually saw the Russian architectural plans for the reactor. While the Soviet Union did limit its support to a research reactor, rather than the comprehensive network of power reactors and monitoring stations that Nkrumah had initially requested, it would seem that they had planned to hold up their end of the bargain.

"A Ring of Secrecy"[81]: The Coup and the Dismantling of GAEC

On February 24, 1966, the National Liberation Council under the leadership of Lieutenant General J.A. Ankrah deposed Kwame Nkrumah in a coup d'état. That day, Nkrumah was sitting down to a lavish banquet in Peking (Beijing), hoping to find ways to end the war in Vietnam.[82] Dramatically terminating the Nkrumah era, the Ankrah coup allowed outsiders a close look at Ghana's nuclear program. Ankrah's government permitted the British physicist Sir John Cockcroft, a Nobel Prize winner and former head of the United Kingdom Atomic Energy

Authority, to come to Ghana, opening all the available information on the reactor plans.

Nkrumah's increased ties with the Soviet Union, including his nuclear reactor program, cost him his presidency. The cozy relationship between Ghana and communist countries led Western powers, including the United Kingdom, France, and the United States, to nurture efforts to destabilize Nkrumah's regime. By May 1965, if not earlier, US President Lyndon B. Johnson's Special Assistant for National Security learned of plans to topple Nkrumah:

FYI, we may have a *pro-Western coup* in Ghana soon ... The plotters are keeping us briefed, and State thinks we're more on the inside than the British. While we're not directly involved (I'm told), we and other Western countries (including France) have been helping to set up the situation by ignoring Nkrumah's pleas for economic aid ... All in all, looks good.[83]

Nkrumah, in a letter to Johnson, personally admonished the United States, and the CIA in particular, for its efforts to undermine his administration. It seems that Nkrumah and Kennedy had hit it off, but Nkrumah did not feel the same level of trust with Johnson after Kennedy's assassination. Nkrumah became increasingly paranoid, particularly after a mysterious bomb attempt on his life in 1964, after which he declared a single-party state and announced that he would be president for life. Nkrumah's departure meant the deterioration of relations not only with the Soviet Union, but also with China, with whom the National Liberation Council and subsequent regimes broke off diplomatic ties until 1972.[84]

It is clear from correspondence between the United Kingdom Ministry of Technology, the United Kingdom Atomic Energy Agency, the Foreign Office, and the Commonwealth Relations office that British officials were determined to shut down Ghana's nuclear reactor program once Nkrumah was out of the picture.[85] Once the Soviets pulled out, either because of choice or friction with the National Liberation Council, the United Kingdom Ministry of Technology felt that, "It would be extremely awkward for any outsider to help the Ghanaians ... it would be preferable for the Ghanaians to do no further work on the reactor."[86] Over the years, this meant that Ghana was essentially held hostage to the Soviets, who kept increasing the cost of reinitiating contact, and to the internal bickering of nuclear powers, as the Ghanaians did not know how to actually construct the reactor. Nor could they order standard parts, including fuel, from another country. Since the United Kingdom was unwilling to create a hybrid Soviet-British design with bespoke parts, the officials in the former colonial occupier worked in the background to make sure that Cockcroft, once the Ghanaians sought his advice, could make a tidy argument regarding the overwhelming cost of maintaining a reactor and put an end to what they saw as a dangerous, unnecessary initiative.

Cockcroft thus took an economic approach in assessing the value of the reactor to Ghana. He felt that it would be best to table the program until Ghana could justify the large expense it entailed. Particularly, he argued the reactor would be a "load on their science budget." The preliminary budget for constructing the necessary infrastructure was at least £3 million, with £200,000 needed yearly for upkeep. First, he recommended the Ghana Atomic Energy Commission needed to be "dissolved." Second, he suggested that the significant infrastructure in buildings, roads, water, and electricity at the campus be repurposed for medical and other research laboratories, light industry, and faculty accommodations. Further, rather than keep nearly 200 engineers and staff members employed to run a reactor, sacrificing a third of Ghana's scientific cadre, Cockcroft recommended that any necessary radioisotopes required for research might be imported from places like the United Kingdom at a cost of 1 percent of the annual reactor budget.[87]

In contrast, Baffour, the chairman of the Ghana Atomic Energy Commission, felt that "the utility value of the Reactor" and "an evaluation of its economic feasibility today would be unrealistic and unwise for the benefits of this Reactor will not be felt in the immediate future, but will have a major impact upon the nation's development" in later years.[88] Baffour likened the legacy of a reactor project to earlier undertakings of the Gold Coast colonial government, including the Achimota Secondary School and Takoradi harbor. In the end he, along with the reactor project, became a subject of intense enquiry for the new government, including his questionable use of a pendulum to settle disputes and his wife's threatening students with her shoe, which emerged as signs of the broad powers afforded Nkrumah's cronies.[89]

Similarly, Lindsay, one of the first Ghanaians to train for his PhD in nuclear physics in the Soviet Union, provided a comprehensive overview of the reactor project after the National Liberation Council took over. He argued that "the Ghana reactor project is about 95% completed." Lindsay felt that it was short-sighted to jettison a project where "practically all the equipment needed, scientific and technical, is already available on site." Unlike Cockcroft, he felt that "most of the structures are [functional], rather highly specialized and their adaptation to other use though not totally impossible, will be technically difficult and perhaps rather expensive."[90]

In place of the Ghana Atomic Energy Commission, the National Liberation Council government set up a Managing Committee, which the chemistry professor J.A.K. Quartey at the University of Ghana, Legon directed.[91] Quartey prepared his own investigation into the past, present, and future of GAEC. Quartey, like the other Ghanaian scientists involved, argued that there was still potential for Ghana to do high-level nuclear physics.[92] Eager for technical advice and financing, Quartey and his associates sought advice from the International Atomic Energy Agency, the United Kingdom Atomic Energy Authority, and the United States Atomic Energy Commission on possible avenues once the Soviet initiative collapsed. Quartey received assurances "that the [International Atomic Energy] Agency is always willing to assist Ghana" even if "the installation of a reactor has been postponed indefinitely."[93] GAEC leaders in turn participated in the creation of a new channel of open communication on nuclear developments with international and Western nuclear bodies.

As a result, despite a dormant nuclear reactor scheme, Ghanaians succeeded in maintaining their position as leaders in nuclear affairs during a period of political and financial instability. Quartey, for example, filled out his term on the International Atomic Energy Agency Board of Governors, completing Ghana's first two-year term in 1967.[94] Ghanaian governors also served in 1969 and 1973, when GAEC began to receive government support once again.[95] Between 1969 and 1973, the management committee received technical assistance for equipment, fellowships, consultants, and a Regional Training Course for Africa from the International Atomic Energy Association, the United Nations Development Programme, and Official Development Assistance from the United Kingdom. Critically, in 1972 the United Nations provided $30,000 for GAEC to import a cobalt-60 source to study ways to irradiate moths that threatened the harvest of cocoa, a staple export for the country.[96] As I describe below, through external support and some domestic funding, GAEC management weathered political upheavals and made several attempts to acquire other reactors, before they successfully imported the GHARR-1 from China in 1994.

"Simple to Operate": Additional Proposed Reactors

During the late 1960s and 1970s, GAEC pursued several avenues to import a reactor to Kwabenya. After the first military coup d'état that removed Nkrumah from political office, the National Liberation Council allowed the Cockcroft Report to sway national policy and disbanded GAEC. One of the earliest subsequent attempts to bring in a reactor dated to 1967, when the new government, under Lieutenant General Joseph Ankrah's National Liberation Council, briefly sought out Cockcroft's advice on a proposal from the Himmelman Associates Company in California to assist in financing Ghana's reactor project. However, in the end, GAEC was unable to secure the necessary financing and political will to install this and other proposed reactors.[97]

The return to civilian rule with the election of Prime Minister Kofi Abrefa Busia and his Progress Party government in 1969 did not improve matters for the nascent class of atomic physicists in Ghana. Unlike Nkrumah, who had written a dissertation in ethnophilosophy but did not fully complete requirements for his PhD from the University of Pennsylvania, Busia finished his doctorate in anthropology at Oxford and had returned to Ghana as a rival and opponent to Nkrumah in the 1950s. During the Nkrumah era, Busia had fled to the Netherlands, fearing for his safety. When he managed to work his way up in the National Liberation Council to take over as prime minister in a national election, the last thing on his mind was recommissioning one of Nkrumah's most controversial "prestige projects." Arguably, the control of Ghana's successive governments by military leaders, social scientists, and lawyers often left science policy in the doldrums. Futuristic projects like Nkrumah's extravagant "science city" and atomic power did not capture their imaginations when faced with a struggle to maintain basic political control, feed the population, and secure foreign currency to maintain infrastructure.

Busia's Right-leaning government, however, did not last, and the country's second military coup in 1972, under Colonel Acheampong, ironically improved the situation for advocates of Nkrumah's failed reactor project. The following year, the director of the Ghana

National Standards Board, R. Oteng, chaired a committee to reconsider the merits of the dormant nuclear program. Other members of the committee included A.K. Ahafia, the Soviet-trained physicist at the University of Science and Technology who would later direct GAEC. While not placing them on his committee per se, Oteng also consulted with key players from the earlier wave of activity on the nuclear program, including Quartey, Baffour, and A.N. May, who headed the department of physics at the University of Ghana, Legon.[98]

Oteng was well aware that nuclear technology in Ghana was "a controversial matter," but he did not want his country to be left behind as other African nations moved forward with atomic power plans.[99] In 1972, the country of Zaire (formerly the Belgian Congo) under Mobutu Sese Seko successfully installed a second nuclear reactor.[100] Zaire secured a 1000kW TRIGA Mark II reactor with Belgian support.[101] Named the TRICO-II, Zaire's reactor stood as a symbol of continued Western dependence on the African country's rich mineral deposits. In the wake of this event, Ghana renewed its efforts to secure a reactor as well. But, as had occurred in the colonial period, Ghana, lacking the bargaining chip of local uranium deposits, had to come up with the financing for any reactor project.

Oteng nevertheless called for the reactivation of the reactor program in 1973 (Figure 4.5). The first order of business was rehabilitating the reactor complex, which as I discuss in Chapter 6 was purposely left intact to mislead the public into believing there was a reactor there. Initially, GAEC sought to reestablish efforts to bring in a reactor through Russian sources at V/0 Atomenergoexport. The Commission hoped to use the original building constructed during the Nkrumah era and some of the Russian-made components for the reactor that they had carefully kept in storage over the previous seven years. The costs of reinstating the Russian design, however, were enormous, and the commission felt it could not shoulder the projected sum of $20–25 million that this would require. It additionally noted that the Soviet proposal "was 4 to 5 times higher than current world prices of similar research reactors of comparable design and thermal power." Scientific equity remained the goal, but the price tag was too high and no one was offering to donate the high-cost machine.

By 1978, the Commission planned to secure a 5,000kW pulstar experimental reactor from the Institute for Resource Management Incorporated (IRM), a private US company. Ghanaian physicists

Figure 4.5 Francis Allotey with GAEC leadership
(*Source*: Ghana Atomic Energy Commission)

needed support in the amount of approximately $5.8 million to cover the costs of the proposal, presumably from the Ghanaian government. The Commission went so far as to sign a draft agreement for the installation. In the lead-up to the decision to import the IRM reactor, the Commission also considered proposals from two other companies, Fairey Engineering Limited in the United Kingdom and Interatom in West Germany. As part of the process for submitting bids, the Commission hosted delegations from all three companies at Kwabenya where they viewed the previously constructed reactor building and cooling towers. The Commission, under the leadership of Francis Allotey, decided to go with the IRM reactor in part because of its low up-front costs and in part because "the pulstor [sic] reactor system (USA model) is simple to operate, reliable, durable, versatile and very low in fuel consumption."[102] In addition, Commission reports noted that the spare parts necessary to maintain the IRM pulstar reactor would be easier to secure than the less-standard components associated with the V/0 Atomenergoexport IRT-M research reactor.

Since the original Russian reactor that Nkrumah had sought to import in the 1960s was also expected to be a medium-sized reactor (under 5,000kW), GAEC saw itself as substituting a similar model in the context of changed circumstances. In this case, GAEC planned to import uranium fuel through IRM's contacts in the United States, expecting a streamlined approval process from "the USA government ... since Ghana is a signatory to the Non-proliferation Treaty."[103] It seems that GAEC was at this point working quite closely with officials at both the US Department of Energy (the successor agency to the US Atomic Energy Commission) and the State Department. GAEC sent representatives to the United States to meet with staff at both departments, where they were assured that it would not be difficult to have the US Congress approve a bilateral agreement to sell the reactor and provide fuel to Ghana. GAEC even thought it was possible that the IAEA might defray some of the $1.7-million uranium fuel costs.

Even with all these promises in hand, however, GAEC could not confirm that the Ghanaian government would meet its end of the bargain: providing the necessary $2 million per year for three years to cover the purchase of the reactor. By 1978, when payments were first due to IRM, GAEC struggled to access the necessary foreign currency during the last unstable year of Lieutenant General Fred W.K. Akuffo's Supreme Military Council's government (1978–1979). The meltdown of the reactor at Three Mile Island in Pennsylvania in March 1979 raised additional doubts among Ghanaian officials outside of GAEC. Economic advisors in the Supreme Military Council government stressed their distrust of American assurances of reactor safety.[104] And before GAEC could convince the government to continue with the scheme, the young leader Flight Lieutenant Jerry John Rawlings staged his first coup d'état on June 4, 1979, the nation's third military takeover. Rawlings reshuffled Ghana's economic affairs yet again, making sure that GAEC was no longer a main priority. Meanwhile, US partners distanced themselves from another untried government in Ghana.

For Ghanaian physicists, the 1970s and 1980s were periods of repeated frustration, when the resources to rehabilitate the nuclear reactor kept slipping away. Benjamin Nyarko, in his capacity as Director General of GAEC, explained:

And when [Nkrumah] was overthrown, the project was abandoned. And so the whole place was closed down, the whole Atomic Energy was closed down. Until the then head of state Col. Acheampong after 7 years of closing it down [reopened it]. So, when the program was revived [there were several attempts to bring in reactors.] I understand too that during President

Limann's time, there was an initiative to bring a TRIGA reactor. That one, too couldn't materialize. Until 1994, that we had the smaller Chinese 30kW.

During a brief two-year return to civilian rule from 1979 to 1981 under President Hila Limann and his Vice President Joseph W.S. de Graft-Johnson, a respected engineer and founding member of the Ghanaian Institute of Engineers, the Commission tried to jumpstart their reactor initiative.[105]

Then, the nation experienced its fourth coup d'état when Rawlings orchestrated his second overthrow of government on December 31, 1981. Rawlings staged public executions of former leaders (including the former leader Colonel Acheampong who had supported and revived GAEC) and many fled the country. During the 1980s, when economic conditions worsened under structural adjustment, the Commission continued to serve a useful purpose in Ghana as a watchdog for radiation safety. Commission scientists continued important research on radiation, as described in the next chapter. But many scientists, like the Soviet-trained physicists Acquah and Fletcher, decided to leave Ghana during this period of political oppression and near-famine conditions. In the end, the dream of installing an actual reactor into the ghostly buildings that Nkrumah had left behind had to be deferred until Ghana's return to civilian rule in the mid-1990s.

GAEC's "New-Found Love"[106]: Chinese Support for a Reactor

Despite best efforts of scientists at the Commission to document the benefits of a reactor to the country, the reactor initiative remained dormant again until the dawn of the "second nuclear era" and the rise of smaller, safer reactors in the last decade of the twentieth century.[107] New manufacturing techniques reduced the size and weight of reactor parts by the late 1980s, with China, India, and South Korea emerging as leaders in supplying the "emerging global market" for what were termed "deliberately small nuclear reactors."[108] According to Amuasi, the Commission under the leadership of A.K. Ahafia was finally able to convince the Rawlings government to consider a reactor some time around 1987. At that point the politician Joyce Aryee accompanied Ghanaian representatives to an IAEA General Conference to begin negotiations for the GHARR-1. Rawlings also strengthened ties with China, who supplied the reactor, when in 1985 he was the first Ghanaian leader to visit China since Nkrumah (he returned in 1995).[109]

In 1990, the Commission submitted a formal request for a nuclear reactor through the International Atomic Energy Agency's (IAEA) Technical Co-operation Program. After the IAEA sanctioned the request, the Ghanaian government defrayed part of the cost ($200,000), renovated a Nkrumah-era structure to sink in the reactor, and accepted additional support through an IAEA grant of over $1 million.[110] Ironically, the reduction in both cost and size of nuclear reactors by the 1990s meant Ghana's first reactor has not been the massive development project that Nkrumah once envisioned. Smaller scales and lower costs made scientific equity and access to nuclear reactors for all finally a more attainable goal after years of limited foreign support and even sabotage.

At the official launch of the reactor on March 8, 1995, the Minister of Environment, Science, and Technology, Christine Amoako-Nuamah, welcomed the Director General of the International Atomic Energy Agency, Hans Blix, to Ghana. He had actually first come to Accra in the 1960s and expressed enthusiasm for the inauguration of a new era in IAEA-GAEC relations. He stressed, of course, the party line around the proliferation of nuclear technology; his role was "to promote the peaceful use of atomic energy to contribute to the health and prosperity of the people of Ghana."[111] In her remarks, Amoako-Nuamah noted how very excited Ghanaian scientists were about the advent of a reactor at long last; she encouraged them to conduct experiments with it. "I know that when you yearn that long for something and you eventually get it, your first reaction is to keep on admiring it and not wanting even to touch it. To GAEC therefore, I would say admire your new-found love by all means, but please don't stretch the Honeymoon period. There is a lot of work to be done, and new frontiers to be explored."[112]

Conclusion: Perseverance on the Road to Nuclear Power

The sunny optimism of scientists and politicians in the 1950s and 1960s about the promise of nuclear energy for the Gold Coast colony and then Ghana began to falter after the emerging country could not secure assistance to import even a low-power reactor. And once the

Ghana Atomic Energy Commission found renewed domestic support in the 1970s, the meltdown at Three Mile Island in the United States in 1979 led to an even more cautious approach to atomic reactors worldwide. Unfortunately, weakening international support for nuclear reactors coincided with political upheaval in Ghana, after Flight Lieutenant Jerry John Rawlings staged successive coup d'états in 1979 and 1981. The nuclear physicists who still hoped to bring a reactor to Ghana were among the many who saw their plans dashed in this period. They still held onto the idea that Ghanaians could be full stakeholders in science and pushed for scientific equity, but their many attempts met successive obstacles.

The development of less expensive, smaller reactors in the early 1990s ushered in a new wave of popular trust in nuclear technologies, and Ghana was lucky enough to finally get the small reactor that Nkrumah had long hoped to have for physicists "to play with."[113] With the waning of the Cold War, the attempts of African countries to build partnerships with nations as ideologically diverse as the United States, China, and Hungary drew less scrutiny and resistance. GAEC strategists like Allotey, Amuasi, and Ahafia can be commended for their perseverance and careful adherence to International Atomic Energy Agency guidelines to allow Ghana this opportunity. In the 1990s, Ghanaian political leadership also stabilized once Rawlings refashioned himself as a democratic leader and he and his wife, the women's leader and humanitarian Nana Konadu, helped broker agreements for the reactor and radiotherapy equipment. Politics and technological shifts aligned to allow Ghanaian scientists access to a reactor at long last.

During the long journey to realize full atomic autonomy Ghanaian physicists conducted their work in close partnership with the International Atomic Energy Agency. The Ghana Atomic Energy Commission fulfilled one of its original promises to the country, to protect the people from the dangers of radiation at hospitals, ports, and mines.

5 | Radiation Within: Monitoring Particles in Bodies

At the school of Nuclear and Allied Sciences at Kwabenya, Virginia Tsapaki walked down the stairs toward the auditorium. She wore a crisp white skirt suit, stray hairs floated from her blond ponytail. Tsapaki, a Greek radiation specialist, took her place at the front table adorned with a lush kente cloth alongside leading scientists and directors at the Ghana Atomic Energy Commission (the Commission). John Amuasi, in a dark suit with golden tie, his white hairs closely cropped, welcomed her to Ghana. It was Tsapaki's first visit to West Africa, though she had been to other parts of the continent, and she was honored to have the opportunity to assist in a week-long training course on radiation protection for operators of X-ray machines from across the country. "I am here for this reason, and this reason only, to help you. And I will also be learning from your own queries," she smiled brightly at the assembled crowd. Brought to Kwabenya through an International Atomic Energy Agency (the Agency) radiation safety project, Tsapaki helped to cement the bond between the two organizations, providing activity and purpose for top Commission officials.

During the long battle to secure a nuclear reactor for Ghana, the Commission performed one of its additional roles as outlined in the initial 1963 Act 204 that established it, monitoring radiation at the nation's X-ray facilities. It was the last of seven key roles described in the Act, after powers related to maintaining ties with the Agency, prospecting and using radioactive minerals, and advising government on atomic energy. At the outset, the Commission was perhaps more eager to "acquire and dispose of land" required for its use than to go forth and "secure the safety and health of persons employed in work in the course of which they may be exposed to the risk of injury from ionising radiations."[1] Yet, as this chapter describes, this role became arguably the Commission's main purpose over the years.

Monitoring risks of ionizing radiations brought the Commission out of its hallowed campus, into the Ghanaian public. Particularly, it gave the Commission a mandate to apply physics to human bodies. In the earlier discussion of radiation in Chapter 2, "Radiation Outside," scientists in Ghana sought to monitor nuclear fallout from colonial French bomb tests in Algeria to determine if strontium levels might impact agriculture and human health across West Africa. In this chapter, scientists at the Commission measured the levels of exposure to ionizing radiation as Ghanaians turned on radiation sources themselves and radiation became an internal, everyday occurrence. Nuclear scientists partnered with radiologists, radiotherapists, and others who administered the radiation to study patterns of exposure among staff and patients. They were concerned with ionizing radiation, which occurs when particles are released from a source, such as an X-ray machine, to essentially take an internal photograph of a body. They knew that to get the image, radioactive particles must penetrate the skin. Ghanaian scientists raised awareness that some particles might remain, gradually decaying and continuing to emit radiation over time.

At the Commission's School of Nuclear and Allied Sciences, workshop participants streamed out of the hall during a break. Agyare Acheampong, an X-ray technician, was excited. "I think I will learn a lot. She's an expert, you know. She has a lot of knowledge when it comes to radiation protection and quality assurance. As a novice, I think I will learn a lot from her." He took his place standing with the other visiting workshop participants behind then-Commission director Edward Akaho and his confidants, most in suit and tie, seated in white plastic armchairs. Tsapaki put on her dark sunglasses, after which she asked Akaho, seated to her right, for his thoughts. Laughing and shaking her head, she opted to go without the shades, squinting in the bright morning sunshine as the photographer captured the event in a group portrait. Each participant carefully crafted their image in the ongoing performance between the Commission and the Agency (see Figure 5.1).

A Nuclear Protectorate: Exchanging Radiation Protection for Nuclear Goods

The dreams of the independence generation in Ghana were deferred for many years, as entry to nuclear nationhood remained elusive. Rather

Figure 5.1 Radiation Protection Seminar, Ghana School of Nuclear and Allied Sciences. Front row (l–r): John H. Amuasi, Edward H.K. Akaho, Virginia Tsapaki, Yaw Serfor-Armah, Cyril Schandorf (*Source*: author photo)

than establishing a nuclear power station, Ghana scientists courted access to technological goods as a protectorate of the International Atomic Energy Commission. Protectorates in African countries trace their historical lineage to the days of European colonial occupations. The term "protectorate" covered, for instance, British jurisdiction over Togo, the former Germany colony adjacent to the Gold Coast. After World War I, the British secured control of German Togoland (part of which voted to join Ghana at independence). As a protectorate, people residing within the boundaries of Togoland had British occupiers as their new protectors. A protectorate implies an infantile state of development, a territory for adult states to manage and oversee the young ones coming up.

In using the term nuclear protectorate, I suggest a domain similarly subservient to the interests of more powerful states, who set the terms of engagement with nuclear technology. After the establishment of the IAEA in 1957, member states participated in a regulatory system for the management and safe passage of radioactive materials used for everything from experimental medical studies to power generation. While Ghana was a member of the IAEA from 1960, it was still vastly dependent on its good will to access any nuclear training courses and technology. Gabriel Hecht has explored the ways in which nuclearity became part of the fabric of colonial and postcolonial African mining life, with clear dependencies on international uranium buyers. Here, I am interested in how, even within a framework of nuclear independence, African scientists had to create strategies for autonomy. Eventually, this meant infiltration of the IAEA at various levels to show the reliability of Ghanaian scientists.

Ghana and the Congo vied for nuclear sovereignty and supremacy among African nations in the early days of independence, even within the IAEA framework. As indicated in the introduction, R.P. Baffour led an IAEA conference in 1962. The next year, Ghanaians learned that should they wish to request small amounts of fissionable materials through the IAEA, they would need to document "health and safety standards and measures" already in place, including any previous evaluations by the IAEA.[2] In keeping with these procedures, the University of Ghana, Legon sent a request for a multi-channel pulse-height analyzer to conduct medical experiments using radioisotopes, analyze radioactive particles in the air, and monitor radioactive contamination of food products like cocoa. The IAEA then suggested Ghanaians might be well served to have a mobile radioisotope laboratory on loan from the United States, as opposed to setting up permanent and costly stations. At the same time, the Congolese, who hosted one of the first reactors in Africa, offered to the IAEA the use of their TRICO as a regional research center for interested African scientists to run experiments. Baffour felt that "Ghana … plans to proceed with a research programme on a more elaborate and extensive scale … Ghana will participate in regional activities based in the Congo and will at the appropriate time request that her own reactor be accepted for the development of regional activities in nearby countries."[3] As it turned out, the wait for the reactor in Ghana was much longer than anticipated and scientists became increasingly dependent on IAEA demands.

Fundamentally, entering into a nuclear protectorate flew in the face of the initial desire, and ongoing struggle, for scientific equity and ultimately nuclear independence. Yet, what choice did scientists in a country like Ghana have, as they yearned for access to expensive and highly secretive nuclear technologies like fission reactors? Indeed, Ghana's relationship with the IAEA over the years allowed it to secure access to technologies related to nuclear technology, like cobalt-60 and other radiation sources, prior to the importing of the actual reactor in 1994.

In turn, Ghanaian scientists at the Commission have focused much of their energies on monitoring radiation and calibrating equipment, both within GAEC and for radiation sources at ports and hospitals. This monitoring is a sign of good faith, to demonstrate that Ghanaians are capable and trustworthy. If Ghanaian scientists could adequately monitor radiation in the nation, then this was a good indicator for that they would properly manage a low-power reactor, and eventually high-power ones to generate electricity.

Providing radiation services allowed the Ghana Atomic Energy Commission to cement relations with the IAEA. Once proper safety standards were in place, Ghanaian scientists could show they were competent to handle larger research equipment up to the 30kW miniature neutron-source reactor. As this chapter shows, a big part of this was the gradual institutionalization of a radiation board from 1971 to 1992. Through a gradual building-up of radiation monitoring capacity, the Commission won the confidence of the IAEA, which first provided smaller radiation sources, including ones for medical diagnosis. The medical physicist and historian John Amuasi (pictured in Figure 5.1) explained:

You see, all of these heavy-duty equipment like the reactor, the radiotherapy machine, the cobalt, and so on, the Agency – the IAEA – spelled it out clearly to us that they are going to assist us, [provided that] right away we have the radiation protection board in place. They are the greater authority, so to speak. They can monitor and we do the right thing. We also fulfilled that bit of their request, putting the radiation protection board in place. Then we were able to get the help that we needed from IAEA.

The IAEA required member countries to participate in its Nuclear Safety Standards Programme, and to follow regulations in a series of codes and safety guides. In the absence of a reactor, Ghanaian scientists still collected these standards, studying them perhaps on hot evenings, dreaming of how they might be implemented someday. A draft description of IAEA reactor safety guidelines circulated at the Commission from 1988 to 1989, long before Ghana was able to import the GHARR-1, when the country was coming out of a period of extreme economic downturn and political instability.[4] While the IAEA put some restrictions on the Ghanaian dream of nuclear energy, they also afforded Ghanaians a degree of autonomy from the changing cast of political leaders in the volatile years after independence.

"Under Tropical Conditions": Memories of Radiation on the Eve of Independence

How did Ghanaians begin to monitor radiation in bodies? Let us move back in time to understand the grievances and challenges of scientists a bit better. Long before the establishment of the Ghana Atomic Energy Commission or the International Atomic Energy Agency, the first X-ray machine arrived in the British Gold Coast Colony. Before its long journey by ship to West Africa, the earliest X-ray machine on record had a circuitous life. The Snook Company in the United States made the machine in 1915, and the New York Red Cross Society presented it as a gift to a hospital in London, where it was well-used. After World War I, the machine was going to be replaced, and the hospital sought a suitable place for it. At that juncture, the new hospital for Africans at Korle Bu in the Gold Coast welcomed this free donation. Unfortunately, the X-ray device was both well-worn and inefficient in a tropical, humid environment near the Korle Lagoons. After it was finally transported to Accra in 1923, it took nearly a year until it was up and running.

By 1926, A. Buckner, the British radiographer who came to take over running of the machine, found that, "I had to spend three weeks repairing minor faults and leaks. Since that date the Department has had to shut down for varying periods of from one hour to eight days for faults of one kind and another."[5] Primarily, Buckner felt that since the Snook Company had insulated their early X-ray machines with "rubber and vulcanite which deteriorates under tropical conditions," a new model designed with tube insulation and porcelain housing might fare better in muggy Gold Coast.[6] Further, the Snook machine used direct current (DC), which was common by 1915 in the United States, but the Gold Coast had taken up the alternating current (AC) standard after the United Kingdom.

Gradually other hospitals in the Gold Coast imported X-ray machines.[7] An X-ray machine in Kumasi acquired for around £250 in 1933 also acted up in "the moist atmosphere." To keep the insulation crisp and dry, the hospital placed a carbon filament lamp inside of the machine.[8] Similarly, the Sekondi African Hospital imported a series

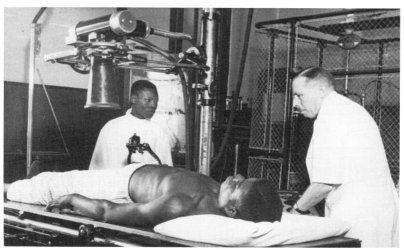

Figure 5.2 X-ray room, the Gold Coast Hospital, Accra, c. 1955
(*Source*: Korle Bu Hospital, 1923–1973: Golden Jubilee souvenir)

of X-ray machines, even soliciting private donations from interested Europeans to help fund the purchase of newer machines. The colonial government solicited suggestions from X-ray operators in tropical environments to develop a set of best practices. For instance, in Malay colonial medical officers reported that "systoflex" did not work well as an insulating material.[9]

In the early days, radiographers in the Gold Coast were white (Figure 5.2). One of the first Ghanaians to train in radiography was Salome Francois. She recalled how European hospital staff relied heavily on African assistants to adjust patients and actually run the machines, but that these assistants were not professionalized. More egregiously, the African staff did not receive adequate training on dangers of radiation and were not always equipped with protective lead aprons. While she initially went to England to train as a nurse midwife, she was fascinated by X-ray technology, particularly the ways that a film could be exposed to create a vision of someone's internal body. However, the colonial office repeatedly refused her request to switch to radiography. A chance meeting with friends of Kwame Nkrumah sent to England to encourage Ghanaian students to take up new fields of study provided the motivation she finally needed to change to an X-ray course. She recalled the struggles she had with

European staff when she returned as the first female African radiographer from the Gold Coast. For instance, she and the X-ray assistants were not permitted to drink tea with whites. She lobbied for a break room, as well as raising awareness about the need for lead aprons. In the end, she explained this may have cost her the lovely hospital bungalow and car initially assigned to her as she was swiftly dispatched to a rural posting after one year.[10]

Francois then made her way back to Korle Bu Hospital, recalling the immense joy she found assisting patients. One time she was on her way home when desperate parents brought her their son who had swallowed a coin. She was able to make the X-ray quickly and surgeons removed the coin, saving his life. Sadly, her career as a radiographer was brief. Concerned over adequate supervision of her three children while she was at work, she opted to leave her post after nine years and nine months in the medical service. Later on, her eldest daughter had developmental delays that she eventually learned from tests in the United States was related to an infection, though initially she was concerned it was due to radiation exposure. She established a world-renowned school for disabled children in Ghana and made a name for herself in Ghanaian high society as a photographer and portraitist, repurposing her knowledge of exposing X-ray films for the darkroom in her home.[11]

Other women followed, and they took senior leadership positions at the Korle Bu radiography department. The Ghanaian Dorothy Mills served as the first female chief of radiography at Korle Bu in the 1990s. Like Francois, she originally studied midwifery in England, at Barat Maternity Home in Northampton after working as a trained teacher in the Gold Coast. "After qualifying, I worked for 2 years as a midwife but as we took patients to the x-ray department, I had interest in it. I saw how they turned on the machines and how they did the x-rays, I was so interested in it so I said to myself I will do this course, too. So, I kept asking questions about it and they were looking for students to do radiography so I went in and I was taken." After studying at St. Bartholomew's Hospital she specialized in angiography, conducting scans of brains, and worked in England before returning to Ghana in 1964 with her Ghanaian husband. After a brief stint at Korle Bu Hospital's radiography department, Mills worked as a radiographer at what was then a newer facility, Ridge Hospital until her return to Korle Bu in 1991. After she retired in 1992, other female chief radiographers including Mrs. Odonokor and Mrs. Duah joined the department and took on leadership roles.

In addition to securing adequate training, the hospitals throughout Ghana suffered from insufficient radiation dose monitoring. The monitoring of radiation exposure in Ghana became more closely regulated over the years, as discussed in the following section. The Korle Bu Hospital in Accra had a laboratory, which housed radiation sources for medical purposes. They required technicians to wear badges that the Department of Physics at Legon had got for them, and checked periodically.[12] According to interviews with Commission staff and radiographers, the monitoring of badges fell to the Commission over time. Mills expressed that when she initially considered training in radiography, a friend tried to discourage her:

She said with the radiation, you won't be able to have children. So I started reading more about it, x-rays, radiation. I told myself if you really protect yourself, it won't be able to get into you. So when I first got married, nothing happened. The first year I got pregnant and had my first daughter, so I have four children now, including my twins.[13]

She recalled how careful she and her colleagues were in the X-ray departments, always wearing lead aprons and badges that were collected monthly for monitoring. In her memory, it was "the Kwabenya people, atomic energy, they were coming for them [the badges]." Mills explained that in the 1960s and 1970s, "they were very creative" in order to get results of a high standard. Unlike the equipment that she had used in England during training, the X-ray machines in Ghana did not have any computerized components, requiring several people in the darkroom to actually expose the X-ray film. Other radiographers recalled that the machines were less accurate than ones at present, often requiring more than one attempt to get a decent image. These repeat exposures put everyone at greater risk.

The trend of placing used X-ray machines in Ghana has continued. Not only has their maintenance been a problem, it is also difficult to secure adequately trained X-ray technicians to run them. In a study of 15 X-ray machines at rural Catholic hospitals, only three of the operators had the required three-year training, and six were trained on the job. Nonetheless, at these rural clinics, the demand for X-rays, especially of the chest and skeleton, was consistently high given widespread tuberculosis, with each machine producing an average of 1500 scans each year.[14] In this way, exposure to radiation and its monitoring became a mundane aspect of life in Ghana as in all parts of the world.

"All Our Five Senses": Monitoring Radiation Doses

By the early 1970s, health officials in Ghana sought to better regulate radiation exposure at health units in the country that housed X-ray machines (see Figure 5.3). In part, this was due to growing awareness from a campaign of the World Health Organization on radiation. Importantly, Ghanaian officials sought to implement changes in alignment with the 24th World Health Assembly Resolution on radiation monitoring, "Development of the Medical use of Ionizing Radiation." The 1971 Assembly sought participation of member states in a three-fold strategy that included studies of medical applications of ionizing radiation, development of best practices to reduce radiation exposure, and the establishment of "radiation protection services."

On September 18, 1971 E.G. Beausoleil, Director of Medical Services, called a meeting of representatives from the Commission, the Korle Bu Teaching Hospital and Ghana Medical School, Department of Physics at Legon, Ministry of Labour, and National Standards Board to discuss "The dangers of ionising radiation and the need for the proper control of sources of ionising radiation in Ghana."[15] As part of this shift in government policy, GAEC became incorporated into a Radiation Protection Board, which oversaw safety concerns at X-ray and radiation facilities. Initially, it was a loosely formed board, which tapped the Ministry of Health as well as GAEC's national nuclear research institute to do somewhat regular inspections at radiation sites across Ghana.

Ghana was one of several African countries investing in radiation protection. To encourage similar efforts on the continent, in October 1975, the IAEA sponsored training on Radiological Health and Safety Measures in Lusaka, Zambia. J.K.E. Amusah, a health physicist and senior scientific officer at GAEC, attended the seminar on behalf of Ghana, with the understanding that the IAEA would meet all costs related to participation. Amusah was well suited to make use of this opportunity. After completing his secondary education at the Prempeh College in Kumasi in 1956, he received his BSc in Physics at the

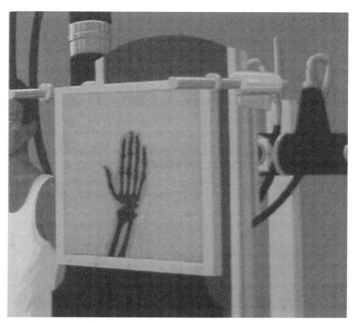

Figure 5.3 Popularizing X-ray machines
(*Source*: Ghana Bureau of Languages Science book: *Atom*, 1964)

University of Ghana in 1963, followed by a postgraduate diploma in Radiochemistry at the Regional College of Technology in Leicester in the UK in 1965 and a Certificate in Occupational and Environmental Safety in the Utilization of Radioactive Materials at the Harvard School of Public Health in August of 1975.[16] While Amusah attended the Lusaka meeting, it appears that the Commission had to purchase his air ticket to Zambia and had quite a bit of hassle actually getting reimbursed from the IAEA, if at all. In this sense, it was not always clear how much the IAEA was actually funding the ambitions of Ghana, its burgeoning nuclear protectorate.

This case notwithstanding, Ghanaian physicists continued to find that the IAEA was an important resource for travel and training opportunities, and access to equipment. For instance, when the World Health Organization teamed up with the IAEA to set up a "Network of Secondary Standard Dosimetry Laboratories (SSDLS)," John Fletcher, then head of the Health Physics Unit at GAEC, who had trained in Minsk in the Soviet Union (Chapter 3), worked efficiently to upgrade the existing Health Physics Laboratory "to enable Ghana become a member of the Network."[17] B.W. Garbrah, the Soviet-trained physicist (Chapter 3) who at that time served as head of GAEC's physics department, agreed that the Commission should team up with the Ministry of Health and the Environmental Protection Council to establish a Secondary Standard Dosimetry Laboratory in Ghana. Particularly, Garbrah noted in 1977 that "It will also improve our Film Badge service to X-ray Units which at the moment is in a very unsatisfactory state."[18] In addition to their role monitoring badges for X-ray technicians, Commission employees were quite concerned about the regulation in Ghana of ionizing radiations overall and felt that it was also a matter for the newly established Environmental Protection Council to oversee.

The professionalization of X-ray technicians and radiographers with IAEA support was critical to improving radiation protection in the country. Working with X-rays was not an obvious career path and the routes to expertise were varied. For instance, the head of the Radiography Department at Korle Bu Hospital, radiographer Steven Boateng, recalled how he initially trained as an X-ray technician "by accident." He graduated from a top school, Presbyterian Secondary School, in 1982, shortly after Flt Lieutenant Jerry John Rawlings led his second coup d'état in 1981: "I had finished 6th form and there were so many things happening in Ghana at that time … there was turmoil in Ghana. Our educational system had been suspended and so many things. Universities had to close down so I saw one advert in the newspaper, they were looking for x ray technicians. This course was being run by the Ministry of Health at the time so I put in an application and we were shortlisted interviewed and then taken (Steven Boateng)." He recalled that not all of the sixteen students on the intensive three-year course enjoyed it: "You really have to be good in maths and physics. People who didn't like physics didn't enjoy the program because you will do a lot of radiation protection and atomic nuclear medicine." Meanwhile, the Commission worked with the IAEA to run training workshops for X-ray technicians and radiographers, as well as to lobby for better laws surrounding licensing of radiation sources.

Physicists in Ghana remained concerned that hospitals did not always follow strict safety protocols around X-ray machines. Of particularly concern, one-time over-exposure to X-rays, or cumulative effects of low levels of regular exposure, were known to cause cancer.[19]

When the Commission conducted a study of X-ray dosages for five common types of tests, they found that more than half of the X-ray rooms examined were subjecting patients to doses of radiation above European Community guidelines.[20]

"Tough Stuff": Ghanaians Infiltrate the IAEA

Others interested in physics found that the best way to survive the unstable economic climate in Ghana over the years was to go work for the IAEA. In this sense, Ghanaians came to provide invaluable manpower not just for their own national nuclear program and related medical physics services, but the global regulatory authority. Their presence there also set a tone for competency among Ghanaian scientists that later may have expedited efforts to bring in a reactor (Figure 5.4). Ghanaians infiltrated the IAEA at all levels of the organization. Some, like the Princeton-trained physicist Kwaku Aning, even served as the Deputy Director General of the IAEA before returning to chair the Board of Governors of the GAEC. Scientists reflecting on their peripatetic careers in nuclear physics show the extent of their resilience in a constantly changing political landscape.

As described in Chapter 3, Isaac N. Acquah trained in physics in Moscow in the early 1960s before completing his PhD in Slovenia. He first joined the Commission in 1974 when the Soviet-trained scientists like Fletcher and Garbrah were able to convince the military regime of Colonel Ignatius Kutu Acheampong (1972–1978) to reactivate the national nuclear program. Acquah's initial task had been to go through all the boxes from the initial reactor project, since he could read Russian, and prepare for a visit of Soviet experts they hoped would be able to assist in getting everything to work again. In late 1975, when it was clear that the reactor might not be an easy fix, Acquah left to do a PhD in Slovenia. There he studied reactor construction in cooperation with an IAEA team. He arrived back at Kwabenya in 1980, just when things became chaotic with further coup d'états, and by 1985 opted to work for the IAEA in Vienna as both an international inspector of reactors and training instructor. Meanwhile, Acquah's colleague Fletcher, another Soviet-trained physicist, went to work in Nigeria and then Libya, sharing his nuclear radiation expertise with Ghaddafi's government in the 1980s.

Figure 5.4 "A delegation from GAEC presented a Traditional Kente Cloth to the IAEA Director General, Yukiya Amano, during the 57th IAEA General Conference and the 50th Anniversary Celebration of the Commission" (*Source*: GAEC 2014 calendar, January photograph)

Acquah stressed that he did not of course inspect nuclear installations for the United States, Russia, France, or the United Kingdom, but did participate in inspections at other signatories to the Non-Proliferation of Nuclear Weapons Treaty (initially established in 1968 and extended indefinitely from 1985). He explained, "The aim is to make sure that the nuclear materials are not used for non-peaceful purposes ... Then, of course, you have to go back. When you go back, you want to see that there has been no change." Individuals like Acquah were extremely knowledgeable about how reactors could be used for both peaceful and non-peaceful purposes and the IAEA seemed to attract them to form teams of international inspectors, as opposed to having them float with their knowledge in unstable regimes. Acquah explained why it was so difficult for a poor country to develop a bomb, and especially under the watchful eye of himself and other inspectors mandated to report suspicious activity to the Security Council. "Enrichment takes a lot of money. It's so tedious. You cannot do enrichment from natural uranium to bomb level. It's not easy. It's not easy. And, you cannot hide it, because you need a lot of centrifuges, thousands, arranged, and then you should have a power station. If your country's a small country which is poor, you would make all this power station to make a centrifuge for uranium [enrichment]. So, it's out. Then, if you want to use plutonium, then you need a reactor. Then, if you build a reactor which is natural uranium, using heavy water. They also cannot hide it."

Reverend Dr. Samuel Akoto-Bamford, now a professor at the Ghana School of Nuclear and Allied Sciences as well as a popular televangelist and senior pastor at the Charismatic Evangelistic Ministry, is another example of someone who came to facilitate IAEA activities and establish Ghanaian prominence in the organization. He studied physics at Kwame Nkrumah University of Science and Technology and joined the Commission as a scientific officer in 1978 on the cusp of an attempt to bring in a reactor through the United States Atomic Energy Agency when there was a sense of possibility once again. But when the 1979 and 1981 coups hit, and the reactor was delayed once again, Akoto-Bamford started a doctorate at the University of Ghana, Legon in atomic physics. He did a three-month laboratory attachment with an IAEA laboratory in Vienna, and then five years later during a meeting for the Commission in Vienna he learned that his supervisor at the laboratory would be retiring and would like him to apply for the position once it was announced. The International Atomic Energy Agency then selected him from among a number of candidates, and he ended up actually getting the PhD from the Technical University of Vienna while working full-time, an experience he described as "tough stuff" for him and his wife and daughter who joined him there.

Akoto-Bamford played a key role in making sure that IAEA-sanctioned goods would actually be effective in contexts like Ghana. With his high technical training, as well as congenial and charismatic personality, Akoto-Bamford worked to test equipment and "adapt technologies" for less wealthy countries, as well as provide training courses for technicians from member states in Vienna and on-site around the world. As he stressed,

We want to make sure, for example, that if I am recommending an equipment to come to Africa, you know, it will suit the conditions ... for example, with an x-ray spectrometry set up, it requires that you have the ability to cool the x-ray tube. In many developed countries, all that you need is to connect it to the mains, the tap. Just open the cold water, and that temperature is cold enough to cool the tube. But, you cannot do such a thing in an African country, because the water that is coming from the tap is at best 35 degrees or maybe 34 degrees Centigrade, you cannot take it further down. So, you need a chiller. Besides, even if you may get water, the pressure may not be good enough to meet the safety requirements.

So, if you are buying such a device and you are bringing it to an African country, then you have to request that an independent chiller which will cool water to cool the plates of the tube is needed. Otherwise, they bring it home, and then within a very short time it is broken down. Sometimes there are some devices too that are very sensitive to humidity and humidity may not be a problem in certain parts of Europe, but you come to Africa, you come to Ghana, you go to so many places then you have to have ways and means of dealing with that humidity aspect, otherwise it affects the quality of the results that you will get from that particular equipment. So, these are some of the things one has to look at, as to is it suitable for the region in which it is going?

A byproduct of Nkrumah's vision for the Ghana Atomic Energy Commission was investment in educational opportunities in the country for people interested in nuclear physics. When some like Akoto-Bamford were unable to fully realize their research, they took advantage of opportunities abroad, including at the IAEA. In the end, they were sensitive to regional differences in technology management and helped to extend scientific equity to other countries hoping to realize robust nuclear research programs. Akoto-Bamford worked to counter the colonial assumptions that continued to linger in the circulation of technology that was inappropriate for tropical environments. While Ghanaians wished to expand their stake in science with the best equipment possible, they also had to contend with the fact that much of it was just not designed with them in mind, no matter how adept they became at using it.[21]

"The Males Become Sterile": Radiation in Plants, Minerals, and Insects

In addition to radiation monitoring, the Commission experimented with applications of radioactive particles in plants and insects with the support of the International Atomic Energy Agency over the years. Research fueled the papers and publications, which the scientists also needed to improve their salaries and status in Ghanaian institutions, so they brokered their expertise as radiation managers to get the necessary equipment. Outside the laboratories at the Commission, rows of maize swayed easily in the breeze during my visits. A short walk from the reactor building, scientists experimented with agricultural products on grounds that once hosted farms for the neighboring Haatso and Kwabenya communities. On the expropriated fields, Ghanaian scientists secured the agricultural future of the nation.

As early as 1967, when the Commission still hoped to swiftly bring in a nuclear reactor, and the empty shell for the Soviet installation led some to believe the reactor had actually arrived, the agricultural research began. The IAEA supported Ghana, Senegal, Tunisia, and other countries in developing higher yields for cocoa, coconut, oil-palm, rubber, groundnuts, sorghum, and olives with nuclear research.[22] A decade later, in 1977, after GAEC received substantial government backing, scientists there began to seriously examine the uses of "Nuclear Science and Technology in solving agricultural problems of national significance."[23] Specifically, a four-year experiment induced mutations in rice, maize, and wheat with radioactive sources to find ways to increase protein and resistance to diseases and pests at the height of the first international "green revolution."[24] By 1993, with support from the IAEA, Amusai, who then served as director of the National Nuclear Research Institute, was happy to announce a substantial upgrade in the research capacity and additional research into plantain, yam, pineapple, and cassava.[25]

Scientists were creative in their use of available radiation sources in the late 1970s and 1980s, including in the mining arena. Akoto-Bamford, the reverend who worked at the IAEA laboratories testing equipment, did a thesis on using nuclear techniques to conduct a multielemental analysis of the gold tailings, or waste products from gold mining in Ghana. He found ways to better extract small trace amounts of gold in what had formerly been materials that were disposed. Akoto-Bamford recalled an interesting use of X-rays and the neutron source to study ant hills, which in West Africa become massive red earth structures taller than people. The scientists were curious to know why after a heavy rainfall or even flood, earth brick homes were sometimes destroyed, but "the ant hill is standing despite the severity of the storm." They found that ants selected soils from quite deep in the earth by the time they got to the top of their dwellings, as compared to mud homes, with a much higher concentration of zirconium, one of the hardest metals on the periodic table. The research could then be used for prospecting for other minerals, including gold, to see the relative concentration of minerals at the top of the ant hill. This approach was relevant to other African countries, including Mali.

Less controversial than other GAEC research, perhaps because it involved insects rather than people or foodstuffs, was an ongoing project to irradiate tsetse flies to counteract sleeping sickness and mosquitoes to reduce the spread of malaria. In 1998, Amuasi touted Ghanaian development of an "insect sterilization technique" at the Biotechnology and Nuclear Agriculture Research Institute to highlight the "peaceful" activities at the Commission.[26] A decade later, Charles Annoh, a senior researcher at the Department of Animal Science, showed me the metal shelves where he and his team bred tsetse flies in round containers in a large blue room. In white cases with netting over them, we could see the mature flies swarming. He explained, "we expose the male flies to gamma radiation to cause them to become sterile."[27] The flies then were released in areas where sleeping sickness was a problem, in the north of the country, to reduce the offspring of female flies who mated with the irradiated males.

"African Scientific Renaissance": Accessing Nuclear Goods under Democracy

In 1992, Ghana entered a time of renewal with the first democratic elections in over a decade. Under World Bank and United Nations pressure, many African countries entered into the democratic enterprise. Sometimes, ethnic tensions rose in the wake of party productions, as the world saw most grievously with the genocide in Rwanda several years later. In 1992, my father was a visiting professor at the (Kwame Nkrumah) University of Science and Technology in Kumasi and we all lived on campus. We discussed the relevance of democracy for African states, laughing when an editorial in the Ghanaian newspapers by Africentric linguist Kwame Ankrah (an old friend of my father from when they were students at the University of California, Berkeley) argued that democracy was actually an African institution, and could be linked to the root word "demon-crazy." My sister Masi and I attended St. Louis Secondary School for girls. Our classmates began to greet one another with shouts of "Akatamanso!" (umbrella) for the ruling party's sign of unity or "Kukurudu!" (call of the elephant) for the main, predominately Asante, opposition based in Kumasi. We all groaned when the esteemed history professor and presidential candidate Adu Boahen, an Asante who lived nearby, gave his final TV address sitting at home and a goat (perhaps one being fattened for a possible victory party) bleated incessantly in the background. While there were only three TV channels in those days, young people in Ghana were becoming increasingly media-savvy and production values seemed to matter. When Boahen lost in Ghana's first democratic elections in over two decades, we discussed the ramifications and implications with our parents and classmates. I remember how the parents of some students got new government appointments and others lamented what might have been in the pro-Asante town.

After the elections, the government implemented a new constitution and it was a time of scrutiny of vestiges of earlier regimes, one of which ended up being GAEC. While the country did not have a new leader, per se, President Jerry John Rawlings, who had come to power after staging two coup d'états in 1979 and 1981 as a flight lieutenant, won the elections, and donned civilian clothing. If the Commission needed to heed concerns of the IAEA, they also found that their own nuclear power rested on convincing the Ghanaian public of the merits of their research and activities. The Commission lobbied government for new laws, including the Legislative Instrument 1559, Radiation Protection Instrument of 1993, which formalized the long-standing Radiation Protection Board.

The Commission was also under new leadership, with the Princeton-trained mathematician Francis Allotey back at the helm. After the disappointment of 1981, when the Commission was on the verge of importing a reactor from the United States, the combination of the Three Mile Island disaster and the second Rawlings coup put their dreams on hold once again; there was a sense that things were finally on the move. Ghana was poised to fully participate in an "African Scientific Renaissance" being promoted through the Organization of African Unity (now the African Union) after a resolution passed in Addis Ababa in 1987. On June 30, 1991, the day set aside as "Scientific Renaissance for Africa Day," Allotey stressed that government financial support was the missing link for African countries to increase "scientific and technological knowledge" and reclaim the dreams of the independence generation.[28] Ironically, while he is often credited with helping to bring in the reactor and radiation sources, Allotey expressed to me his sincere interest in other forms of renewable energy, including the solar panels he had installed on his own residence.

Allotey and his colleagues set to lobbying the country, donors, and the IAEA for the necessary funding and legal backing to realize Nkrumah's vision for the Commission. Speaking to the media in 1991, Cyril Schandorf (pictured in Figure 5.1), then a senior nuclear research scientist and the head of the National Nuclear Research Institute, stated, "[radiation protection legislation] would also enable GAEC to implement its programmes in conformity with the demands of the International Atomic Energy Agency (IAEA) of which Ghana is a member."[29] The subsequent head of GAEC, Amuasi, who authored the commemorative history for the commission, stayed as true to the original plans for the Commission as possible, seeing through the final importation of a reactor, always mindful of IAEA requirements. In the end, the Commission secured IAEA support for a radiation laboratory, and significant funding from the Ghanaian government by 1993. In this atmosphere, the Commission brought on board additional staff, including engineers, chemists and physicists, animal breeders, laboratory technicians, welders, and administrative assistants.[30] After many years of steady cooperation with the IAEA on radiation protection, they were winning access to scientific goods and establishing scientific equity for what Rawlings touted as the "Fourth Republic." In addition to the reactor, the country strengthened its commitment to radiation protection.

To put in place the groundwork for a reactor, the Commission established an actual Radiation Protection Institute (RPI) to further its work in radiation monitoring across the country. In 1993, PNDC Law 308 allowed the Commission to officially set up additional institutes, in addition to the original National Nuclear Research Institute founded thirty years prior.[31] Emmanuel Darko, while serving as a deputy director of RPI, expressed that it was challenging to find the necessary resources to carry out the expectations of the new laws that precipitated the founding of RPI. "Over the years, what we normally do, is to develop project areas, and then some of these projects are funded by the IAEA. That is how we get our equipment and also how we get people trained." From Darko's perspective, "there have been some improvements in the activities of the [Ghana] regulative authority now," through liaisons with the IAEA. He also hoped that the modest support from government might also be enhanced.[32] In order to maintain the Commission, the scientists depended on both government financing and occasional grants and loans from the international community.

The Commission, through the RPI, worked with the IAEA to secure the safe passage of radiation sources, such as cobalt-60 sources, checking to see if permits were secured before importation into Ghana, and transporting across the country to the selected installation site. With Article 588 in 2000, government permitted the Commission to engage in commercial services for fees. The number of radiation sources was rising in the country and there was a clear need for the Commission to charge some fees for consultancies. Gradually, the Commission realized that it would be difficult to adequately fund research solely on government support. With this new policy, the RPI staff had a mandate to visit facilities, inspect them for safety, and collect regular data on dosimeter readings. They also issued licenses to allow the operation of X-ray and other radiation equipment. Darko expressed that "Before that, people were not aware of the dangers caused by ionizing radiation sources; there are a lot of radiation sources and x-ray machines all over the country." He was especially concerned with the health and safety of the operators "working with these sources as well as the environment."[33]

Commission employees monitored radiation at sources located outside hospitals and clinics. A chief technologist at the Commission, Michael Kojo Asare Obeng, led a periodic radiation monitoring exercise at the Tema Port along the Atlantic coast.[34] Train tracks headed to the interior of the country lined the road. Stacks of blue, red, and yellow shipping containers pulled off of nearby ships lingered in every direction. Some of the containers were already loaded onto trucks. These trucks pulled up into the Nick TC scanner. The trucks idled in long lines, with drivers milling around. A red light spinning on the side indicated when the scanner was on. A brass plate with a black symbol for radiation and Chinese letters was nailed to the side of the scanner entrance. Holding a yellow RADOS meter, Obeng and his colleagues walked along the perimeter to measure the amount of radiation and identify whether the scanner remained properly calibrated. During a discussion inside, the operators mentioned some challenges they faced.[35] An instruction manual for the scanner, in Chinese, lay on a desk nearby. Afterwards, as they stood outside to chat in the cool sea breeze, the fresh white lab coats of the GAEC visitors sparkled in the sunshine.

"This Will be Good"[36]: Nuclear Medicine and Radiotherapy

While radiation could cause harm, in a controlled setting it could also heal. During the wait for a reactor, scientists continued to look to peaceful applications of nuclear physics, including human exposure to a cobalt-60 source. Medical uses of radiation in turn necessitated further monitoring, providing work for the Commission.

At the Korle Bu Nuclear Medicine and Radiotherapy Unit the women sat in rows beneath the high ceiling. They faced forward, looking expectantly. Most were quiet, with a certain sadness, no mobile phones in view. They were dressed primarily in kaba and slit, made up of printed fabrics, all with a bright scarf over their head. In front, there was a high desk with a few individuals clustered around. From time to time, a nurse stepped into the back of the large hall and mentioned a name. A woman – it seemed they were mostly women – got up and disappeared with her guide behind a door. It was here that individuals from across Ghana, not just Accra, but even as far as Tamale in the north of the country, traveled to receive radiotherapy. According to Professor Opoku, most were in the later and end stages of cancer.[37] But a doctor, a friend, perhaps someone whose cancer has been "healed," referred them to Korle Bu. So they sat quietly in rows at the cathedral of nuclear medicine awaiting treatment (Figure 5.5).

It was not always so. When I was younger, I heard the acronym "CA" whispered when someone had a growing tumor. Noni juice was one cure a healer told me about, imported from the South Pacific. Perhaps, a wealthier relative might be able to take advantage of the National Health Service in England. Transport would be arranged, family and friends in London sorted a place for them to stay while they received treatment. Or perhaps a trip to South Africa. But cancer remained highly visible, with tumors and growths bulging from the afflicted until they were crushed.

During the 1980s, scientists trained in nuclear medicine in Ghana were frustrated that IAEA provided technology for diagnosis of tumors, but not for treatment, according to John Humphrey Amuasi, who did his degree in medical physics in the United Kingdom, followed with a postdoctoral fellowship at Trieste. In the early 1990s, then-First

Figure 5.5 Under construction: improvements underway to the National Centre for Radiotherapy and Nuclear Medicine at Korle Bu in 2017 (*Source*: author photo)

Lady Nana Konadu-Rawlings made cancer therapy a *cause célèbre* as part of the activities for the nationalist women's organization that she ran, the 31st December Women's Movement. She was instrumental in raising awareness and hope, and the Commission tapped her enthusiasm to further their funding and projects. The IAEA provided training fellowships to individuals with a physics background to travel abroad. Eventually, a Hungarian cobalt-60 source arrived in the capital. A second cobalt source traveled to Kumasi, where a second radiotherapy unit began operation as well. These complemented a private Swedish clinic in Accra that provided treatment for cancer with a linear accelerator.

Samuel Yaw Opoku, who headed the Radiography Department at the Korle Bu Teaching Hospital from 2009, traveled to Howard University where he studied radiography for a BSc. He later went to City University of London in England to augment his studies in radiography to the PhD level. He now oversees the training of students receiving BScs in radiology, radiotherapy, and related fields at the

University of Ghana Medical School. Opoku is quite reserved and proper. There is a guarded air to him. Yet, he is patient and compassionate, considering the magnitude of the problem before him and his colleagues. Since most patients receiving radiotherapy arrive in the later stages of the development of their cancers, the atmosphere at the nuclear medicine unit is often one of false hope.

People provided their own payment for treatment. Opoku and his colleagues faced dilemmas when a patient might benefit from further exposure, yet could not afford to receive additional treatment. "And that is also one of the challenges because the patient comes to you and you know that this will be good for the patient but the patient can't afford so even you as a health worker, you are thrown into a state of not knowing what to do because you know what may be good for the patient but the patient can't afford it. Sometimes the patient will start treatment and then half-way they have to forgo the treatment because they can't find a place to stay, they can't accommodate themselves, they can't feed themselves. We have this challenge that sometimes you as a health worker if you are not very careful, you also feel down."

Or, a patient might arrive from the Western Region and require accommodation in Accra for the duration of their treatment. All individuals were outpatients – some might be able to find a room at the on-site Korle Bu hostel, but there were neither nurses nor dedicated medical staff to attend to them and they needed to find their own meals. Occasionally, a patient received successive doses in a twenty-four-hour period and might be admitted for a night to a special ward attached to the radiotherapy facility. Even some might return to their towns with analgesics or morphine. The radiotherapists hoped to work with community nurses to better monitor the pain management of those who often returned home to die with little follow-up or medical care. And yet, some survive and it is seeing the recovery cases that propels the medical staff and scientists to continue.

Behind the scenes, the Commission monitors and helps to calibrate the radiography equipment at Korle Bu, Okomfo Anokye, and other hospitals. They now use thermoluminescent dosimeter or TLD badges, which require special equipment to read. Each technician, radiologist, and radiographer who normally worked with radiation sources as a routine part of their jobs was assigned TLD badges that it was their responsibility to wear while at work. At one point in my research, staff at Korle Bu were threatening to go on strike as a missing part at the Commission was preventing timely inspection of the badges. Steven Boateng, who was in charge of the radiographers at Korle Bu, explained some of the practical complications of the system:

We have TLD badges [thermoluminescent dosimeter], monitoring badges, but I will tell you our monitoring has reached a very bad stage. Personal monitoring is not good now. For now, it is Atomic Energy who is responsible for monitoring us. One, the TLDs we are told are always in short supply. They are supplied by IAEA. We have occasionally been told these are in short supply. Even the machine they have at Atomic used in monitoring us has broken down so for the past two months we are not being monitored and my people are annoyed. I am just coercing them [the staff] small small but they will stop work because radiation is not colored blue or red for you to see so when it is getting to you, you don't see it but it's killing you. So, our radiation protection is not the best in Ghana. Once it [this monitoring problem] is here, it's all over the country. Yes, quote me, you can quote me that for 2017, for the first half of 2017. According to Atomic Energy their monitoring equipment has broken down and personnel in Ghana are not being monitored.[38]

In response, I spoke to staff at the Commission, as Boateng requested, and learned that a senior member there had recently been to Vienna and brought a part back from the IAEA meant to address this issue. Another radiologist suggested that perhaps there was also a hierarchy of who was being monitored, with radiologists more likely to have their badges inspected than less senior members of the team. But for emergency situations like this, Boateng suggested a reasonable idea, "If that thing is broken down, they should have an alternate way of doing it for us, a special way of maybe collecting the monitors sending them by DHL somewhere and bring it back to us."[39]

"We Prefer to be Left Behind"[40]: Irradiation and Public Monitoring of the Commission

On occasion, the public also felt that they needed to monitor the Commission. Around the same time that the country was putting in place better standards to protect the public from radiation sources at hospitals and clinics, a dispute erupted over the Commission's research on irradiation of foodstuffs. In this period, Ghanaian scientists partnered with WHO and IAEA to develop food supplements from local crops in African countries to combat malnutrition in kids with HIV. G.Y.P. Klu explained the Commission was "in a unique position to provide scientific information on the nutritional value of foods."[41]

Further, Ghanaians learned in the newspapers of innovations at GAEC to preserve foodstuffs with irradiation. "Nuke Energy for Food Storage," one headline declared.[42] For scientists involved, the scheme was absolutely critical for the Commission to establish further legitimacy through the IAEA. The pilot experiments allowed them to participate more fully in globally accepted practices for modern food preservation. At this point, scientists were also paving the way to import an actual reactor, at long last, into the country in 1994.

The leading physicist, Victoria Appiah, oversaw the irradiation project as head of the Department of Food Science and Radiation Processing at the Commission, and some of the less enthusiastic comments seemed to bring her gender into the debate over its legitimacy and safety record. One critic, Carl Mutt, in his opinion piece "Nuke Energy for Whose Belly?" dared "the good lady" to go on T.V. "to explain whatever discovery she and her colleagues have made."[43] He was especially unconvinced that zapping the foodstuffs with "nuclear energy and radiation et all the atomic cetera" would have any impact on the weevils that tended to deteriorate rice or corn.[44] During the fervor, the journalist Charles M. Gbedemah went to visit "Ghana's 'radioactive' village," to see for himself.[45] There, he spoke with Appiah, who explained how irradiation actually worked, and confirmed its wide acceptance by a swath of organizations globally, including the American Medical Association and World Health Organization. Gbedemah was a big proponent of African foods and cultures, and though he valued the potential of time-honored traditions like dehydration in the sun to cure foods, it was hard for him to argue with the complete neutering of bugs and eggs in irradiated fresh produce, when he was shown a cob of corn at GAEC that dated to the 1980s but was still looking quite tasty. He was especially impressed with the potential of bombarding onions with gamma rays from a cobalt-60 source; "irradiation also inhibits sprouting of bulbs and tubers (this is where shallots from Angola, onions from Bawku, *puna* and *ponja* from Bimbilla and *afase* or *apoka* from Kete Krachi also appear."[46]

Opposition to irradiation had two strands. The first concern was over the safety of bombarding food "with radio-active material," lest consumption lead to detrimental health consequences. Commentators like Mutt argued, "Time marches on; and so does science and we in this country must not be left behind; but we certainly prefer to be left behind [as opposed] to contaminating our already bacteria and viral 'saturated' environment with radio-active human waste."[47] The second concern was over the cost and feasibility of implementing irradiation in Ghana on a wide scale. "[A]re they ordering ten [machines] … one for each region, so that the farmers will carry the onions, garden eggs, cowpeas et cetera to the depot (or agricultural radiation 'hospital') for treatment before they take their wares to the markets or barns?"[48] The possibility that irradiated food might have some radioactive particles still stuck inside, making it an unhealthy choice for consumption or handling, loomed large for Ghanaians who heard about the pilot program. Appiah had to make appearances in the media to explain that irradiated food did not have enough particles in it to be considered radioactive.[49]

Fundamentally, it was an argument about whether Ghana was ready to experience the innovations enjoyed elsewhere, including safe storage of irradiated foods. In terms of the origins of the technology itself, commercial irradiation of food began around the time of Ghana's independence in 1957 with the first creation of irradiation facilities in Germany for spices.[50] In fact, scientists at GAEC had been hoping to implement irradiation on a wide scale since the 1970s. By 1980, scientists there found that as much as 50 percent of food harvests had to be disposed of due to insect infestations post-harvest within the first two months of storage. After four months of storage, average losses of harvest were more than 80 percent![51] One considers what might have happened had Ghana been able to implement the irradiation scheme by 1980, given the near-famine conditions of 1983–1984. By the early 1990s, it still remained a relatively costly initiative for a country entering a new decade and civilian regime after years of scarcity. IAEA offered at least $200,000 in training and equipment to bolster the irradiation program, with the Ghanaian government budgeting at least 300 million cedis for GAEC to use toward the project.[52] The IAEA supplied the cobalt-60 source and the Hungarian Academy of Science's Institute of Isotopes directed its installation in Ghana, but more equipment would be necessary for the entire country to participate.

When I went to the School of Nuclear and Allied Sciences to speak with Victoria Appiah, then retired from the Commission itself but lecturing the next generation, I learned of her incredible personal sacrifices to bring irradiation technology to Ghana. She studied agriculture at the Kwame Nkrumah University of Science and Technology, although she had originally hoped there would be space for her in a pharmacology course at the Faculty of Pharmacy. It was there that she learned of the research underway at GAEC. She decided to apply for a national service internship and stayed on as what may have been the Commission's first female research scientist. In the late 1970s, she was selected to participate in an eighteen-month training course in the Netherlands. As it turned out, she was expecting a child and had a three-month-old baby when it was time to begin the program. While another Ghanaian participant, a man, was allowed to bring his family to the Netherlands, she was asked to leave her child behind with her husband. Her mother and relatives raised the child in her absence; she did not see her daughter until her return to Ghana after eighteen months. She stoically described how the child did not at first recognize her, though an older child of hers had vague recollections.

The Commission actually started construction on an irradiation facility around 1976–1978 during the revitalization period under Colonel Acheampong's military councils, according to Appiah. But it was a long process to actually roll out irradiation on a commercial scale, in part because of additional military coups in 1978, 1979, and 1981. Hungary assisted in the installation of a new cobalt-60 source in 1994 after the reestablishment of democracy in Ghana in 1992. To popularize the new irradiation technology, Appiah ran a food festival. She said one man came to have his yams treated with radiation and then stored them until the harvests of his competitors were rotten, though he never told them his margin of profit. Politicians were invited to taste irradiated food to indicate the level of safety. Other options for the irradiation source included sterilization of medical products with the gamma radiation, which would reduce the need for a costly chemical that needed to be imported. However, by 2007, the Commission began to give up hopes of ever installing commercial-grade irradiation facilities across the country for processing foodstuffs ahead of exports given lack of government financing. Then-GAEC director Akaho appealed to the media in a bid to get government support, even allowing government officials to be photographed in front of the research reactor.[53] The IAEA was able to assist in an upgrade to the smaller irradiation center from the 1990s in 2010, with one focus on medical sterilization. In a conversation in 2015, Appiah contemplated on the still-hoped-for agricultural irradiation facilities: "I came here a young lady, now I am old. And still we haven't seen what we were hoping for."

"World Super Power Nation Assisting Ghana"[54]: Monitoring Radioactive Waste

The proliferation of radioactive sources in Ghana and the West Africa region overall led to an increase in radioactive waste. In 1994, when he served as head of the Radiation Protection Board, the medical physicist Cyril Schandorf helped to set up Ghana's first National Radioactive Waste Management Centre to reduce risks of radiation exposure.[55] But the prospect of radioactive waste in the neighborhood emerged as a further area for public scrutiny at the Commission.

Inside the Commission's research campus, which comprised laboratories, administrative bloc, cafeteria, and the research reactor, stood a double-height white cement building with pretty lattice ventilation holes at the top. GAEC scientist Yvette Aggrey, wearing a white coat, stood before a dark green door emblazoned with red radioactive symbols. She and her colleagues, including Mawurtorli Nyarko and Abdalla M. Dawood, demonstrated the radiation monitoring devices that they used to maintain a secure storage facility for radioactive waste. Carefree as their white coats swung in the breeze, they held up a RadEye device, about the size of a mobile phone, and proudly pointed to the digital dosimeters on their pockets. The substantial storage building behind them housed materials collected from industrial sites, including Ghana's vast mining, medical, and transportation sectors. According to Gustav Gbeddy, one of the scientists at the Radioactive Waste Management Centre, this included about twenty types of unstable atoms or radionuclides, mostly americium-241, cesium-137, strontium-90, radium-226, and californium-252. The Commission sent a radioactive waste collection team with clearly marked vehicles to different sites to collect these byproducts of industrial and medical activities.[56]

Beginning in 2011, GAEC had significantly expanded this structure to allow room for more waste, increasing risks of encroachment on the Commission's property. Under the leadership of then Director Akaho, Ghana accepted $300,000 from the United States Department of Energy to build an addition onto the small white cement structure in use for the past fifteen years. Improvements included sloping metal roofs, and a large ramp and driveway for deliveries.[57] At the inauguration of the facility, which the US Ambassador attended, Akaho assured those assembled "that nuclear safety and security will not be comprised whilst we (the Commission) pursue the development and promotion of nuclear technology."[58] The Commission also adopted a strategy for borehole storage, or underground storage, of radioactive waste at a new site close to the research campus.[59]

Again, assuring "world powers" and the IAEA that Ghana could adequately safeguard radioactive waste brought the Commission closer to its goal of installing high-power reactors capable of producing electricity. Yet, not everyone was convinced. In a prescient opinion piece warning against larger reactors, Kofi Thompson simply stated, "No one in this country can convince me that public officials in Ghana will be able to supervise the storage of radioactive waste effectively – so as to ensure the safety of present and future generations of Ghanaians. Ever." As evidence, Thompson pointed to "the number of abandoned underground fuel tanks in defunct petrol filling-stations leaking fuel ... as a result of the inability of an inadequately-resourced regulatory body like the EPA to police the industry and enforce ... regulations. A nation in which such things occur must never contemplate building nuclear power plants."[60]

Conclusion: Tropicalization and the Ghanaian Way of Nuclear Physics

One of the initial mandates for researchers at the Ghana Atomic Energy Commission was to monitor radiation in the country. They were also tasked with finding applications of radioactive matter. In order to further their careers, and justify their existence at Kwabenya, GAEC employees needed to maintain safeguards on any equipment brought in with the International Atomic Energy Agency. Further, they took up a key role in monitoring radiation exposure at medical facilities and industrial scanners.

Ghanaian scientists made key contributions to the adaptation and calibration of devices to the tropical environment with warmer tap water and higher degrees of humidity. From the colonial period, X-ray operators had struggled to get their equipment to work in the muggy coastal environment of Accra, Sekondi, and Cape Coast. After independence, Ghanaians trained as X-ray technicians, radiographers, and radiologists, finding ways to get high-quality results with limited equipment. They lobbied for newer, computerized equipment including computed tomography (CAT) scanners. They set up nuclear medicine centers at the two main hospitals in Accra and Kumasi. Ghanaians like Akoto-Bamford were picked by the IAEA to calibrate equipment for them in Vienna and set up standards for use in many other countries with similar environmental and economic conditions. In this way, he extended scientific equity globally.

In the long wait for the reactor, Ghanaian scientists at GAEC tried as much as possible to give the IAEA the impression that they were a respectable bunch, despite the five successful military coups from 1966 to 1981. Part of this entailed monitoring radiation exposure at any radiation source in the country, including the rising number of X-ray machines. Between 1971 and 1993, they established a formal Radiation Protection Board to promote this work. All the while, they were very much dependent on IAEA support, even requiring their assistance to obtain every single TLD badge used in the country and parts for the machine to read them.

The Ghanaian way became one of measured, creative resilience. Scientists looked at anthills for clues to gold mining, zapped flies to reduce disease, and considered ways to forestall a food crisis with irradiation (sadly unrealized, with near-famine coming swiftly after). When opportunities in Ghana dried up, they moved into other countries, often continuing to use their physics expertise. Nationalist physicists like Acquah did inspections for the IAEA, based in Vienna. At times it was their children who carried the nuclear physics flame, showing that indeed Ghanaians could be trusted to manage power reactors. For instance, Duanyo Doh, my husband's cousin whose father was a nationalist mathematician in exile in France, ended up working at French nuclear power plants for Areva. Gradually, Ghanaian scientists became indispensable in international scientific management. They channeled the harmonious, calm approach to peaceful uses of nuclear physics that Baffour had used when he represented Ghana for the IAEA. Indeed, during the decade that the Ghanaian lawyer Kofi Annan headed the United Nations, 1997–2006, he furthered the Ghanaian brand of stability and diplomacy that these scientists embraced. Ghanaian scientists like the former IAEA Deputy Director General Kwaku Aning gained strong international reputations for reliability and intelligence. As the mathematical physicist Allotey described himself, "African Scientist, World Citizen."[61]

The question remained, however, whether or not the many years of hard work would lead to a nuclear power station. And while the scientists worked hard to realize the dream of scientific equity and nuclear independence, and promoted best practices in radiation protection, there was a danger of leaving behind ordinary Ghanaians in the quest for nuclear science. A lot of misinformation circulated in the Atomic Junction area as nearby residents settled the nuclear neighborhoods. They often did not have a clear picture of activities on the expansive grounds of the Commission. Nor did they fully understand the relative low risk of the reactor or the exact timing of its installation. It is the question of encroachments and conflicts on Atomic Energy Commission lands that we turn to next as we move outside the gates.

6 | *Atomic Lands: Risks on a Nuclear Frontier*

Let us walk over to Atomic Junction. We converse with a group of men sitting at the GOIL filling station on the southwestern side of the busy intersection leading to the Ghana Atomic Energy Commission. Atomic Junction is where the Haatso-Atomic Road and Legon Road meet. Cars honk all around, people buy and sell at kiosks set up along the road. An older gentleman in a white-and-black polo shirt with the word "Monarch" explains how the area has changed. "The name of Atomic Junction?" he answers our query. "Our first President Dr. Kwame Nkrumah wanted to establish something like Atomic Energy, that place [points toward the Commission]. They wanted to build some bombs [sic] etc. You understand. That time, that road [points behind] from here to Aburi was a narrow road, it was a feeder road. Then, the government wanted to lay this road here for the Energy Company. Then, they put some gates here, nobody was allowed to pass here unless [an employee on the way to work] at Atomic Energy. That road was purposefully for atomic workers." In the staff bungalows down the Haatso-Atomic Road, two senior Commission employees confirmed it was tough enough to get a ride from the junction that workers and their families might hitchhike or walk. They would pass a few small villages where long-term residents lived in compact earth-brick dwellings among their farms. Elders in these villages described how their mothers would walk barefoot with their crops in baskets balanced on their head to sell at the coast on market days. There was no informal mass transport like you would see now with the minivans or "trotros" shuttling people in every direction (Figure 6.1).

But, gradually, the barriers came down and the lanes off the Haatso-Atomic Road proliferated as newcomers settled the lands that local villagers leased and sold to them, all in the shadow of the Nkrumah-era reactor building. From 2008 to 2018 when I worked over my summer and winter holidays with Ghanaian filmmaker Eyram Amaglo to document the Atomic Junction area, the government reconstructed

139

Figure 6.1 Author walking past Atomic Junction Service Station at intersection of Haatso-Atomic Road and Legon Road
(*Source*: author photo)

the junction itself into a flyover with a roundabout underneath to ease congestion. The Haatso-Atomic Road still had one lane in each direction and moved at a slow pace with lots of activity on all sides. One day, we filmed a mechanic sitting on the ground as he tried to repair an engine deposited on the curb. We observed how someone might unpack a bundle of imported goods – jeans or hubcaps – and set them up between a few trees to make a temporary store along the road. We tracked down village elders and ageing Commission workers, getting confused on where to find each home before the government introduced road signs at every bend, since the directions from their friends and colleagues seemed to reference one of innumerable fueling stations on the Haatso-Atomic Road and its tributary lanes (note the filling stations in Figure 6.2).

Most of our research days concluded at the Haatso Total to refuel my (mother-in-law's) car and a trip to Stages Spot, a popular "chopbar" or restaurant that attracted loyal patrons from miles away, one of whom was Kofi, a family friend who drove us on our rounds as the project

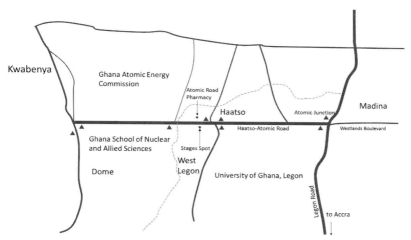

Figure 6.2 Map of Haatso-Atomic Road and environs. Triangles represent petrol (gas) filling stations; dotted line represents the riverbed
(*Source*: drawn by the author)

developed (see Figure 6.2). Here, a buffet of steaming soups and a variety of meats were on offer on a shady lot on the Haatso-Atomic Road, where regulars savored their favorite combinations and chatted on their mobile phones. Yet, what "atomic workers" did every day remained a mystery to many of the people circulating through the area. The atomic workers for their part cultivated an air of secrecy as a way to keep people from building on the vast Commission landholdings at the center of a thriving suburb.

We learned that underneath the gleaming facades and aspiring shops was a highly contested landscape filled with historical intrigues of competing families. This chapter probes the shifting interpretation of risk on "Atomic Lands" (as in property held by the Commission) through a historical tour of the Haatso-Atomic Road. The introduction of a nuclear exclusion zone in the 1960s complicated preexisting conflicts in this borderland area. Commission staff used the potential risk of radiation from the reactor (real and imagined) to limit encroachment on the borders of the campus and outmaneuver claims of their neighbors to ancestral lands. They faced scrutiny from these nearby residents who wondered if they were fully exploiting the fertile fields, since much of Atomic Lands remained empty at the time of my research. In response, Commission officials periodically demonstrated their mandate to maintain a buffer zone around the reactor through successful court battles and demolitions. In 2009, the Commission partnered with the Ministry of Lands to reclaim property set aside five decades before. They hired bulldozers to raze homes and businesses; several people reportedly died of shock watching their life investments destroyed.[1]

In early 2012, when a Ghanaian-Chinese venture, Anaina International, began to construct a large commercial complex on part of the campus without authorization, Commission staff set the construction site ablaze. Highlighting the apparent risk of siting a shopping mall near a reactor, the director-general at the time, Edward Akaho, explained: "GAEC remains committed to utilize nuclear science and technology to address socio-economic problems and has the responsibility to protect the people from radiation. Therefore, any form of encroachment on lands earmarked for the Commission will not be tolerated."[2] The Commission and popular media focused on the relative dangers associated with a nuclear installation. However, it was the explosion of a petrol tanker near Atomic Junction on October 8, 2017 that brought into sharp relief the risks surrounding rampant siting of petrol stations in urban areas (Figure 6.7). The story of the Ghana Atomic Energy Commission is incomplete without a close reading of the fast-moving urban landscape outside its gates.

Atomic Lands: A New Risk in a Contested Landscape

Ghanaians popularly refer to the disputed area near Atomic Junction (now modified into an overpass) as "Atomic Land(s)," meaning property claimed by GAEC that lines the Haatso-Atomic Road. Indeed, nearby residents even contest public claims to the land under the road itself, recalling how their sons constructed it as day laborers, filling it in with gravels from their roadside villages. Here, I investigate how Ghanaians link their term to the broader phenomenon of "atomic land"' emerging in African countries and beyond.[3] People who live and work near the Commission have a common set of experiences with others residing near atomic lands. They are participants in a nuclearized frontier zone where local populations lose access to territory through new regulations and secret scientific activities. Like New Mexicans who navigate the realm near the secret headquarters of the US nuclear industry, Haatso and Kwabenya residents have experienced secrecy surrounding the research and activities at the reactor and other radiation sources at the Commission.[4] Importantly, due to new Ghanaian laws surrounding nuclear installations, they have lost pieces of territory that currently, or may someday, contain radioactive materials. This extended loss happens through state expropriation of land and recurring legal cases where it is clear that "nuclear materials are sources of invisible power," which amplify the authority of scientists in the area and allow them to claim land rights.[5] Simultaneously, Ghanaians living near Atomic Lands graft national and international regulations for atomic zones onto prior understandings of land ownership, including the importance of occupation to confirm a claim.

Atomic lands are places where real or *potential* radioactive contamination inhibits land use and timeworn pathways and roads. While the Ghana Research Reactor Number One (GHARR-1) is safe, the potential for catastrophe consumes the public's imagination and animates those who run the reactor. Terrain around the world is increasingly infused with radioactivity from reactor accidents, nuclear waste, and bomb tests. In Africa, this includes Reggane in Algeria, where France tested atom bombs in the early 1960s.[6] Most notably, 8.9 percent of the land in Ukraine and 30 percent of the land in Belarus absorbed dangerous levels of radioactive materials after reactors exploded at Chernobyl in 1986.[7] Forests, farmland, and even ocean waters gained radioactive isotopes, including cesium-134 and 137, after an earthquake and tsunami in 2011 destabilized Japan's Fukushima Daiichi (Fukushima Plant No. 1).[8] For these "nuclear wastelands," as historian and physicist Peter Galison and filmmaker Robb Moss document, contamination can open up new possibilities for biodiversity to flourish when people abandon toxic territory.[9]

Conflicts over Atomic Lands at Kwabenya present a new filter for viewing land ownership and use in Ghana. Controversies like GAEC's arson of a shopping mall (which I describe in more detail in the final section) are significantly different from other land disputes because Ghana's nuclear installations – real and imagined – have shifted the value of empty terrain. Since 1963, "unused" and "unoccupied" land signifies not real estate, farmland, mining concessions, nor even a wildlife park, but a potential buffer zone designed to limit radiation exposure.[10] However, despite education on the risks of atomic lands, vacant land remains valuable land, whether for physicists operating radiation sources, families who lost farmland, or entrepreneurs eager to "develop." All of these actors have found various ways to visibly occupy Atomic Lands to show that they have a claim to them.

Historians and sociologists of science have examined the creation of atomic lands in places like the United States, Russia, France, and India, emphasizing the roles of physicists.[11] Here, I examine how citizens in an African context imbued a territory with atomic qualities, including possible radiation, during and after the siting of a fission reactor. Presently, Ghana hosts one low-power reactor, but expansion plans indicate increased potential for radioactive landscapes either at the GAEC campus or in other parts of the country. Importantly, for both Ghana and the International Atomic Energy Agency, the pilot reactor is a test case for how Ghanaians will monitor larger reactors and higher volumes of radioactive waste as the nuclear program expands. Though the stakes may seem low today, Ghana's plans to install larger power reactors to generate electricity suggest the politics of the public understanding of atomic lands will become increasingly contested and high-risk.[12]

A fundamental difference is the way in which people understand "occupation" and use of land in Ghana. A culture of occupation helps people to show ownership of land when written documentation of long-standing family claims is scarce. People put up walls, buildings, or plant any kind of vegetation in neat rows to stake a claim. Once Nkrumah expropriated the land for the Ghana Atomic Energy Commission, the culture of occupation in the area shifted. The Commission maintained buildings and planted crops on the vast campus, but generally argued that the empty areas past the gates were necessary to provide a buffer zone. To understand the history of occupation in this nuclear borderlands, I trace the history of occupation disputes in the area back to one of the first recorded cases, a family scuffle regarding a grove of palm trees.

The Palm Trees Matter: A Landmark Case on the Akuapem-Ga Border

The land in the Kwabenya-Haatso area was not always atomic, but it has long been a site of intense land battles. If today people are burning down shopping malls on the Commission's campus, a century ago they were chopping down disputed palm trees on contested property. The Atomic Junction area is at the crossroads of Ga, Guan, and Akan community life, and intermarriage has led to conflicting recollections of land ownership in the area for generations. The Haatso-Atomic Road is a well-worn vein that has long connected communities. The earliest transcripts of conflicts in this area emerged in the colonial period, when British surveyors and their African assistants sought to inscribe land boundaries on paper maps.[13] In 1901, a family argument between the Martei brothers over rights to a grove of palm trees bordering Kwabenya and Haatso erupted into a landmark case heard before the Supreme Court of the Gold Coast.[14] A brief overview of the case allows us to ground later debates on Atomic Lands within competing histories of settlement in the area.

In the colonial period, rival owners supervised the inscription of differing boundaries. Their descendants then used these competing maps and testimonies as evidence in later court cases concerning Atomic Lands along the Haatso-Atomic Road. At the Ghana Public Records and Archives Administration Department, people who believed they could trace their ancestry to the early settlements at Haatso, Kwabenya, Dome, and surrounding areas commonly came in to peruse handwritten court records from the early twentieth century to bolster their claims. The Archives would then gladly produce a certified copy with a red seal for them to present to their rivals. When I first asked Bright Botwe and other staff members at the Archives for documents on Atomic Lands, they had become so accustomed to requests on this choice area that they quickly brought me a stack of books and pointed right to the cases in question. Indeed some cases, including the Martei brothers' dispute, were so popular that archive staff had made photocopies of the original handwritten testimonies and typed up transcripts and bound them in books for search room use. As Sara Berry noted for property disputes in rural areas, "Both indirect rule and subsequent competition for power among African elites fostered debates over the legitimacy of competing claims to power which turned on multiple interpretations of history."[15]

In the pivotal case that started a written trail of claims, Kofi Martei accused his brother, Doku Martei, of chopping down palm trees he cultivated and owned on a parcel of land at Oncassi, on the border of Kwabenya and Haatso (now Commission property). Kofi Martei, "a Teschi [Ga] man," whose Akuapem mother was originally from Berekusu and bore children on the disputed land, gave a portion of his harvests to K. Bosumpim, Chief of Djabeng, who paid the King of Akuapem (or Akwapim) periodically in livestock.[16]

In the absence of written records, people in the colonial period pointed to trees, stones, and rivers to demarcate boundaries.[17] They held up Ga names for the land as signs that Ga-speakers had lived on the land for "three hundred years." Osabu, another defendant in the case, expressed a point that would circulate in court battles up to the present: "Odai Nto founded that village. This I have been told. Ashong, his son, married my aunt Akwele."[18] Rejecting Ga claims that Odai Nto "hunted elephants" on the land, another witness expressed, "This property is not property of Defendant's ancestors … it is Akwapim land. I am an Akwapim and I claim the land to be Akwapim land."[19]

These and similar disputes dependent on oral recollections demonstrate that what is now a nuclear borderland was, by 1900, a multiethnic, colonial realm, riddled with footpaths where family lines crossed.[20] While the land was not government property at the time, the Supreme Court adjudicated this gray zone between customary land holdings and private property increasingly recognized under British colonial law. People in Kwabenya tended to ascribe to private property held among families, not stool (tribal) lands, inspired by efforts of the Danish-Ga Reindorf family to codify local history with "drawn boundaries."[21] In the end, the presiding chief Justice, Sir W. Brandford Griffith, determined the case in favor of Kofi Martei, who identified as Ga (an Accra citizen), largely on the basis of his "undisturbed possession" of the land for many years:

The land in dispute is on the borderland between Akwapim and Accra. There probably never has been a fixed boundary between the people of these two tribes and the land of each tribe probably extends as far as its members have farms. Occupation is the greatest test in cases of this sort.[22]

Giving birth to children, farming, and constructing buildings were increasingly signs of consistent land use needed to establish ownership under British rule. In this case, Kofi Martei asserted ownership of a plot of land through "occupation," a viable tactic for navigating colonial courts when chiefs disagreed.

Similarly, as historian Robert Addo-Fening described for Akyem Abuakwa, seat of a colonial gold rush, "first occupation" coupled with continuous settlement solidified rights to stool or royal lands.[23]

The inscription of Kofi Martei's battle in the Supreme Court records made his claims more widely available for subsequent generations, in contrast to Akyem Abuakwa and other Ghanaian kingdoms that managed intra-family disputes in indigenous courts under indirect rule. His purported descendants turned to this borderlands case again and again after the introduction of nuclear activity to the area. Yet, as with the Martei family, even once laws changed, occupation endured as a viable way to claim Atomic Lands despite increasing risks.[24]

"We Built the Road": Making the Road to Nuclear Power

By the 1960s, the area Nkrumah's government expropriated for the Ghana Atomic Energy Commission and the Haatso-Atomic Road was still a porous borderland between Akuapem and Ga kingdoms. What is now "Atomic Lands," the popular term for Ghana Atomic Energy Commission property, once housed several villages including Kwabenya and Haatso. The village of Haatso moved a little bit to the east and "donated" land for the road to Atomic (hence the name Haatso-Atomic Road). Much of their properties was then given to "strangers" from different Ghanaian ethnic groups for rent and purchase as the area gained popularity. By the early twenty-first century, a vibrant community that traces its heritage to the original settlers commonly meets up at a palace on a small field hidden amongst the urban sprawl.

To reach Haatso proper from Atomic Junction, travel along the Haatso-Atomic road westwards. You pass a hectic scene of more fuel stations, lots of construction of multi-story buildings, kiosks close to the road, goods strung up between trees for sale, and people walking on foot to buy, sell, or return home (Figure 6.3). Before you cross the river on Haatso-Atomic Road, turn right down Royal Street and you will find the Haatso community palace tucked off a side street. Here, elders at the Haatso palace explain to us the meaning of the word Haatso. It is synonymous with a type of thorny tree that is found in the area. Outside, a short walk behind the palace, they show us a grove of *haatso* trees. They call our attention to the sharp pricks along the spine of its branches: "See the thorns? You cannot touch it. When you put your hand in, to pull it out it's not a joke!" Nii Amarh Sogbla, the hunter who is said to have discovered this area "over three hundred years ago" and brought over his extended family, met the *haatso* tree. People came to use it to reference his settlement; "*haatso* was here before."

Figure 6.3 "Recharge your Energy," Vitamilk billboard with footballer Stephen Appiah on Haatso-Atomic Road
(*Source*: author photo)

Haatso community members trace their ancestry to the Ga ethnic group and commonly highlight their ties to the larger Ga enclaves on the coast. One elder was born in Osu, a historical Ga town adjacent to historical Accra on the coast, but moved back to Haatso as a child. He then schooled in Osu, spending time in Haatso to visit relatives and attend community events. In the 1980s he moved back permanently to Haatso and was appointed as one of the key community leaders, a kingmaker responsible with a group of elders for determining successive kings (chiefs) of the town.[25] Another elder, Lawrence, explained how he was also born in Osu. Around 1966, when the coup against Nkrumah took place, he opted to move to Haatso village where he had family ties to reduce his commute to the University of Ghana, Legon, where he worked. From the village he could walk to Legon in about forty minutes. He witnessed the migration of Haatso farmers away from the Atomic Lands at a time when the palace area was surrounded by forest and villagers built small mat homes with thatched roofs. Farmers cultivated cassava, okra, peppers, tomatoes, and other staples, which they would load into a car once a week to take to the market at Accra to sell. Even the women who sought to sell were normally expected to walk on foot for several hours to get to the coast. Before a school was situated in the town of Haatso and cars were more common, people walked with their children between one to three hours through underbrush each way to attend schools near Achimota and other surrounding areas.

Lawrence recalled how the Legon road to Aburi was actually in a different location but moved further to the east over time. This made it more necessary to improve the dirt path to Kwabenya and the burgeoning Ghana Atomic Energy Commission. Haatso leaders met with Commission delegates to agree to the terms for a road, and Haatso granted permission. Elders expressed that even gravel on the Haatso-Atomic Road was brought from their fields, giving them a keen sense of ownership of the road. "They took part of our land to prepare, to make that route."[26] For them, the name of the road is perhaps more Haatso than Atomic. Further, young men from Haatso went to work on Atomic Lands, not as farmers but as day laborers assigned to clear fields for science buildings.

Until 1972, when pipe-borne water came to Haatso through a government initiative, people got their water from several ponds in the area. Perhaps in part due to this new addition to the landscape, "elders sat down, had a meeting" to discuss a process where newcomers could sign a covenant to lease land in the area. Lawrence expressed that "after 1974 we started giving some portions to strangers to come and live with us, so from then going building started rushing on us here in Haatso. And, it started spreading northwest to east, to west, and south."[27] According to the elders, the initial plans were well organized, with clear designs for a layout of streets, amplifying interest. My father-in-law in Accra told me that it was especially wealthy government ministers who sought land in the area during the 1970s, but the Haatso elders with whom I have spoken dispute this claim. They said it was just ordinary people from all over Ghana, as they did not discriminate by "tribe" (and perhaps class).

One day, before we could speak with Haatso town leaders, we waited while the king and his entourage reviewed plans from a team of developers. Several charming young men presented their plans to transform the palace into a modernized complex with a hospital, historical reference library, and museum, plus accommodation for the royal household. Elders (all men) clustered around a laptop screen to view mockups and visuals of what the multi-story building could look like. There would be an emergency entrance for patients in distress, as well as residential entrances. We marveled amongst ourselves how in fact all of those impressive components would be integrated into a relatively small area. At that time, the palace was a low, squat building with a kitchen outside and a number of rooms. Later, we watched the king take his meals and sip a refreshing beverage under a shady stand of trees with a few companions, though we were not allowed to take any photographs of him consuming food.

Through historical performance and celebration, Haatso has found ways to reclaim the land and roads lost. The elders invited our team to document the Homowo (harvest) celebration. Eyram Amaglo moved into the kitchens with women preparing a community feast of yam and palm oil with meats and seafood, and sat with community members dressed in vibrant yellow. The king led his community on foot throughout the neighborhood, first to pour libations on thaves of those who had gone before. The women closest to him, sporting more detailed dresses, adorned in massive amounts of gold, toyed elegantly and conspicuously with fancy mobile phones. Drummers and singers twirled around the festive parade as it poured into the streets, reclaiming lands that had once belonged to the Haatso people. A few men sparked ancient guns presumably dating to the days of the slave trade smokily into the air. This emphasized their historic claims to the area and the battles fought in the past. The elders, including Lawrence, in a dark cloth slung over his shoulders like a toga and carrying a carved staff, walked prominently within the crowd. The Homowo festival celebrates the end of the annual ban on noise in historically Ga neighborhoods. Each year, communities that trace their heritage to Ga-speaking original settlers on the coastal area in Ghana fight with the "strangers" they have allowed to settle among them to preserve the noise bans and their joyful aftermath. Exuberant crowds then spill into the streets during colorful Homowo events across the city in a performance of reoccupation.

Occupying a Nuclear Frontier: Government Expropriation for Atomic Energy

Moving from Atomic Junction, past Haatso, you will see signs of where the lands become Atomic. If you are traveling in a vehicle, and

Figure 6.4 "Energy Fast": intersection of Haatso-Atomic Road and Beta Avenue, with Atomic Police Station in the background. Note the sign to the Ghana Atomic Energy Commission Hospital with a Lucozade drink advert at bottom
(*Source*: author photo)

traffic is not at a standstill on the two-lane road, in a few moments the hectic bustle will give way to the relatively sparsely populated Commission grounds. First, on your right, you will see the gates to the reactor and research campus. You then come to staff accommodations, Kwabenya Atomic Police Headquarters, and the Commission hospital (Figure 6.4). These are the hotly contested Atomic Lands that used to belong to residents of Haatso and Kwabenya.

The independent government led by Kwame Nkrumah introduced a significantly new way to use land in the Haatso-Kwabenya environs when it expropriated land through the 1963 Atomic Energy Commission Act 204. Parliament decided the Commission had a right to "acquire and dispose of land" in "the public interest." Three additional laws on the administration of state lands, Acts 86, 123, and 125, provided legal muscle for the expropriation. Act 204 required the Commission to compensate "any person" affected through its acquisition of land out of its internal budget. It further stipulated the Commission would ensure "no *nuclear damage* results from anything on any premises *occupied* by them ... anything which is in the course of carriage on their behalf to or from such premises, or any waste discharged."[28] It gave the Commission two broad mandates: first, to set up research, education, and policy on the "peaceful uses of atomic energy," and second, to distribute and monitor radioisotopes for the medical profession. The Act tasked the Commission with involving the International Atomic Energy Agency in their plans and activities.

With the creation of the Atomic Energy Act, Nkrumah's government invented Atomic Lands. Nkrumah expressed that an atomic energy power station would become operational in the very near future, providing a clear justification for the size of the land parcel. Act 204 implied that "any nuclear installation operated in Ghana under the supervision of [the Commission]" would be located on the land at its original base at Kwabenya.[29] Of course, the Commission remained an aspirational enterprise after the fall of Nkrumah, with no reactor located in Ghana for many years.

Ghanaian physicists, however, refused to leave the site, propagating the myth that Nkrumah installed a reactor on GAEC property. Scientists and their families continued to live near the original reactor site in a planned community with staff bungalows. They included individuals like Benjamin Garbrah, the expert in gamma-ray spectroscopy and radioisotopes who had traveled to the USSR, learned Russian at the Moscow State University, and completed his PhD in the UK after the coup.[30] They kept the flame of nuclearity alive, dreaming of Nkrumah's proposed "metropolis of science, learning, scientific agriculture and philosophy."[31] Reflecting on this period, when he served as the officer in charge of GAEC from 1966 to 1972, Garbrah recalled, "there have been a lot of misconceptions. Unfortunately, some of the [Ghanaian] scientists have to accept some of the blame because they make it appear that something wonderful is happening there, or was going to happen ... but many of them didn't really know what was going on."[32]

In the staff quarters, the families of employees created their own community support structures. One example was my father's cousin, who worked with the maintenance team at the Commission for several decades. His wife set up a nursery school in their staff accommodations, which she ran with their daughter. At nap time, all of the kids lay down quietly on mats packed tightly across the floor. They played outside in the dusty yard with children of other Commission employees. On a line strung through some trees she hung brightly tie-dyed clothes that she made to sell. She gifted me with a blue-and-white piece the color of the sky. For someone like their daughter, Alice, who had grown up near the research center, it was clear what was going on. She explained to me, "GAEC is a something like a science community."

Other relatives of Commission employees set up shops in a small market area near the staff housing. You could buy smoked fish, tomatoes, and other staples spread out on the concrete floor of a simple stall opposite a gravelly parking area. There was also a beauty salon with hand-painted portraits in rainbow hues of women sporting different styles. Opposite, a woman sold bulk provisions like tinned meats, rice, and soap. She explained that researchers at the Commission conducted important experiments with practical relevance. "You know *biari* (yam)," she explained hurriedly while taking a break from tending to her many customers. "It grows close to the ground, but the researchers are trying to see if they can make it a climbing plant."

For those less intimate with the activities within the walled research areas, Ghanaian scientists participated in "boundary work," to establish authority over Atomic Lands.[33] They deployed secrecy and some degree of subterfuge to demarcate a private space only accessible to GAEC employees. As nuclear physicists, they participated in the "culture of secrecy" that Hugh Gusterson notes "segregates laboratory scientists as a privileged but somewhat isolated elite" at US atomic research centers.[34] Once Nkrumah lost power and the Soviet-sponsored reactor scheme faltered, Ghanaian nuclear physicists found strategies to justify their occupation of Atomic Lands.[35] Ghana received a donated cobalt-60 gamma-ray source in February 1972 from the United Nations Development Programme.[36] Officials stressed the need for the large campus, despite the relatively compact laboratories at the center of the site, in hopes of someday importing an actual reactor.[37]

Above all, GAEC cultivated a phantom reactor to sustain control over its campus for more than five decades. Even today, there is a common perception that Atomic Lands has long hosted a nuclear reactor. From the main road, local residents can see large cooling towers and the empty, uncompleted warehouse designed to store the reactor. Ironically, the fictive nuclear facility that attracted residents from the 1960s through the 1980s complicated local relations with GAEC once a real reactor materialized in the 1990s.

Upon receiving the reactor in 1994, the Commission agreed to abide by international regulations on radiation protection. They recommended that the "area containing the reactor" needed to be "defined by a boundary and under effective control of the reactor management."[38] While Commission officials debated the reactor's buffer requirements, they generally agreed some sort of exclusion zone was necessary. Emmanuel Ofori Darko, director of the Commission's Radiation Protection Institute, acknowledged, "Though they say the reactor is very safe, there should be at least a 5 km safety zone."[39] Low-power research reactors around the world, however, lack noticeable areas of fallow land; they are often sited on busy campuses close to residential areas.[40] The Nigerian 30kW reactor (NIRR-1), also a Chinese miniature neutron-source reactor, is located right on the Ahmadu Bello University campus in Zaria state.[41] International Atomic Energy Agency documentation asserts that, "for a research reactor, the reactor building is the ultimate barrier for ensuring confinement."[42] While reactor buildings generally form an appropriate buffer, the Commission's official position is that the GHARR-1 is not sufficiently deep in the soil to attenuate all risks and so a barrier of at least 2 km is advisable.[43]

Despite these concerns, the GHARR-1 is a very small, "inherently safe" research reactor, as GAEC employees stress in their publications.[44] It was originally supplied with a ten-year fuel supply of 980.40 grams of highly enriched uranium, which the Commission replaced with low-enriched uranium in 2017 to eliminate any possibility of using the original fuel in a small radioactive weapon.[45] For the nuclear engineers who worked so hard to obtain it, the reactor at the center of the complex is almost a sacred space, even if it has been effectively neutered. It mimics the sacred shrines found in town centers throughout West Africa, including the Kwabenya village nearby.

"Our Ancestors Lived There": Displacements and the Phantom Reactor

Moving past the grounds of the Commission and staff housing, we come to the Kwabenya residential area. On an early visit in 2008, we were hoping to find the village of Kwabenya itself, but no one could give us clear directions to the palace and shrine. I am not sure who saw the woman first. Cassandra Appiah, then a student at Legon, and Eyram Amaglo, who had just graduated from the National Film and Television Institute, were in the car with me that day. Mr. Afari, a driver at the University of Ghana, Legon with a steady manner, slowly rolled his aging vehicle close to the curb after we turned off toward the Kwabenya market. We looked out from the right of the car and saw a woman with white chalk on her face as she was paying for a beverage from a vendor in a small kiosk. She looked like a priestess! Was this the Kwabenya priestess? Amaglo and I debated turning on the small discreet videocamera but opted against it since we had not sought permission. We got out of the car and approached Naa Opoku. Yes, she was the priestess, and if we parked our car, she could lead us into the village.

On our first visit, everyone was dressed casually in t-shirts, in jeans or khakis mostly for men, and wrapped fabric skirts with t-shirts for most of the women. But there were signs of their strong commitment to connecting Kwabenya to an earlier time. Elders greeted us cordially outside a cluster of trees with a small white fence around it. Inside the white fence they explained there was a small animist shrine, the spiritual center of the village. They casually mentioned that a woman on her period should not come too near the shrine. When we returned to film the head of family and his advisors, everyone was dressed in fine clothes, with jewelry and royal footwear (Figure 6.5). We offered symbolic gifts, including schnapps, and watched as an elder poured some on the ground in respect to the ancestors. After our discussions, several younger men showed us where you could see the Opoku hill off in the distance, the source of further spiritual power for the community.

When we interviewed the acting chief, his sister, who served as queen of the youth, his linguist, and others, they explained that there was no running water or flushing toilets. This was a big difference from the Haatso palace, which had boasted of running water since the 1970s. On a common area outside near the palace, we noticed a young boy who was watching his sister as she washed his school uniforms. He seemed visibly agitated. From the pocket of a pair of shorts, he rescued a sheet of paper and spread it out to dry. It was a science test he had taken from another school to study beyond what had been offered him at his own. He read it out loud for us, perking up that we were showing interest in the forgotten paper. Here was a vestige of Nkrumah's project to bring science to the masses. Yet, the two-page sheet pointed to a school system dependent on rote memorization without laboratories:

Figure 6.5 Town leaders, Kwabenya
(*Source*: author photo)

Section A: Question 1: Which of the following is not a branch of
   science?
   (a) Chemistry

   | (b) History |

   (c) Biology
   (d) Physics...

Section B: Question 6: Which of the following does not form part of
   the three basic particles of matter?
   (a) Atom

   | (b) Iron |

   (c) Molecule
   (d) ---- [washed out]...

Section B: Question 3: What is energy?

   [Handwritten]

   *Energy is the ability to do work: Liquid Energy, Sound Energy,
   Electrical Energy, Chemical Energy, Solar Energy from the*

Sun, Biogas, Electricity, Potential Energy, Kinetic Energy
$KE = \frac{1}{2} mv^2$

Here was a young boy living a stone's throw from the Ghana Atomic Energy Commission without access to running water, who was taught to let his sister wash his clothes according to "traditional" gender norms. We asked him about the questions and what he thought of the Atomic Energy Commission nearby. Energy was in the air, on the school exams, even if nuclear energy had ironically been omitted from this test. His dreams were big; he hoped to be a physician someday. He commented that nearby on the Haatso-Atomic Road we could find the Atomic Commission Hospital; perhaps he could see himself working there one day.

For their part, the elders in Kwabenya expressed cynicism about Nkrumah's decision to site the Commission near them. One expressed, "at that time, our father of the nation, Dr. Kwame Nkrumah, he passed the law that he has the power to take any land which he feels is good and can be used for public interest. So he just takes it, by that law." He reflected that even while Nkrumah was espousing, "I forgot, what do you call it? Pan-Africanism," he was essentially stealing valuable land from Ghanaian citizens. "How can you at the same time tie the hands of your own people behind them?"[46] I asked each of the members assembled what benefits the Commission had brought to the neighborhood. Queen of the youth, sister to the chief, could hardly contain her disgust. "No benefit. Absolutely nothing has come of it."[47] Arguably, the community of Kwabenya lost more of their properties overall to the Commission than Haatso, squeezing into a smaller parcel on the western perimeter of Atomic Lands. While families in Kwabenya received compensation, there have been ongoing efforts to obtain further monies from government for members who felt they had not received a fair allotment.

Simultaneously, many of the men assembled were enthusiastic that their neighborhood had received national and international attention over the years. The shift in their prospects came in 1973, when Col. I.K. Acheampong's regime (1972–1975) began funding GAEC again. The government purposely left the structures set up under Nkrumah's regime intact: "any modifications to the buildings which are found to be necessary should be carried out in such a way as to preserve those existing features which are essential for a reactor, so that they would be available when the country is in a position to afford a reactor."[48] Nkrumah's government had paid £3 million to a team of Soviet experts, Ghanaian architect Mr. Amartey, an Indian surveyor, and Ghanaian construction company Messrs. A. Lang Limited to construct the "reactor complex," and Acheampong was not prepared to destroy this significant investment.[49] With renewed support in the early 1970s, Ghanaian scientists continued to live and work on the Commission campus, under the leadership of Francis Allotey, the Princeton-trained mathematician.[50] Physicists and their families lived in a remote suburb, then located along a "bushy feeder road" where a gate prevented non-GAEC employees from traversing the four-mile Atomic-Haatso road, and the occasional car offered rides to staff.[51]

As Accra expanded, private ventures became keenly interested in Atomic Lands and its periphery. The prospect of lucrative sales brought families who held rights to land in this area into conflict, both with each other and with the Commission and the Lands Department. Dissatisfied with three payments from the Lands Department, members of the Odai Ntow family of Kwabenya went to court in the late 1970s seeking further compensation. The defendants (descendants of an adopted grandson of Odai Ntow and Odai Ntow's adopted daughter Koko Dugba) presented a map certified to be "carefully and correctly modernised from the 1904 Martei" chart. Justice of the High Court K.A. Agyepong ruled the compensated members owed 500 cedis to the descendants of Anteh Kwadwo, one of Odai Ntow's original three sons, and all needed to be in agreement prior to any further sales of land that they might claim.[52]

Even after successive payments from the Lands Department to various family members, other factions attempted to reclaim "unused" land expropriated for the Commission. To combat this, GAEC allowed people to remain confused about the presence of a reactor on site. The oral testimonies of families in the town of Kwabenya to the west of GAEC, whose lands were among those Nkrumah's government expropriated through eminent domain, convey this misconception. According to Nii Akrade Annan Oti II, acting chief of Kwabenya and head of the Opoku family, the reactor had been on site since the 1960s:

AOA: But how long have they actually had a reactor there?
OTI: It was acquired in 1962.
AOA: But since those days, has there been a reactor there?

OTI: [joined by others] Oh yes. That is what they are using for their research purposes. And they have a university on there.[53]

In fact, Nii Tettey Commey II, the chief's advisor, explained that this reactor was directly responsible for the growth of the surrounding community:

When Kwame Nkrumah built the atomic reactor, the name Kwabenya started to travel all over the world, even to other remote areas in Ghana. So people became interested, "Eh, I would like to live somewhere closer to it." So, people started to come ask of land, to build. Through this process that is why you see buildings all over. Just a few years ago, before the development, you would only see the reactor, in the bush, and you would see bush [makes road motion with hand] until you came to the village. But now, because the reactor brought in so many people from all parts of Ghana, they have shown interest to stay here. Our family through the *abusia panyin* [head of family] has granted them a whole lot of leases. And most of them have built up, you see. Yes, that is why.[54]

To our surprise, like their counterparts in Kwabenya, elders in the town of Haatso also thought that there was a nuclear reactor in Ghana earlier than 1994. "Atomic [Energy Commission] came in after Kwame Nkrumah and acquired lands in these areas to establish atomic energy. Somewhere around the 1970s [sic] they came and erected the reactor. Up till now it is there." As long-term residents, they recalled how Commission representatives during the Nkrumah era advised them to relocate the village to the other side of the Onyasia River to avoid exposure to radiation, "So, we pushed over to the more eastern side."[55]

The insertion of a reactor into the landscape at Kwabenya raised concerns about radioactivity both among the local populations and the scientists managing the reactor. Local leaders were unfamiliar with the safety features of the GHARR-1, primarily because they did not understand it to be new. Oti, acting chief of Kwabenya, explained his concerns over possible radiation from what he viewed as an aging reactor dating to the 1960s. "Our problem with Atomic Energy [Commission] is that we know of Chernobyl in Moscow [Russia] where there was a leakage in an atomic reactor. It caused a disaster. So some of us are suggesting to government, now that the land has been encroached upon, why couldn't the state think of relocating the atomic reactor."[56] This would also give Oti more land to sell. But the Commission also valued the land on which this nonexistent reactor supposedly sat and never planned to "move" it. The empty warehouse and cooling towers built during the Nkrumah era now dwarf a real reactor that occupies a low-slung building nearby. Given the falling cost of nuclear energy, made possible in large part by the availability of relatively inexpensive, portable reactors made in China, Ghanaian officials hope to eventually construct a nuclear power plant, most likely at a new site.[57]

In the absence of an actual reactor until 1994, and now in the planning stages for a power plant, land has become the main pre-occupation of the Commission. Land was the most important resource Ghanaian nuclear engineers had in their quest for nuclear access and scientific equity. It became their primary goal to secure the boundaries of the campus in order to maintain the dream of atomic energy and they stressed the risk of nuclear exposure before and after the siting of the reactor. In the meantime, the nearby inhabitants merely saw themselves as losing out on access to land. They were less invested in the scientific agenda and merely lamented the sacrifice that politicians from Nkrumah's era had expected of them.

"This Road Leads to Atomic!": Where Commerce and the Commission Meet

Along the Haatso-Atomic Road there are a number of landmarks, including the Maxxon and Total petrol stations and UTC Bank. Another spot that pops out is the Atomic Road Pharmacy under some trees. When we spoke with Uriel Andoh, whose mother established the pharmacy, we asked how they came up with the name. She laughed and simply said, pointing further down, "This road leads to Atomic!" With rapid development in the surrounding areas, the remaining empty land reserved for scientific purposes emerged as the biggest asset of the Ghana Atomic Energy Commission and something they actively worked to secure for their research. The Commission, alongside local royal households from Kwabenya, published notices in newspapers alerting the public to legitimate owners in an atmosphere of keen interest in real estate near Atomic Junction.

In fact, the Ghana Atomic Energy Commission has faced incursions on its sizeable campus since 1963. The nuclear frontier on Ghana's

Atomic Lands is a porous one. Not only does radiation not respect boundaries, nearby residents cross onto the borders of the campus and even set up farms, residences, and businesses. The Commission's head of security, Major Samuel Kuleke, recently estimated 30 percent of 2000 acres of their property has been re-appropriated.[58] Uriel Andoh, the pharmacist who managed the Atomic Road Pharmacy, explained, "When we came here it was all bushy. We didn't see the place like this where we are now having petrol stations and supermarkets and shops all over. I think it's better now."[59] Newcomers have made their own claims to the Atomic Junction area, taking up the afrofuturistic monikers as a marketing device and geographic designator. Their Atomic Junction is a vibrant, commercial hub where mobility along the road brings customers and economic promise. Hawkers fry plantain and turn kebabs as people on foot, in cars, on motorbikes, and on buses buy, sell, and chat on the many lanes criss-crossing this popular suburb.

In contrast to entrepreneurs, the Commission's administration saw growth in the neighborhood as a real threat; periodically, the agency announces planned demolition exercises. In a 2005 advertisement in the main newspaper, the *Daily Graphic*, GAEC reiterated the agency's claims to the land, stating, "The public is informed that the land is not lying fallow. It is within GAEC's *exclusive zone for the management of any radiological accidents*.'" They further expressed that "the government has not released any portion of the Ghana Atomic Energy Commission land to any person or family."[60] In 2007, GAEC sponsored a dramatic demolition effort to dismantle walls and buildings on the outskirts of the campus (Figure 6.6).

While the Commission publicly plays up the relative danger of the current reactor, incursions suggest their neighbors are growing less fearful. Below the Nkrumah-era buildings, observers of Atomic Lands see a lot of "fallow," highly desirable land. In fields behind the administration block, maize sways easily in the breeze as part of agricultural experiments. Neighbors note Commission staff live within the "exclusive zone." How necessary is it to keep non-employees off the land? They watch as, every day, people go near the reactor to work. Furthermore, Kwabenya and Haatso families still live close by and can walk over to recall burial grounds or hunt, in contrast to people resettled far from a "radiation zone" of thorium deposits in Indian fishing villages.[61] Increasingly, residents may not conflate the risk

Figure 6.6 Demolition on Atomic Lands in 2007; photo by Emmanuel Onoma-Barnes. Original caption: "Some workers of the Ghana Atomic Energy Commission busily demolishing some of the unauthorised structures" (*Source*: Kingsley Asare, "GAEC Demolishes Unauthorised Structures," *Daily Graphic*, January 16, 2007, p. 29)

of the research reactor with atomic lands elsewhere, like the health dangers for trespassers and workers who moved within the exclusion zone before and after the meltdown at Chernobyl.[62] And while some locals equate the reactor site with nuclear weapons research, careful observers like an elder in Haatso note, "They have not been using it for the actual bombs and for what it was supposed to do, but for agricultural and medical research and training."[63]

To limit encroachment, the Commission has constructed a large School of Nuclear and Allied Sciences along with a new Ghana Space, Science, and Technology Center on the main road opposite the campus housing the reactor.[64] Statements from entrepreneurs along the Atomic Road spanning Haatso and Kwabenya suggest that this has been an effective strategy to demonstrate full use of these contested lands, which were not part of the initial expropriation. Pointing down the road to the new school, Charles A. Ocran, a welder, expressed,

I stay at Haatso. Sometime ago, whenever you pass through the Atomic Road you see that [GAEC] is like an abandoned place ... But now you can

see that a lot of projects are going on. Especially, they have started reno-
vating the abandoned buildings. And you can see a big signboard there [for
the school], trying to tell the public about the things that they do. So now, to
me, I can tell that it is taking a new shape.[65]

Paradoxically, a purported goal of the School for Nuclear and Applied
Sciences is to train scientists with the assistance of the International
Atomic Energy Agency to run a future nuclear power plant that will
undoubtedly be located at a different site where there is a larger source
of water nearby.[66]

In constructing an attractive school with large white buildings,
prominent statues, and tidy grounds visible from the road, GAEC
deployed occupation to bolster its claims in the area. Land occupation
remains a popular tactic, even with new laws to encourage registration of land and proper usage. The 1986 Land Title Registration Law
(PNDCL 152) allows individuals, families, neighborhoods, and royals
to receive paper documentation for long-standing claims in major
cities like Accra and Kumasi. However, since a large group can acquire
a title, its many members often vie for authority to manage the land
in question.[67] The new 1992 Constitution addresses concerns over
vacant state lands that remain highly contested. Clause 5 of Article 20
states "property compulsorily taken possession of or acquired in the
public interest or for a public purpose shall be used only in the public
interest or for the public purpose for which it was acquired." Clause
6 of that same article indicates government lands acquired after 1992
but not used for their intended purpose can be resold to the original
owners at current market prices.[68]

During President John A. Kufuor's tenure (2001–2009), popular
media reports suggested government was returning unused state
lands throughout Accra to Ga owners, including part of the GAEC
holdings. People living near Kwabenya interpreted the new policy to
mean "[Atomic] lands acquired by government, but not put to their
intended purpose for the acquisition, must automatically be returned
to their original owners."[69] Tasked with examining these issues from
2002, George Ofosu-Amaah, law professor and former Chairman of
the Greater Accra Regional Lands Commission, expressed, "at no time
were the GAEC lands included in these deliberations."[70] Regarding
the extent to which GAEC was actually exploiting land for the public
as intended, Ofosu-Amaah considered that, first, a radiological buffer
zone served public interest and, second, the (belated) installation of

a reactor fulfilled the original mandate for nuclear research. Third, should reversion take place, even though the land was acquired before 1992, nothing about it would be "automatic."

Still, the slim possibility of original owners or their descendants being able to reclaim any land in Accra fueled a bout of real estate speculation in the Kwabenya area. In the *Daily Graphic*, Naa Korkoi Ashalley, Head of the Family in Kwabenya, stated:

I wish to assure the public that Nii Abbey Okanfra is not the recognized chief of Kwabenya ... Kwabenya lands are family lands belonging to ODAI NTOW, NII KWAO BLENYA, OTUOPAI, OKANJA GBEKE and NEEFU families, but never stool land ... [Okanfra] is a self-styled chief and has no land at Kwabenya to [sell] ... His claims are therefore null and void. We are therefore advising our numerous customers that anyone who acts in accordance with his claim, does so at his/her own risk.[71]

As they had for many decades, rival family factions traded in names, like Odai Ntow, that had been enshrined in official maps and court records since 1904.

Demonstrating legitimate occupation of land in a nuclear exclusion zone presented a new legal quandary for Ghanaian physicists. First, GAEC was caught within a situation where "a plurality of land tenure and management systems (i.e., state and customary) prevail ... and increasingly cause problems of contradiction and conflict."[72] Second, popular interpretations of land laws for government property pushed the agency to maintain structures to show use.[73] Third, GAEC recognized international codes regarding the need to maintain a buffer zone for future reactor expansion, limiting what they might construct on the land. Further, beginning in 2011, GAEC significantly upgraded its nuclear waste storage facility, increasing risks of encroachment on Atomic Lands. Under the leadership of then-Director Edward Akaho, Ghana accepted $300,000 from the United States Department of Energy to expand the small building on the GAEC campus used to house radioactive waste collected from the National Nuclear Research Institute, hospitals, laboratories, and other sites across Ghana. At the inauguration of the facility, which the United States Ambassador attended, Akaho assured those assembled "that nuclear safety and security will not be comprised whilst we (GAEC) pursue the development and promotion of nuclear technology."[74] So although GAEC held legitimate titles for the bulk of Atomic Lands, albeit contested ones, and enjoyed support from the International Atomic Energy Agency and foreign governments, it scrambled alongside other academic institutions in Ghana that anxiously occupied land for which they have virtually no right and no registered title, including Winneba College and the Central University College.[75]

Thus, attempts to break ground or put up cement blocks on Atomic Lands held huge significance, as a recent occupation highlights. The Anaina International Company claimed that it had secured a parcel of 164 acres along the Dome and Kwabenya borders for construction of a "state-of-the-art International Business District" that would employ more than 50,000 Ghanaians at its "casinos, supermarkets, departmental stores, recreational facilities and parks, banks, bus stations and a host of other infrastructure."[76] Costing over half-a-billion US dollars, the initiative engaged substantial Chinese investment and Chinese contractors. When Akaho saw signs of construction in January 2012, he reacted forcefully. Moments after Akaho directed staff to set fire to an Anaina administrative block under construction, and just after firefighters put out the resulting "fireball," he exclaimed to rapt reporters in front of the Atomic District Police Station:

We must exercise control over this land because we want to make sure that people do not build very close to nuclear facilities. Ghana has signed international conventions and if there is any accident we have to do evacuations. We have to protect the public and the environment so we cannot allow any encroachment in any form ... [I]t is only a country where people do not respect laws that will allow a foreigner to build hotels, build apartments and shopping mall very close to a nuclear facility. This kind of thing can never happen in China.[77]

Private enterprise with foreign investment threatened to dwarf what was once the pinnacle of Nkrumah's plans for a socialist Ghana. Ironically, Chinese entrepreneurs working with Ghanaian partners compromised the security of the Chinese-made reactor. Indeed, the Anaina dispute mirrored rising public frustration in Ghana over families selling land and providing mining concessions to new Chinese migrants.

The Ghana Atomic Energy Commission establishment benefited from misunderstandings over reactor safety and was able to successfully outmaneuver family claims in this instance. The Public Service Workers' Unions in Accra "cautioned members of the public that it *was dangerous for one to live around the atomic energy restricted zones* not to mention about health implications in case of disasters and other chemical and radioactive emissions as a result of the activities of GAEC."[78] The Commission went to court against the Onormorkor-Adain family, who had reportedly sold the land to Anaina International. According to media reports, the Lands Commission received a court order to return land to the family, but the Onormorkor-Adains "went ahead to allocate to themselves a portion of the land that would suit them." Acting on behalf of the family, Arthur Hammond Tetteh Quarcoo sued the Commission and sought compensation for damages when Akaho ordered the demolition. The judge dismissed the case and rather required the Onormorkor-Adain family to compensate the Commission with 500 Ghana cedis.[79]

Nor was it the last fire that the Atomic Fire Brigade would have to put out within a few kilometers of the reactor. In October 2017, a petrol tanker was offloading at the government-owned GOIL when a fire broke out.[80] It was there that I had first sat to hear locals chat about the history of the Junction. I could see T.K. in his pristine white shirt, "this area used to be a bushy feeder road." As if an exploding tanker at a station was not enough, the fire at the GOIL had jumped to a cooking gas depot next door. From my quiet street in Texas, I had been on WhatsApp earlier with my cousin who lived off Legon Road. Had Henrietta made it back home yet? We soon were on a conference call with my husband's aunt, who was debating whether or not to drive with her household into the hills near Aburi to escape the flames approaching her home in Haatso. It was just jumping from place to place; people were literally running with their families for miles to escape the heat. On the news it sounded like the Atomic Fire Brigade had rushed over and quickly gotten it under control, but could the reports be trusted with all of those underground petrol tanks in that area? In fact, it had started raining heavily in what many saw as an act of God and this had helped them tremendously in their efforts to get the rolling fire under control. Still, at least seven people died and ten times as many were injured as they passed through the busy area. Within minutes, Eyram Amaglo, the filmmaker partnering with me to document the area, sent me videos from people who witnessed the explosion from a house nearby. She and my brother in Tema both

Figure 6.7 Viral photo of October 8, 2017 explosion of petrol tanker at the GOIL station by Atomic Junction
(*Source*: Twitter, WhatsApp)

sent me the photo of the mushroom cloud taken from a high-rise that became viral from the day on the WhatsApp messaging service (Figure 6.7).

On the ground, the rumor across Accra was that the red clouds billowing out of Atomic Junction were related to the reactor. I assured my colleagues and friends sending me messages from around the world that the fire was actually not near the Ghana Atomic Energy Commission itself. For Ghanaians, the trauma from the fire was intense and stirred up painful memories. Just two years before, a dramatic flood in Accra turned fatal when a large crowd sought refuge under the overhang of a petrol station at the Danquah Circle interchange, another quickly expanding transportation hub closer to downtown Accra. As the waters rose above their waists and panic was already at fever pitch, a leak below ground in the petrol station led to a tremendous fire and explosion, killing at least 150 people. This new petrol station explosion at Atomic led to calls to improve regulation of underground petrol tanks and to reconsider their frequent siting in tightly packed urban areas. The next day, thousands assembled on the flyover at Atomic Junction to observe the destruction for themselves and to watch Ghana's Vice President Alhaji Dr. Mahamudu Bawumia, who had the night before been on a tour with President Nana Addo Dankwa Akufo-Addo in the Northern Region of the country, survey the damage and reassure the community.

From the conflicts over palm trees, to the fights over shopping malls, to the mushroom cloud hovering over the exploding GOIL, these contests on the Haatso-Atomic Road are symbolic of Africa's nuclear futures. We are at a chaotic junction, where we see modernity, we construct all the signs, but it is a fragile performance that can be tipped off-balance at the simplest provocation. An hour of rain when all the open gutters overflow and traffic comes to a halt. Or a fire or two. How can Ghana's nuclear program exist in such a precarious location? And yet it does.

Conclusions: Atomic Lands and Relative Risks

On Ghana's nuclear frontier, new regulations surrounding nuclear installations have exacerbated long-standing family disputes over territory. Conflicts at Kwabenya-Dome date to at least 1904, when the Supreme Court of the British Gold Coast Colony judged that there was no "fixed boundary between" the Ga and Akuapem ethnic groups in this area. Conflicting testimonies over property rights proliferated once the Ghana Atomic Energy Commission expropriated land for a large scientific research campus in 1963. Multiple claims led to dissatisfaction with government compensation, re-sales, and squatting on the Commission's "Atomic Lands." Since the 1963 Atomic Energy Act, the Commission conflated the dangers of Ghana's reactor program with exclusion zones elsewhere to control property.

The Commission tacitly allowed nearby residents to believe they had a reactor from the 1960s, greatly exaggerating radiations risks once the GHARR-1 was critical from 1994. Nkrumah's promise of a reactor provided the Commission with invisible power.[81] To indicate atomic power, both real and foretold, the Commission did not demolish uncompleted buildings from the 1960s, and it created additional signboards, walls, and schools visible to the public from outside the exclusion zone. The Commission periodically destroyed structures built by encroachers, asserting its legal claims to state lands. The arrival of an *actual* reactor in the 1990s catalyzed more volatile conflicts on the Atomic Lands stretching along the Haatso-Atomic Road.

Scientific equity for the nation writ large has meant different levels of disenfranchisement for people proximate to the reactor campus. While the nationalist government set out to establish a science city where "men of learning" would propel Ghana's future, they managed to trample on residents of Kwabenya or Haatso whose own sons and daughters have not always seen the fruits of the scientific enterprise. Yes, Ghanaian scientists have worked tirelessly to realize the dream of a nuclear reactor and the promise of atomic science, but as my investigations have shown, they have oftentimes kept their activities a mystery to those nearby to enhance their own status and reputation and thereby secure land. In their quest to protect the small nuclear reactor at Kwabenya, they turned attention away from the growing number of filling stations along the Haatso-Atomic Road. Ultimately, it was to be the petrol stations and the moving tankers that filled them that brought a horrifying mushroom cloud to Atomic Junction. The question remained whether the road would take Ghana to nuclear power.

Epilogue: Nuclear Power at the Crossroads

When I first met J.J. Fletcher, the affable professor at the Ghana School of Nuclear and Allied Sciences who trained in Minsk in the Soviet Union, he was wearing a Ghana Nuclear Society polo shirt. I immediately knew I needed several of my own and spent the rest of the afternoon chasing down students from the Ghana Nuclear Society with Eyram Amaglo, the filmmaker documenting Atomic Junction with me. We found a very entrepreneurial female student who went off to search for the stash of shirts in a room in the student hostel named after the former director of the Commission, Francis Allotey. While we waited a little longer for our new fashion statements, we chatted with a recent male graduate of the Ghana School of Nuclear and Allied Sciences. He seemed absolutely forlorn and provided a disappointing conclusion to a long day filled with inspiring chats with his teachers.

He explained that there was a government hiring freeze, so now that he had finished his Master's degree he would return to his hometown in the north of the country until he was called for a job. How depressing! But you are in Accra for a few more days, the American in me responded. Why not circulate your CV and visit a few companies? Surely someone would want to hire you. But I knew that without connections, it would be tough. Even the small number of scientists at the Ghana Atomic Energy Commission benefited from connections, for instance, a nephew of Allotey was already a stalwart among a group of young Commission scientists who we met up with another day. The female student returned and sold us all the shirts we could carry. I asked her how she was enjoying her program and knew she would survive; she was already doing a side hustle selling shirts and was full of positive energy. The offspring of Ghana's nuclear program stood at the crossroads with several directions they might turn.

I first began this project in an effort to better understand the nuclear neighborhood that had grown in an afrofuturistic landscape. Atomic Junction, Proton Lane, Gamma Avenue. What was happening beyond the gates of the Ghana Atomic Energy Commission? Was it true that there was actually a reactor over there? There has been some speculation about the prospects of nuclear energy production in African countries, but little attention to the history of different nuclear programs from the perspective of black scientists in key countries including Ghana, Nigeria, and the Democratic Republic of Congo. The North African situation, including Libya and Egypt, has often been folded into the geopolitical discussions in the Middle East, while the South African case has been seen as an anomalous story given white-led nuclear research and the higher consumption of electricity in the country overall. The time is ripe to continue historical examinations of African nuclear programs.

Ghana's experience with nuclear power has been one of challenges and persistence. Kwame Nkrumah's vision for a nuclear program in an independent African country opened a new chapter of afrofuturism. It may be back in vogue to imagine some new modernist, high-tech reality for African nations, but afrofuturism has a longer history linked to independence struggles. While European colonial scientists in Ghana, Nigeria, or Congo projected the possibility of conducting nuclear reactions on the continent, Nkrumah's approach provided a space for black African researchers to be at the helm of scientific work themselves. This was important, given a legacy of colonial efforts to delegitimize the intelligence and mental capacity of African colonial subjects. And yet, in the independence moment, the prospect of a nuclear-charged African intelligentsia led to peak anxiety in London and Washington. British and American scientists and politicians conspired to destabilize Nkrumah's regime. British intelligence reports, as described in Chapter 4, indicated efforts to limit access to nuclear information and equipment in Ghana. Even the Soviet Union, which purported to be a friendly supporter of Nkrumah's agenda and the prosperity of independent African countries, refused nuclear aid once Nkrumah's regime was toppled. When a new government made overtures to the Soviets a decade later, little was done to propel the Ghanaian nuclear vision forward.

Yet, to dwell on the empty buildings for the desired reactor that have haunted the Kwabenya landscape for so long misses the point. It breeds a distinct brand of afropessimism and despair. What this book has sought to do is keep the lives of Ghanaian scientists at the center of the story, to show their specific hopes, dreams, and struggles. Nkrumah and Baffour may have provided a spark for the nuclear program. However, it was the many scientists who have taken on the call and animated the project. Indeed, African scientists have always had the intellectual capacity to engage in nuclear research, whether in Ghana, Nigeria, or Congo, for example. While this book acknowledged the pessimistic arguments against nuclear energy in African countries, it aimed to primarily document an afrorealist view of the actual trajectory of events and the afrofuturistic dream and vision that has been at its core. Rather than vaguely pointing to prospects for nuclear futures in African countries, I traced the series of events and perspectives of key actors to see where we have been so far.

Across Africa, nuclear physicists have traversed long, dusty hallways nurturing dreams of nuclear power for more than half-a-century. A major aim of the Nkrumah generation was to actually train Ghanaians in nuclear physics. Initially, they sought information from the Soviet Union. When Nkrumah lost power, they were equal opportunists and expanded their training wherever they could, from Ukraine to the United Kingdom. If Nkrumah had not stressed the potential of Africans to manage nuclear reactions themselves, sent Baffour and others to approach the Soviet Union for an atomic power reactor, or sponsored the training of Ghanaian scientists at Moscow State University, the International Atomic Energy Agency would not have had a cadre of motivated African scientists to tap in coming years. Nkrumah's vision of scientific equity, where Africans might be stakeholders in technological affairs, did create a tight-knit community willing to devote their lives to securing a reactor, even if it met tremendous resistance from Western powers.

In one direction, the road to nuclear energy in Ghana remains clear. There may indeed be a need to hire the many young men and women still training in nuclear physics at the School for Nuclear and Allied Sciences in the foreseeable future. At the time of writing this book, Ghana has set up an independent Nuclear Regulatory Authority as required through the International Atomic Energy Agency. Granted, it is still a very modest affair set up in a former student hostel at the School of Nuclear and Allied Sciences with computers and data managed in small bedrooms near a set of open showers. The International Atomic Energy Agency regularly commends Ghana for safe management of its equipment. Surveys are underway to identify additional sites for nuclear reactors large enough to generate power. Ghanaians have proven that "manpower" is not a major limitation on expanding their nuclear program and land can be found. It will be a question of equipment and the initial startup costs. Like their counterparts at nuclear programs in Nigeria and Tanzania, they have explored memorandums of understanding with partners to import larger reactors.

Through strong relationships with the International Atomic Energy Agency, Ghanaian scientists find ways to beat the challenges of sourcing and maintaining equipment in tropical environments. Products of Ghana's nuclear establishment have actually been at the helm of tropicalization efforts at the Agency. Ghanaian scientists have monitored reactors in other countries and are tech-savvy. They find creative ways to bring in necessary equipment to maintain the nation's radiation badge monitoring system. If people in African countries have robustly adopted mobile phones, microwaves, and cars despite challenges of accessing electricity and fuel, it is believable that nuclear reactors are on the table, too. Indeed, the surrounding neighborhood thrives on the Atomic moniker and believes anything is possible, from the Atomic Road Pharmacy to the Atomic Modern Clinic to the Atomic Junction Petrol Station.

There is certainly evidence from Ghana and other African countries that the importing of high-tech equipment while on one level is a sign of extending scientific access and proclaiming national status, it can also be a terrific avenue for graft with little financial planning for maintenance and repair of broken parts. Nkrumah's pet project of the Soviet reactor scheme was an easy target after his regime fell as a potential place for unfair contracts aimed to benefit a few. Concerns do linger with regards to recent contracts set up in Tanzania, Kenya, and Nigeria for nuclear power plants given limitations of existing power grids and cost of nuclear power production versus actual demand and need. And the high costs around power stations still can lead to economic dependencies at the very juncture where Africans seek autonomy.

There remain other directions for Africa's nuclear future that point to other avenues for sustainable energy. In Ghana, many questions still linger on Atomic Lands, including safety and security, with implications for the siting of future reactors and the longevity of the Commission. The fires and explosions off the Haatso-Atomic Road in recent years were definitely worrying. Urban density and the fight for real estate and petrol stations to fuel the growing numbers of cars in the Atomic Junction area made it harder for the Commission to hold onto its large campus. Recent decisions to upgrade an above-ground radioactive waste site and to maintain the reactor with a new fuel supply made sense from the perspective of scientists but seemed out of place given the hectic Haatso-Atomic Road outside the gates.

Ghana's "nuclear borderlands," to use Masco's term, continue to be porous, contested terrain.[1] Research on African land disputes stresses escalations between traditional leaders, government officials, and land-less citizens.[2] Multinational land grabs, either through out-right purchases or extended leases, further destabilize governments.[3] Despite recent land legislation in Ghana that distinguishes between customary land managed through chiefs and public land owned by the state, observers continue to note the "uncertainty" of Ghana's land market and the rise of sometimes violent land disputes due to "multiple sales, administrative lapses, registration problems, corruption, delays, frustrations, unreliable estate agents, disregard for laws, encroachment, implementation of weaknesses and lack of information."[4]

Nor can one rule out regional competition and a nuclear arms race down the road. At the time of writing, Ghana had removed fuel rods that could be used to make a weapon and swapped in safer versions. At the center of national quests for nuclear power has been the urge to gain information and know-how prior to a nearby regime. We see this for India and Pakistan, Iran, Israel, Egypt, and Libya. The sagas of Nigeria and the Democratic Republic of Congo (DRC) are part of the story of Ghana's journey for nuclear access. Initially, Kwame Nkrumah and Baffour spoke of nuclear power in Ghana as a way to prevent Western imperialism. They also suggested it as a way to unify Africa. Simultaneously, there was a competitive element: would Ghana surpass Congo's nascent nuclear program? On the eve of inde-pendence, would Ghana get a reactor before the rival British colony Nigeria? There is tremendous wealth in private hands within West Africa; perhaps someone will fund a project to make some kind of nuclear weapon, or at the least radioactive waste byproducts from industry and medicine will be repurposed for ill.

As other African countries increase their nuclear capabilities, the potential for disputes on nuclear lands expands. Like Ghana, Nigeria also initiated a process to import a nuclear reactor from China in 1996. With ten research reactors in six other African nations, and larger power reactors planned, atomic lands management near exclusion zones warrants further investigation. Over thirty African nations have joined the African Regional Cooperative Agreement for Research, Development and Training related to Nuclear Science and Technology since 1990. Inspired by South Africa's power reactors, these nations seek to expand their nuclear programs through support from the International Atomic Energy Agency.[5] Rising populations, urbanization, and industrial needs return governments to the potential of nuclear energy for generating electricity.

Debates over possible radiation at Kwabenya have global resonance. Dissatisfaction in Ghana around the siting of a pilot reactor echoes international concern over the management of atomic lands elsewhere. At one point, I thought that the meltdown at the Fukushima Daiichi reactor in Japan after a tsunami in 2011 would be the death knell to African nuclear programs. Once news of Fukushima Daiichi reverberated in Ghana, officials at the Commission reassured Ghanaians that the research reactor was secure, although Accra is built along an earthquake fault and near the sea. The Commission then proceeded to work with the International Atomic Energy Agency to implement a power station by 2020, taking such steps as the establishment of an independent Nuclear Regulatory Authority Board alongside replacing the fuel supply for the GHARR-1 (Figure 7.1).[6] While some countries, including Germany, have delayed or stopped nuclear power programs in the wake of the Fukushima meltdown, there is little to suggest that African countries in the post-Fukushima era plan to reconsider their nuclear futures.

Nkrumah's vision of scientific equity for Ghana and the African continent continues to be upheld. Ghanaian nuclear scientists have emerged as highly skilled individuals who are taking a leading position in African atomic affairs and within the International Atomic Energy Agency. Despite efforts to literally undermine their autonomy and nuclear ambitions from racist experts brought in at various times to "advise" the country on nuclear prospects, they have just carried on. Deftly outwitting the constraints of the nuclear protectorate, they have sought to understand the latest in nuclear technology and radiation protection and extend this knowledge to other Ghanaians and fellow African researchers. Indeed, a cousin, the son of a Ghanaian mathematician, worked for Areva managing nuclear reactors for France while I conducted my investigations. If Ghanaian scientists run nuclear

Figure 7.1 Dr. Kwaku Aning, GAEC Board chairman with H.E. Mrs. Sun Baohong, Chinese Ambassador to Ghana, on August 10, 2017, after a successful core conversion of the GHARR-1
(*Source*: GAEC 2018 calendar, March, hanging on wall of in-law's kitchen)

reactors in Europe surely they have the intellectual capacity to do so in Ghana, too.

Still, global and local inequalities exist. Ghana does not yet have reactors large enough to generate electricity. And the relative success of the Ghanaian nuclear physicists does not happen in a vacuum. Their nearby neighbors also seek access to science for their own children, and question empty land used to secure the small fetish object of the nuclear scientists. As we stand at the crossroads to nuclear power, we are reminded that enshrining nuclear science to prove African expertise can be a way to also trample on the lives and careers of those who are still standing just outside the atomic gates.

Notes

1 Introduction

1 Kwame Nkrumah, "Nuclear War is an Economic and Political Suicide – Kwame," *The Ghanaian Times*, June 23, 1962.
2 Kwame Nkrumah, "Osagyefo Dedicates Atomic Reactor: Science City for Ghana," *The Ghanaian Times*, November 16, 1964.
3 "Osagyefo Dedicates Atomic Reactor: Science City for Ghana."
4 On the rise and fall of Baffour, see PRAAD ADM 5/3/145 Report of the Commission of Enquiry, University of Science and Technology, Kumasi, 1966.
5 Letter from R.P. Baffour, Chairman, Ghana Atomic Energy Commission, University of Science and Technology, Kumasi, Ghana to Mr. S. Addo, Secretary Education Review Committee, Parliament House, Accra, July 16, 1966 in PRAAD RG 3/6/1167 Ghana Atomic Energy Commission.
6 IAEA GC(VI)/OR.72 Official Record of the Seventy-Second Plenary Meeting Held at the Neue Hofburg, Vienna, on Wednesday, September 26, 1962, at 3.20 p.m. President: Mr. Baffour (Ghana), 1962.
7 *Ibid.*
8 On afterlives of the independence moment in Asia and Africa, see Christopher J. Lee, "Between a Moment and an Era: The Origins and Afterlives of Bandung," in *Making a World after Empire: The Bandung Moment and Its Political Afterlives*, ed. Christopher J. Lee (Athens, OH: Ohio University Press, 2010), 4. On the legacy of Nkrumah, see Jeffrey S. Ahlman, *Living with Nkrumahism: Nation, State, and Pan-Africanism in Ghana* (Athens, OH: Ohio University Press, 2017). On race and afterlives, see Ruha Benjamin, "Black Afterlives Matter," in *Making Kin Not Population*, ed. Adele Clarke and Donna Haraway (Chicago: Prickly Paradigm Press, 2018). See also Kwame Anthony Appiah, "Is the Post- in Postmodernism the Post- in Postcolonial?" *Critical Inquiry* 17, no. 2 (Winter, 1991): 336–357.
9 Abena Dove Osseo-Asare, "Scientific Equity: Experiments in Laboratory Education in Ghana," *Isis* 104, no. 4 (2013): 713–741.

10 Christopher O. Justice et al., "Climate Change in Sub-Saharan Africa: Assumptions, Realities and Future Investments," in *Climate Change and Africa*, ed. Pak Sum Low (Cambridge; New York: Cambridge University Press, 2005); Joel Rolim Mancia and Denise Gastaldo, "Editorial: Production and Consumption of Science in a Global Context," *Nursing Inquiry* 11, no. 2 (2004): 65–66.

11 "Editorial: Production and Consumption of Science in a Global Context," 66. Joel Rolim Mancia and Denise Gastaldo, "Editorial: Production and Consumption of Science in a Global Context," *Nursing Inquiry* 11, no. 2 (2004): 65–66.

12 "Editorial: Production and Consumption of Science in a Global Context," 66.

13 *Ibid.* Scientific equity as a concept has also been used in discussions of the need for more diverse scientific research studies that reflect a wider level of experience.

14 Nkrumah, "Osagyefo Dedicates Atomic Reactor: Science City for Ghana."

15 The Phelps-Stokes Fund in the United States argued in an infamous and influential study for the "Improvability of Africans"; Thomas Jesse Jones, *Education in Africa: A Study of West, South, and Equatorial Africa by the African Education Commission, under the Auspices of the Phelps-Stokes Fund and Foreign Mission Societies of North America and Europe* (New York: Phelps-Stokes Fund, 1922), 5–6. See also Helen Kitchen, ed., *The Educated African: A Country-by-Country Survey of Educational Development in Africa* (New York: Frederick A. Praeger, 1962); Leonard John Lewis, *An Outline Chronological Table of the Development of Education in British West Africa* (Edinburgh: Thomas Nelson and Sons Ltd. [1953?]); Leonard John Lewis, *Education and Political Independence in Africa, and Other Essays* (Edinburgh: Nelson, 1962); Leonard John Lewis, *African Education: A Study of Educational Policy and Practice in British Tropical Africa* (Oxford: Oxford University Press, 1953).

16 Allan Nunn May, *The Atomic Nature of Matter: An Inaugural Lecture Delivered on 29th January, 1970 at the University of Ghana, Legon* (Accra: Ghana Universities Press, 1971), 19.

17 Cheik Anta Diop, *Physique Nucléaire Et Chronologie Absolue* (Dakar: Institut Fondamental d'Afrique Noire (IFAN), 1974); *Nations Negres Et Culture* (Paris: Présence africaine, 1955); Cheik Anta Diop, E. Curtis Alexander, and Mwalimu Imara Mwadilifu, *Cheikh Anta Diop: An African Scientist: An Axiomatic Overview of His Teachings and Thoughts*, Pan African Internationalist Handbook (New York: ECA Associates, 1984).

18 Julius Kambarage Nyerere, *The Second Scramble* (Dar es Salaam: Tanganyika Standard [1962?]).

19 Oye Ogunbadejo, "Africa's Nuclear Capability," *Journal of Modern African Studies* 22, no. 1 (1984): 19–43; Avner Cohn and Terence McNamee, *Why Do States Want Nuclear Weapons?: The Cases of Israel and South Africa* (Oslo: Institutt for forsvarsstudier, 2005); Frank V. Pabian, "South Africa's Nuclear Weapon Program: Lessons for U.S. Nonproliferation Policy," *The Nonproliferation Review* 3, no. 1 (1995): 1–19; J.W. de Villiers, Roger Jardin, and Mitchell Reiss, "Why South Africa Gave up the Bomb," *Foreign Affairs* 72, no. 5 (1993): 98–109; Ronald W. Walters, *South Africa and the Bomb: Responsibility and Deterrence* (Lexington, MA: Lexington Books, 1987).

20 Itty Abraham, *The Making of the Indian Atomic Bomb: Science, Secrecy and the Postcolonial State* (London; New York: Zed Books, 1998).

21 Ali A. Mazuri, *Niger-Saki: Does Nigeria Have a Nuclear Option?* (Lagos: The Nigerian Institute of International Affairs, 1981), 18.

22 Alondra Nelson, "Introduction: Future Texts," *Social Text (special Issue on Afrofuturism)* 20, no. 2 (2002): 1–15. She has examined "technophilia" in African American scientific communities: *The Social Life of D.N.A.: Race, Reparations, and Reconciliation after the Genome* (Boston, MA: Beacon Press, 2016); *Body and Soul: The Black Panther Party and the Fight against Medical Discrimination* (Minneapolis, MN: University of Minnesota Press, 2011).

23 Paraphrase from Osseo-Asare, "Scientific Equity."

24 Gabrielle Hecht, "Rupture-Talk in the Nuclear Age: Conjugating Colonial Power in Africa," *Social Studies of Science* 32, no. 5–6 (2002): 691–727; *Being Nuclear: Africans and the Global Uranium Trade* (Cambridge, MA: MIT Press, 2012).

25 "U.S. Lends £10m for Big Volta Project, They Make Conditions," *Daily Graphic*, August 20, 1960; Thomas J. Noer, "The New Frontier and African Neutralism: Kennedy, Nkrumah, and the Volta River Project," *Diplomatic History* 8, no. 1 (1984): 61–79; "Soviets to Build a Railway Line from Kumasi to Upper Volta," *The Ghanaian Times*, February 2, 1962; *Volta Resettlement Symposium Papers*, ed. Robert Chambers, trans. Accra Volta River Authority and Kwame Nkrumah University of Science and Technology Faculty of Architecture, Kumasi, Ghana, Volta Resettlement Symposium (Kumasi: University of Science and Technology, 1965); Emmanuel Kwaku Akyeampong, *Between the Sea & the Lagoon: An Eco-Social History of the Anlo of Southeastern Ghana C. 1850 to Recent Times* (Oxford: James Currey, 2001); A.E. Kitson, *The Possible Sources of Power for Industrial Purposes in the Gold Coast, British West Africa* (London: n.p., 1928).

26 By the 1970s, Letitia Obeng, the prominent Ghanaian etymologist and one of the first women with a science PhD, examined the environmental legacy of the Volta Lake and sounded the alarm at the dramatic rise in the prevalence of the snail-borne disease schistosomiasis (bilharzia) to as high as 70 percent for some nearby residents. Letitia Obeng, "Should Dams Be Built? The Volta Lake Example," *Ambio* 6, no. 1 (1977): 46–50. The ramifications of the Volta Dam or "Nkrumah's baby" are the subject of extensive study by the historian Stephan Miescher, including a documentary film he co-produced with Lane Clark, "Electric Dreams"; Stephan F. Miescher, "'No One Should Be Worse Off': The Akosombo Dam, Modernization, and the Experience of Resettlement in Ghana," in *Modernization as Spectacle in Africa*, ed. Peter Jason Bloom, Stephan F. Miescher, and Takiywaa Manuh (Bloomington, IN: Indiana University Press, 2014); "'Nkrumah's Baby': The Akosombo Dam and the Dream of Development in Ghana," *Water History* 6, no. 4 (2014): 341–366; Stephan F. Miescher and Dzozi Tsikata, "Hydro-Power and the Promise of Modernity and Development in Ghana: Comparing the Akosombo and Bui Dam Projects," *Ghana Studies* 12/13 (2009/2010): 55–75; Stephan F. Miescher, "Building the City of the Future: Visions and Experiences of Modernity in Ghana's Akosombo Township," *Journal of African History* 53, no. 3 (2012): 367–390. British anthropologist Thomas Yarrow has emphasized "ruination" and the "afterlives" of uncompleted infrastructure in the Volta Dam resettlements. Thomas Yarrow, "Remains of the Future: Rethinking the Space and Time of Ruination through the Volta Resettlement Project, Ghana," *Cultural Anthropology* 32, no. 4 (2017): 566–591. On the positive side, the Ghanaian American political scientist Naaborle Sackeyfio has argued that the relatively sizeable output of the Volta hydroelectric dam made Ghana's electrical grid more robust than that of South Africa or Nigeria over time. Naaborle Sackeyfio, *Energy Politics and Rural Development in Sub-Saharan Africa* (Cham: Palgrave Macmillan, 2018).

27 *The Consolidation Development Plan*, 2 vols (Accra: Government Printer, 1958); *Second Development Plan, 1959–64* (Accra: Government Printer, 1959).

28 *Seven-Year Plan for National Reconstruction and Development: Financial Years, 1963/64–1969/70* (Accra: Office of the Planning Commission, 1964); *Seven-Year Development Plan: A Brief Outline* (Accra: Office of the Planning Commission, 1963).

29 *Seven-Year Development Plan: Annual Plan for the Second Plan Year, 1965 Financial Year* (Accra: Office of the Planning Commission, 1965), 155.

30 PRAAD RG 11/1/298 Radio Isotope Research Project, 1961.

31 (p. 11) PRAAD RG 5/1/389 Ministry of Works: Electricity Organisation, 1957.

32 See, "Section A: Education and Manpower," in *Seven-Year Plan for National Reconstruction and Development: Financial Years, 1963/64–1969/70*. Manpower was a term with currency in Africa during the period; see, *Ethiopia: A Study of Manpower Needs, Educational Capabilities, and Overseas Study* (New York: Education and World Affairs, 1965); Richard Jolly, "Planning Education for African Development: Economic and Manpower Perspectives" (Nairobi: Published for the Makerere Institute of Social Research by East African Publishing House, 1969).

33 Daniel Kwasi Asare, scientist, Biotechnology and Nuclear Agriculture Research Institute, Ghana Atomic Energy Commission, July 22, 2008.

34 Letitia Obeng, *A Silent Heritage: An Autobiography* (Surrey: Goldsear, 2008); launch of her autobiography, Ghana Academy of Arts and Sciences, Accra, July 7, 2008.

35 James Ferguson, *Global Shadows: Africa in the Neoliberal World Order* (Durham, NC: Duke University Press, 2006).

36 Walter Rodney, *How Europe Underdeveloped Africa* (Washington, DC: Howard University Press, 1981).

37 Interview with Samuel Akoto-Bamford, reverend, professor, School of Nuclear and Allied Sciences, August 3, 2015.

38 Noémi Tousignant, *Edges of Exposure: Toxicology and the Problem of Capacity in Postcolonial Senegal* (Durham, NC: Duke University Press, 2018). Interest in African medical workers has been especially high: Claire L. Wendland, *A Heart for the Work: Journeys through an African Medical School* (Chicago: University of Chicago Press, 2010); John Illife, *East African Doctors: A History of the Modern Profession* (Cambridge: Cambridge University Press, 1998); Julie Livingston, *Improvising Medicine: An African Oncology Ward in an Emerging Cancer Epidemic* (Durham, NC: Duke University Press, 2012); Adell Patton, *Physicians, Colonial Racism, and Diaspora in West Africa* (Gainesville, FL: University Press of Florida, 1996).

39 J.H. Amuasi, *The History of Ghana Atomic Energy Commission 1963–2003: Forty Years of Nuclear Science and Technology Applications in Ghana* (Accra: AGOL Gh. Ltd., 2003); Lawrence Arthur, "History of Radiography in Ghana," Ghana Society of Radiographers, http://ghanasor.org/history-of-radiography-in-ghana/.

40 Robert S. Anderson, *Nucleus and Nation: Scientists, International Networks, and Power in India* (Chicago; London: University of Chicago Press, 2010); M.V. Ramana, *The Power of Promise: Examining Nuclear Energy in India* (New Delhi: Penguin, 2012); F. Khan, *Eating Grass: The Making of the Pakistani Bomb* (Palo Alto, CA: Stanford University

Press, 2012); Malfrid Braut-Hegghammer, *Unclear Physics: Why Iraq and Libya Failed to Build Nuclear Weapons* (Ithaca, NY: Cornell Press, 2016); Hannes Steyn, Richardt Van Der Walt, and Jan Van Loggerenberg, *Nuclear Armament and Disarmament: South Africa's Nuclear Experience* (Lincoln, NE: iUniverse, 2005); Walters, *South Africa and the Bomb: Responsibility and Deterrence*; Pabian, "South Africa's Nuclear Weapon Program: Lessons for U.S. Nonproliferation Policy."

41 "Science, Technology – Vital Basis of Our Development," *The Ghanaian Times*, November 24, 1965.

42 Reclaiming the mind and asserting African intelligence is a theme of anticolonial and Pan-African discourse. In 1937 Marcus Garvey expressed, "We are going to emancipate ourselves from mental slavery because whilst others might free the body, none but ourselves can free the mind. Mind is your only ruler, sovereign." This was echoed in the lyrics of Bob Marley's "Redemption Song," from the album *Uprising* (Chris Blackwell, producer; Island Records, 1980). See also the song lyrics for Fela Kuti, "Colo Mentality," *Sorrow Tears and Blood* (Kalakuta: 1977). Ngũgĩ wa Thiong'o, *Decolonising the Mind: The Politics of Language in African Literature* (London: James Currey, 1992).

43 Homi Bhabha, "Of Mimicry and Man: The Ambivalence of Colonial Discourse," *October* 28 (1984): 125–133; Dipesh Chakrabarty, *Provincializing Europe: Postcolonial Thought and Historical Difference* (Princeton, NJ: Princeton University Press, 2000); "Postcoloniality and the Artifice of History: Who Speaks for 'Indian' Pasts?" *Representations* 37 (1992): 1–26.

44 Osseo-Asare, "Scientific Equity"; Suman Seth, "Putting Knowledge in Its Place: Science, Colonialism, and the Postcolonial," *Postcolonial Studies* 12, no. 4 (2009): 373–388; Warwick Anderson, "From Subjugated Knowledge to Conjugated Subjects: Science and Globalisation, or Postcolonial Studies of Science?" *Ibid.*: 389–400.

45 My interest in the connections between postcolonial theory and the social study of science stems from my early work from 1996 with physicist Abha Sur, who trained me in independent tutorials at Harvard; Nicholas B. King, my undergraduate thesis advisor who had been a student of Warwick Anderson; and Kwame Anthony Appiah, with whom I read for a field in Postcolonial Theory and African Diaspora Studies in 2000 for my PhD exams. Abha Sur, "Aesthetics, Authority, and Control in an Indian Laboratory: The Raman-Born Controversy on Lattice Dynamics," *Isis* 90, no. 1 (1999): 25–49; Nicholas B. King, "Security, Disease, Commerce: Ideologies of Postcolonial Global Health," *Social Studies of Science* 32, no. 5–6 (2002): 763–789; Appiah, "Is the Post-"; A.D.

Osseo-Asare, "Bioprospecting and Resistance: Transforming Poisoned Arrows into Strophanthin Pills in Colonial Gold Coast, 1885–1922," *Social History of Medicine* 21, no. 2 (2008): 269–290; Osseo-Asare, "Scientific Equity."

46 On blurred lines between reality and afrofuturism in fiction, film, and history, see Aaron Bady, "Things to Come," *The New Inquiry*, March 6, 2015; Naunihal Singh, "What 'Black Panther's' Wakanda Can Teach Us About Africa's History – and Its Future," *Washington Post*, February 28, 2018; Lisa Yaszek, "Afrofuturism, Science Fiction, and the History of the Future," *Socialism and Democracy* 20, no. 3 (2010): 41–60; Nelson, "Future Texts"; Melody Jue, "Intimate Objectivity: On Nnedi Okorafor's Oceanic Afrofuturism," *Women's Studies Quarterly* 45, no. 1 & 2 (2017): 171–188; Timothy Burke, "District 9," *Easily Distracted*, September 2, 2009; Nnedi Okorafor, "My Response to District 419 ... I Mean District 9. :-)," *Facebook*, August 23, 2009.

47 I first explored the socioeconomic and political divides between African scientists and non-scientists in my book *Bitter Roots: The Search for Healing Plants in Africa* (Chicago: University of Chicago Press, 2014), 1.

48 Itty Abraham, "Geopolitics and Biopolitics in India's High Natural Background Radiation Zone," *Science, Technology & Society* 17, no. 1 (2012): 105–122.

49 Kate Brown, *Plutopia: Nuclear Families, Atomic Cities, and the Great Soviet and American Plutonium Disasters* (New York: Oxford University Press, 2013).

50 Clapperton Chakanetsa Mavhunga, "Energy, Industry, and Transport in South-Central Africa's History," in *Energy (and) Colonialism, Energy (in) Dependence Africa, Europe, Greenland, North America*, ed. Clapperton Chakanetsa Mavhunga and Helmuth Trischler (Munich: Rachel Carson Center Perspectives, 2014). Also, *Transient Workspaces: Technologies of Everyday Innovation in Zimbabwe* (Cambridge, MA: MIT Press, 2014).

51 J. Hart, *Ghana on the Go: African Mobility in the Age of Motor Transportation* (Bloomington, IN: Indiana University Press, 2016); Ato Quayson, *Oxford Street, Accra: City Life and the Itineraries of Transnationalism* (Durham, NC: Duke University Press, 2014); Gabriel Klaeger, "Introduction: The Perils and Possibilities of African Roads," *Africa* 83, no. 3 (2013): 359–366; "Dwelling on the Road: Routines, Rituals and Roadblocks in Southern Ghana," *Africa: Journal of the International African Institute/Revue de l'Institut Africain International* 83, no. 3 (2013): 446–469; K. Beck, G. Klaeger, and M. Stasik, *The Making of the African Road* (Leiden: Brill, 2017).

52 Hecht, *Being Nuclear*, 3.

2 Nuclear Winds

1 Kwame Nkrumah, "Speech by the Hon. Dr. Kwame Nkrumah, Prime Minister of Ghana," in *Conference of Independent African States: Speeches Delivered at the Inaugural Session, 15th April, 1958* (Accra: Government Printer, n.d.), 7.

2 "A French Bomb – Not Only for France?," *Manchester Guardian*, July 10, 1959.

3 "Reporter: A Doctor of Science: Death Dust: There Is Danger Ahead!" *Evening News*, February 26, 1960.

4 Here, I focus on the scientific findings and diplomatic interventions. For more on the efforts of the Saharan Protest Team, see Jean Allman, "Nuclear Imperialism and Pan-African Struggle for Peace and Freedom: Ghana, 1959–1962," *Souls: A Critical Journal of Black Politics, Culture, and Society* 10, no. 2 (2008): 83–102; Rob Skinner, "Bombs and Border Crossings: Peace Activist Networks and the Post-Colonial State in Africa, 1959–62," *Journal of Contemporary History* (2014): 418–438.

5 On Malian disdain for the tests, see Vincent Joly, "The French Army and Malian Independence (1956–1961)," in *Francophone Africa at Fifty*, eds. Tony Chafer and Alexander Keese (New York: Manchester University Press, 2013), 80.

6 K. Frimpong-Manso, "Sahara Protest Team Send Message to Ghana: An Appeal to the Youth of Africa," *Evening News*, January 4, 1960.

7 "One Atom Bomb Smashes Four Square Miles of Hiroshima," *Gold Coast Independent*, August 11, 1945.

8 "The Defeat of Japan," *Gold Coast Independent*, August 18, 1945.

9 "The Atomic Bomb Entirely Sweeps Another City into River," *Gold Coast Independent*, August 25, 1945.

10 For example, "Radio Today: Wednesday December 24, 1952," *The Daily Echo*, December 24, 1952.

11 John Tully, "London Letter: Atom Bomb," *Daily Graphic*, October 14, 1952.

12 "Total Ban on Atomic Weapons: 'Matter of Principle with India,' Tests Must End First," *The Times of India*, October 7, 1957.

13 Steven L. Simon and André Bouville, "Radiation Doses to Local Populations near Nuclear Weapons Test Sites Worldwide," *Health Physics* 82, no. 5 (2002): 706–725; Robert Jacobs, "Nuclear Conquistadors: Military Colonialism in Nuclear Test Site Selection During the Cold War," *Asian Journal of Peacebuilding* 1, no. 2 (2013): 157–177.

14 Mervyn O'Driscoll, "Explosive Challenge: Diplomatic Triangles, the United Nations, and the Problem of French Nuclear Testing, 1959–1960," *Journal of Cold War Studies* 11, no. 1 (2009): 28–56.

15 Tawia Adamafio, *French Nuclear Tests in the Sahara* (Accra: C.P.P. National Headquarters, Bureau of Information & Publicity, 1960).

16 UK House of Lords debates, November 18, 1959 in PRO DO 35/9340 Ghana Protest at Proposed French Atomic Explosion in the Sahara, 1959.

17 "France: Stop This Hell Bomb Test," *Evening News*, February 10, 1960.

18 Several cartoons are also analyzed and reprinted in Allman, "Nuclear Imperialism and Pan-African Struggle for Peace and Freedom: Ghana, 1959–1962," 87, 93.

19 Adamafio, *French Nuclear*, 2. Adamafio was a close associate of Nkrumah who was later indicted in the 1962 attempt on the leader's life; see: *By Nkrumah's Side: The Labour and the Wounds* (Accra: Westcoast Publishing House, 1982).

20 Adamafio, *French Nuclear*.

21 Jeffrey S. Ahlman, "The Algerian Question in Nkrumah's Ghana, 1958–1960: Debating 'Violence' and 'Nonviolence' in African Decolonization," *African Today* 57, no. 2 (2010): 66–84.

22 "Ghana Envoy on His Recall," *The Times*, April 5, 1960, p. 10. On debates in Ghana over nonviolence and the Algerian conflict, see "The Algerian Question in Nkrumah's Ghana, 1958–1960," *Africa Today* 57, no. 12 (2010): 67–84.

23 On Nkrumah's efforts to bring together Africans in the diaspora and on the continent in this period, see K.K. Gaines, *American Africans in Ghana: Black Expatriates and the Civil Rights Era* (Chapel Hill, NC: University of North Carolina Press, 2006).

24 Ama Biney, "The Intellectual and Political Legacies of Kwame Nkrumah," *The Journal of Pan African Studies* 4, no. 10 (2012): 127–142; "We Can't Help but Embrace the United States of Africa: British Press Reaction to Nkrumah's Revolutionary Stand," *Evening News*, January 13, 1960.

25 Telegram: Al-Shab: French A-Bomb Test Genocide, received July 14, 1959 in PRO FO 371/138609 France's Atom Bomb Tests in the Sahara.

26 Telegram: Al-Shab: French A-Bomb Test Genocide, received July 14, 1959 in PRO FO 371/138609.

27 Telegram: African TU Congress: Ivory Coast Vote Against Sahara Tests, received September 1959 in PRO FO 371/138609.

28 "A French Bomb – Not Only for France?" in PRO FO 371/138609.

29 "Extract from 5th–18th February 1960, Ghana Fortnightly Summary, Part I," in PRO DO 35/9340.

30 Quoted in Adamafio, *French Nuclear*.

31 Bill Sutherland and Matt Meyer, *Guns and Gandhi in Africa: Pan African Insights on Nonviolence, Armed Struggle and Liberation in Africa* (Trenton, NJ: Africa World Press, 2000).

32 Allman, "Nuclear Imperialism and Pan-African Struggle for Peace and Freedom: Ghana, 1959–1962," 90. The Ghanaian members wrote news articles and appeared in photographs; for instance, Frimpong-Manso, "Sahara Protest Team."

33 "Sahara Protest Team."

34 F. Stephen Miles, Office of the High Commissioner for the UK, Accra to Richard B. Dorman, Commonwealth Relations Office, London, November 9, 1959 in PRO DO 35/9340.

35 V. Intondi, *African Americans against the Bomb: Nuclear Weapons, Colonialism, and the Black Freedom Movement* (Palo Alto, CA: Stanford University Press, 2015), 58; Allman, "Nuclear Imperialism and Pan-African Struggle for Peace and Freedom: Ghana, 1959–1962," 88.

36 F. Stephen Miles, Office of the High Commissioner for the UK, Accra to Richard B. Dorman, Commonwealth Relations Office, London, November 9, 1959 in PRO DO 35/9340.

37 A photograph of Pierre Martin reading the *Evening News* from bed appears below the article, "British Imperialists Again Misfire! Fresh Attack on Nkrumah, Africa! Africa!! Africa!!! Be Warned," *Evening News*, January 5, 1960.

38 Extracts from Official Reports of British House of Lords in PRO DO 35/9340.

39 Kennett Love, "African Nations Ask Nuclear Ban," *The New York Times*, April 23, 1958.

40 Max Frankels, "Khruschchev Suggests Trip to Soviet [Union] by Eisenhower," *ibid.*, February 6, 1959; Audra J. Wolfe, *Competing with the Soviets: Science, Technology, and the State in Cold War America* (Baltimore, MD: Johns Hopkins University Press, 2012).

41 French Embassy in Ghana, January 25, 1960, "The Sahara Test," in PRO DO 35/9340.

42 French Embassy in Ghana, January 25, 1960, "No Danger in the French Atomic Test," in PRO DO 35/9340.

43 Simon and Bouville, "Radiation Doses to Local Populations near Nuclear Weapons Test Sites Worldwide," 722.

44 B. Baggoura, A. Noureddine, and M. Benkrid, "Level of Natural and Artificial Radioactivity in Algeria," *Applied Radiation and Isotopes* 49, no. 7 (1998): 867–873.

45 P.R. Danesi et al., "Residual Radionuclide Concentrations and Estimated Radiation Doses at the Former French Nuclear Weapons Test Sites in Algeria," *Applied Radiation and Isotopes* 66, no. 11 (2008): 1671–1674.

46 Remarkably, the atom bomb did not feature in the history of colonial science in Africa prior to this point. For instance, Helen Tilley does not discuss atomic weapons in her exhaustive study; see Helen Tilley,

Africa as a Living Laboratory: Empire, Development, and the Problem of Scientific Knowledge, 1870–1950 (Chicago: University of Chicago Press, 2011).

47 V. Wassiamal, Ministry of External Affairs, Ghana, to A.H. Ward, Department of Physics, University College of Ghana, Achimota, June 18, 1959 in PRAAD RG 14/4/210 Nuclear Weapons Test, 1959–1961.

48 A.H. Ward and J.D. Marr, "Radioactive Fall-out in Ghana," *Nature* 187, no. 4734 (1960): 299–300.

49 Memo from A.H. Ward, Radio-Isotope and Health-Physics Unit, Physics Department, Legon to Mr. R.M. Asiedu, Asst. Registrar, "University Calendar," March 24, 1964 in PRAAD GAEC 4/SF1 International Atomic Energy Technical Aid (Equipment), 1963–1964.

50 "Radioactive Fall-out in Ghana," 299. These techniques were first used elsewhere; see, Merril Eisenbud and John H. Harley, "Radioactive Dust from Nuclear Detonations," *Science* 117, no. 3033 (1953): 141–147. On Merril Eisenbud see Emory Jerry Jessee, "Radiation Ecologies: Bombs, Bodies, and Environment During the Atmospheric Nuclear Weapons Testing Period, 1942–1965," Montana State University, 2013 (PhD dissertation).

51 L.J.D. Wakely to Mark E. Allen, Commonwealth Relations Office, London, November 7, 1959.

52 J.A.T. Dawson, "Confidential: Note on a Visit to Ghana," March 21, 1960 in *DO 35/9342 Reappraisal of United Kingdom policy in regard to French Atomic tests.*

53 G.M. Edington et al., "The Acute Lethal Effects of Monkeys of Radiostrontium," *Journal of Pathology and Bacteriology* LXXI (1956): 277–293.

54 "The Acute Lethal Effects of Monkeys of Radiostrontium," 288.

55 "Report of the United Kingdom/Nigerian Scientific Committee, 1st Draft," in PRO DO 35/9340.

56 Jessee, "Radiation Ecologies," 209.

57 W.B. Ramsay, "The Use of Numerical Weather Forecasts for Radioactive-Fallout Predictions," *Journal of Geophysical Research* 64, no. 8 (1959): 1120–1121.

58 United States. Congress. Senate. Committee on Foreign Relations, *The International Claims Settlement Act: Hearing before a Subcommittee, Eighty-Sixth Congress, First Session, on S. 706. May 29, 1959* (US Government Printing Office, 1959).

59 Ward and Marr, "Radioactive Fall-out in Ghana," 299–300.

60 "Radioactive Fall-out in Ghana," 300.

61 Wright and Ward, Confidential Report, "Radioactive Fallout No. III," February 23, 1960 in PRAAD RG 14/4/210.

62 PRAAD RG 14/4/210.
63 J.S. Annan, Principal Secretary for Minister of State for Defence to Rt. Hon. Prime Minister, March 16, 1960 in PRAAD RG 14/4/210.
64 Quoted in letter from A.C. Copisarow, Scientific Ataché at UK Embassy, Paris to Dr. J.F. Loutit, Radiobiological Research Unit, Harwell, UK, March 26, 1960.
65 Howard Green, Canadian Secretary for External Affairs, "The Study of Nuclear Radiation," statement presented at UN General Assembly, November 17, 1959 in PRAAD RG 14/4/210.
66 A.H. Ward, senior lecturer, University College, Legon to Principle Secretary, Ministry of Food and Agriculture, December 1, 1960, "Radioactive Fallout Samples," in PRAAD RG 14/4/210.
67 Chief Agricultural Officer, Agricultural Division, "Priority on Ghana Airways Flights Tamale-Kumasi-Accra," to F. Ribeiro-Ayeh, Principal Secretary, Ministry of Defence in PRAAD RG 14/4/210.
68 Nkrumah, "Speech by the Hon. Dr. Kwame Nkrumah, Prime Minister of Ghana," 7.
69 Handwritten note from Raymond Wright, professor of physics, University College, Ghana to Mr. Ribeiro-Ayeh, Principal Secretary, Ministry of Defence, December 28, 1960 in PRAAD RG 14/4/210.
70 Letter from W.G. Penney, UK Atomic Energy Authority, Harwell to Rt. Hon. Alan Lennox-Boyd, Secretary of State for the Colonies, London, September 21, 1959 in PRO CO 937/474 Possible Diversion of Aircraft Due to Atomic Tests, 1959.
71 J.A.T. Dawson, "Confidential: Note on Visit to Nigeria (February 13th–February 20th, 1960)," in PRO DO 35/9340.
72 B.J. Greenhill to D.W.S. Hunt, April 12, 1960, in PRO DO 35/9340.
73 Cypher Telegram from Accra to Commonwealth Relations Office, London and Secret Telegram from the Secretary of State for the Colonies to Sir J. Robertson, Federation of Nigeria, April 8, 1960, in PRO DO 35/9340.
74 Perth to Selwyn Lloyd, Nigeria, March 25, 1960.
75 "Secret: Results of Fall-out Measurements," in PRO DO 35/9340.
76 "Our Science Correspondent: Focus on Ghana Atomic Reactor Project: Nuclear Research in Ghana," *The Ghanaian Times*, November 14, 1966.
77 "Focus on Ghana."
78 Note from R.J. Vile to Mr. Sheffield, October 22, 1959 in PRO CO 937/474.
79 Adamafio, *French Nuclear*.
80 Secret letter from T.W. Keeble, Deputy High Commissioner, Nigeria to G.P. Hampshire, Commonwealth Relations Office, London, November

14, 1960 in PRO FO 371/149450 U.N. General Assembly Ghana's Proposal on an Atom and Base Free Africa, 1960.

81 T. Choy, *Ecologies of Comparison: An Ethnography of Endangerment in Hong Kong* (Durham, NC: Duke University Press, 2011).

82 "Extract from 5th–18th February 1960, Ghana Fortnightly Summary, Part I," in PRO DO 35/9341 Ghana Protest at Proposed French Bomb Test, 1959.

83 A.W. Snelling to Daniel, Office of the High Commission for the UK, Accra, 4 April, 1960, in PRO DO 35/9340.

84 Government of Ghana to Embassy of France, Accra, 1 April, 1960, in PRO DO 35/9340.

85 Government of Ghana to Embassy of France, Accra, 1 April, 1960, in PRO DO 35/9340.

86 M.E. Allen to Mr. Keeble and Mr. D.W.S. Hunt, 1 October, 1959 in PRO DO 35/9340.

87 On Nkrumah's increasing paranoia, see A. Biney, *The Political and Social Thought of Kwame Nkrumah* (New York: Palgrave Macmillan US, 2011), 95.

88 "France: Atomic Club Member," *West African Pilot*, February 15, 1960.

89 Telegram from Khartoum to Foreign Office, London, p. 27, February 15, 1960 in PRO DO 35/9340.

90 Broadcast quoted in "Bomb Explosion Can't Intimidate Africa," *Evening News*, February 26, 1960.

91 "Bomb Explosion Can't Intimidate Africa."

92 Adamafio, *French Nuclear*.

93 Confidential inward Telegram to Commonwealth Relations Office from Accra, cc to other bodies including UK Atomic Energy Authority, Colonial Office, and UK Office of the Minister for Science, April 2, 1960.

94 Allman, "Nuclear Imperialism and Pan-African Struggle for Peace and Freedom: Ghana, 1959–1962," 94.

95 "Ghana Envoy on His Recall."

96 A.W. Snelling to Daniel, Office of the High Commission for the UK, Accra, April 4, 1960, in PRO DO 35/9340.

97 Confidential Telegram from Rabat to Foreign Office, 7.20 pm, March 31, 1960, in PRO DO 35/9342 Reappraisal of United Kingdom Policy in Regard to French Atomic Tests.

98 B.G. Plummer, *In Search of Power: African Americans in the Era of Decolonization, 1956–1974* (New York: Cambridge University Press, 2013), 79–81; O'Driscoll, "Explosive Challenge"; Miloud Barkaoui, "Managing the Colonial Status Quo: Eisenhower's Cold War and the Algerian War of Independence," *The Journal of North African Studies* 17, no. 1 (2012): 125–141.

99 Quoted in "Graham Mum on French Atom Test," *Evening News*, January 25, 1960.

100 Intondi, *African Americans Against*, 58; Allman, "Nuclear Imperialism and Pan-African Struggle for Peace and Freedom: Ghana, 1959–1962," 88.

101 B.J. Greenhill to Mr. Keeble and Mr. D.W.S. Hunt, March 18, 1960, in PRO DO 35/9342.

102 Confidential Outward Telegram from Commonwealth Relations Office, "French Tests in Sahara," in PRO DO 35/9342.

103 D.W.S. Hunt to Sir Alexander Clutterbuck, 22 March 1960, in "Innovation and Technology Transfer."

104 Dictation from D.S.W. Hunt to Sir Alexander Clutterbuck, March 29, 1960, in PRO DO 35/9342.

105 D.W.S. Hunt to Sir Alexander Clutterbuck, March 22, 1960, in PRO DO 35/9342.

106 Secret from Foreign Office to Paris, 8.42 pm March 30, 1960, in PRO DO 35/9342.

107 Confidential Outward Telegram from Commonwealth Relations Office to Ottawa, Canberra, Wellington, Cape Town, Delhi, Karachi, Colombo, Accra, Kuala Lumpur, Salisbury, April 1, 1960, in PRO DO 35/9342.

108 Outward Telegram from the Secretary of State for the Colonies to Sir J. Robertson, Federation of Nigeria, March 30, 18.30 hours, and Confidential Inward Telegram to Commonwealth Relations Office from Accra, 18.16 hours March 31, 1960, in PRO DO 35/9342.

109 April 2, 1960 Permanent French Mission to the United Nations, NY, "L'Experimentation Atomique Francaise," in DO 35–9342.

110 A.W. Snelling to Daniel, Office of the High Commission for the UK, Accra, April 4, 1960, in PRO DO 35/9342.

111 Secret Outward Telegram from Commonwealth Relations Office to Accra, April 1, 1960, in PRO DO 35/9342.

112 A.W. Snelling to D.W.S. Hunt, Commonwealth Relations Office, March 25, 1960, in PRO DO 35/9342.

113 Secret Outward Telegram from Secretary of State for the Colonies to Sir J. Robertson, Federation of Nigeria, March 31, 1960, 22 hours, in PRO DO 35/9342.

114 Secret letter from Selwyn Lloyd to Rt. Hon. The Earl of Perth, March 31, 1960, in PRO DO 35/9342.

115 Inward Telegram to Commonwealth Relations Office from Lagos, 18.35 hours May 18, 1961, in PRO EG 1/685 Military Research and Production: French Atomic Tests in the Sahara.

116 "Nigeria Breaks with France," *Daily Graphic*, January 7, 1961.

117 "French Atom Test in Sahara: Nigera Will Take 'Strong Action' If…" *Daily Graphic*, January 3, 1961.

118 Robert A. Divine, *Blowing on the Wind: The Nuclear Test Ban Debate, 1954–1960* (New York: Oxford University Press, 1978).

119 "Extract from speech by Dr. Nkrumah to the General Assembly on 23 Sept. 1960," in PRO DO 182/13 Ghanaian Proposal for an Atom and Base Free Africa, 1960.

120 Secret draft letter to H.C. Hainworth, Foreign Office from G.P. Hampshire, November 4, 1960 in PRO DO 182/13.

121 Secret letter from C.W. Wright to H.C. Hainworth, Foreign Office, November 8, 1960 in PRO DO 182/13.

122 Secret Cypher from UK Foreign Office to UK Mission to the United Nations in New York, November 19, 1960 in PRO DO 182/13.

123 G.P. Hampshire, January 27, 1961, note to Mr. Pritchard in PRO DO 182/13.

124 Confidential Foreign Office telegram No. 2305 Saving to UKMis New York in PRO DO 182/13.

125 *Ibid.*

126 R.R.G. Watts, Commonwealth Relations Office to J.T. Fearnley, Lagos, January 19, 1961 in PRO DO 182/13.

127 Mr. R. Watts to B.A. Flack Accra and J.T. Fearnley, Lagos, January 11, 1961 in PRO DO 182/13.

128 William Epstein, "A Nuclear-Weapon-Free Zone in Africa?" *The Stanley Foundation Occasional Papers* 14 (1977): 5–26.

129 "Nuclear-Weapon-Free," 6.

130 Peter Braestrup, "France Will End Tests in Sahara: Nuclear Facilities in Desert Are Being Dismantled," *The New York Times*, March 16, 1964; Craig R. Whitney, "France Ending Nuclear Tests That Caused Broad Protests," *ibid.*, 1996.

131 G.K. Reddy, "Astounding Success of Bandung Meet: New Pattern Set for Co-Existence," *The Times of India*, April 26, 1955; Braut-Hegghammer, *Unclear Physics*; Lee, "Making a World," 17.

132 IAEA GC (II)/INF/10/Rev.5 Members of the Agency: List of 20, September 1958, 1958.

133 IAEA GC(III)/83 Scale of Members' Contributions: Revised Scale for 1959, 1959.

134 Quotation in letter from R.P. Baffour, Kwame Nkrumah University of Science and Technology to Mr. Adu, General Secretary, Ghana Academy of Sciences, August 16, 1965 in PRAAD GAEC 1/Vol. 8, Ghana Atomic Energy Commission, 1965–1966.

3 Scientific Equity

1 H.B. Shepards, Secret Memo to Hainworth, June 23, 1960 in PRO DO 35/8330 Atomic Energy Development in Ghana, 1956–1960.
2 G. Stephenson, *Atom*, ed. Ghana Bureau of Languages (London: Longmans, Green and Co., Ltd., 1964, 1966), 1.
3 Michael D. Gordin, *Scientific Babel: How Science Was Done before and after Global English* (Chicago: University of Chicago Press, 2015).
4 Francis Agbodeka, *Achimota in the National Setting: A Unique Educational Experiment in West Africa* (Accra: Afram Publications, 1977).
5 For more on this, see Osseo-Asare, "Scientific Equity."
6 Previously, I have argued that the Science Centre scheme was moderately successful, reaching thousands of students, continuing through the twenty-first century as Science Resource Centres, rather than an utter failure of "scientific equity." See a contrasting view of the Ghana educational service during this period: Jonathan Zimmerman, "'Money, Materials, and Manpower': In-Service Teacher Education and the Economy of Failure, 1961–1971," *History of Education Quarterly* 51, no. 1 (2011): 1–27. On the Entebbe scheme: J.C. Williams, *Ghana: Scientific Instrumentation Centre April 1969* (Paris: UNESCO, 1969); Grace A. Alele Williams, "The Development of a Modern Mathematics Curriculum in Africa," *The Arithmetic Teacher* 23, no. 4 (1976): 254–261.
7 "'In All Things Scientific and Technological, Ghanaians Are on the Run'," *The Ghanaian Times*, November 30, 1964.
8 "New Museum for Ghana," *The Ghanaian Times*, June 14, 1962, p. 1.
9 Mike Anamzoya, "Osagyefo: Let's Not Use Science to Destroy," *The Ghanaian Times*, June 14, 1962.
10 Phone interview with Sam Bortei-Doku, November 11, 2010.
11 *Ibid.*
12 Wayland Young, "Mosquitoes in Accra," *Bulletin of The Atomic Scientists* 18, no. 7 (1962): 45–47.
13 "Mosquitoes," 45.
14 Kwame Nkrumah, "'The World without the Bomb' Accra Assembly: A New Thinking on the Issue of Man's Preservation Is Demanded, Full Text of the Osagyefo's Speech at the Opening of the Accra Assembly," *The Ghanaian Times*, June 22, 1962.
15 Osseo-Asare, "Scientific Equity."
16 G.L. Moss, Science Officer, August 3, 1965, internal memo and "Science Centres: Proposed Programme for First Year of Operation," in PRAAD RG 3/1/496 Science Centres: Curricula, Syllabuses, Teachers Notes, 1964.

17 PRAAD RG 3/1/496.

18 "Emphasis on Science Is Praised," *The Ghanaian Times*, December 1, 1962.

19 R.W.H. Wright, "University Physics in Developing Countries," *Physics Education* 2 (1967): 35–39. *Directory of British Scientists, 1966–1967* (London: Ernest Benn Limited, 1966), 744.

20 "'Auntie Mansa': The Wonders of Science," *The Ghanaian Times*, June 1, 1962.

21 Gordin, *Scientific Babel*, 6.

22 "Hausa-Russian Dictionary to Be Published Soon," *Ghanaian Times*, April 3, 1962.

23 Maxim Matusevich, *No Easy Row for a Russian Hoe: Ideology and Pragmatism in Nigerian-Soviet Relations, 1960–1991* (Trenton, NJ: Africa World Press, 2003), 5.

24 "Poison Cloud Hangs over Africa," *Evening News*, February 16, 1960.

25 Vasily Solodovnikov, "The Soviet Union and the African Nations," *Political Affairs* 47, no. 7 (1968): 41–53.

26 "Soviet Union."

27 "Ghanaian Poetry Gets Big Audition in Moscow," *The Ghanaian Times*, April 16, 1962. "Profile of the late Prof Atukwei Okai," *Ghana Web*, July 14, 2018.

28 "Pushkin, the Great Afro-Russian Poet," *The Ghanaian Times*, February 19, 1962.

29 "We Can't Fan the Embers of Tribalism," *The Ghanaian Times*, August 31, 1963.

30 "USSR To Set up Friendship of Nations University," *Evening News*, March 12, 1960.

31 *Ghana Atomic Energy Commission Status Report 1962–1973* (Accra: Crown Press Limited, 1973), 5.

32 RGAE 365/3/975 Соглашения, Протоколы, Письма Между Ссср И Ганой И Проекты Указанных Документов [Protocol Letters between USSR and Ghana], 1964; RGAE 365/2/466 Материалы Об Оказании Экономического И Технического Содействия Гане, Гвинее, Дагомее, Индонезии, Ираку, Йемену, Камбодже, Кении, Корее, Кубе, Кувейту (Просьбы, Ноты, Памятные Записки, Справки, Переписка) [Materials About Rendering Economic and Technical Co-operation (Questions, Notes, Correspondence) for Ghana], 1964.

33 Agreement on Cultural Co-operation between the Republic of Ghana and the USSR in PRAAD RG 17/1/60.

34 Protocol on cultural exchange between the Republic of Ghana and the USSR in the years 1960–1961 in PRAAD RG 17/1/60.

35 Executive Secretary, National Research Council to E.A. Allman, Department of Pharmacy, College of Science and Technology, Kumasi, "A World List of Institutions Concerned with Atomic Energy," in KNUST FP/R1/199 E.A. Allman Correspondence, Faculty of Pharmacy, 1961–1962.

36 Letter from A.H. Ward, Acting Director, Radio Isotope and Health Physics Unit, Department of Physics, University of Ghana at Legon to Dr. Wilson, January 29, 1963 in PRAAD GAEC 8 Finances: Ghana Atomic Energy Commission, 1963–1964.

37 Letter from A.H. Ward, Acting Director, Radio Isotope and Health Physics Unit, Department of Physics, University of Ghana at Legon to Dr. Wilson, January 29, 1963 in PRAAD GAEC 8.

38 PRAAD RG 11/2/35 Special Appointment: Dr. A.N. May, 1961–1965.

39 R.P. Baffour, University of Science and Technology to Yaw A.L. Adu, Office of the President, October 7, 1961 in PRAAD RG 11/1/298.

40 Agenda of Emergency Meeting of the National Research Council Meeting scheduled for August 5, 1961 in PRAAD RG 11/1/345 Ghana Academy of Sciences Educational Research Committee 1961.

41 From the datebook of M. Zalutskii, August 30, 1961 in RGAE 365/2/277 Аписи Бесед С Представителями Ганы, Гвинеи, Гдр, Индии, Индонезии, Ирака, Йемена [Notes from Meetings with Representatives], 1961.

42 Letter from F.K.A. Allotey to R.P. Baffour, Vice-Chancellor, Kwame Nkrumah University of Science and Technology, Kumasi, March 14, 1962 in Asie Mirekuwa Allotey and Francis Kofi Ampenyin Allotey, *The Saga of Professor F.K.A. Allotey "the African Scientist"* (Accra: Institute for Scientific and Technological Information, 2002), 98.

43 Francis K.A. Allotey, "Effect of Electron-Hole Scattering Resonance on X-Ray Emission Spectrum," *Physical Review* 157, no. 3 (1967): 467–479; "Effect of Threshold Behaviour on Calculations of Soft X-Ray Spectra of Lithium," *Solid State Communications* 9, no. 2 (1971): 91–94.

44 Francis K.A. Allotey, "African Physicist, World Citizen," in *One Hundred Reasons to Be a Scientist* (Trieste: The Abdus Salam International Centre for Theoretical Physics, 2005). Interview with Allotey, Mathematical physicist, former GAEC director, Allotey Residence, Accra, July 30, 2008.

45 R.P. Baffour, Vice-Chairman Atomic Energy Commission, Kwame Nkrumah University of Science and Technology, Kumasi to Osagyefo the President, Flagstaff House, Accra, February 5, 1962 in RG 17/1/88.

46 James Bailey, Snr. Technical Assistant, Electrical, GAEC to Commissioner of Enquiry into the Affair of GAEC, April 22, 1968 in PRAAD RG 3/6/184 Ghana Police Docket, 1966-1968.

47 J.H. Amuasi, *The History of Ghana Atomic Energy Commission 1963-2003: Forty Years of Nuclear Science and Technology Applications in Ghana* (Accra: AGOL Gh. Ltd, 2003), 6.

48 Interview with Isaac N. Acquah, professor, School of Nuclear and Allied Sciences, August 3, 2015.

49 Interviews with Benjamin Woarabae Garbrah, Very Reverend Professor, former director, Ghana Atomic Energy Commission, Garbrah residence, Nyanyiba Estates, July 30, 2015; January 18, 2006.

50 Interview with Benjamin Woarabae Garbrah, Very Reverend Professor, former Director, Ghana Atomic Energy Commission, Garbrah residence, Nyanyiba Estates, January 18, 2006.

51 RGAE 365/2/3369 Обращения И Заявки Правительств Афганистана, Болгарии, Венгрии, Ганы, Гвинеи, Гдр, Индонезии, Монголии, Оар, Польши, Румынии, Сомали, Сирии, Чехословакии, Эфиопии, Югославии О Командировании Советских Специалистов За Границу И Приеме На Обучение В Ссср Иностранных Специалистов [Address and Requests from the Government … of Ghana for Sending Soviet Specialists Abroad and Receiving Education in the USSR. Foreign Specialists] (Trans. Rhiannon Dowling Fredericks), 1963.

52 William Anti-Taylor, *Moscow Diary* (London: Robert Hale, 1967), 11.

53 Patton, *Physicians, Colonial Racism, and Diaspora in West Africa.*

54 Julie Hessler, "Death of an African Student in Moscow: Race, Politics, and the Cold War," *Cahiers du Monde Russe* 47, no. 1–2 (2006): 33–63; Anti-Taylor, *Moscow Diary*, 11.

55 *Moscow Diary*, 14–15.

56 Interview with John Justice Fletcher, Professor, School of Nuclear and Allied Sciences, August 4, 2015.

57 PRAAD RG 11/1/201 The Academy of Sciences of the USSR, 1961–1962.

58 A.J. Millican, Ministry of Education, Accra to Principal, University College of Ghana, Achimota, cc to Secretary to the Prime Minister, Government House, January 16, 1969 and letter from J.N.O. Lamptey, Principal's Secretary, University College to Dr. J.G. St. Clair Drake, University College, July 3, 1959 in UG 1/3/8/5/6 Visits of Russian Scientists and Exchange of Professors, 1958.

59 Letter from P.I. Kupriyanov, postgraduate student of the Moscow Oriental Institute, c/o Liberian Commission for UNESCO to Mr. R.H.S. Stoughton, Principal, University College of Ghana, June 26, 1959 in UG 1/3/8/5/6.

60 Letter from S.P. Tolstov, Corresponding-Member of the USSR Academy of Science to Prof. Stoughton, Principal of the University College of Ghana in UG 1/3/8/5/6.

61 RGAE 365/2/3369.

62 Letter from K.A. Obese-Jecty, Registrar, University College of Cape Coast to the Secretary, National Council for Higher Education, November 5, 1962. Letter from V.O.D. Twum-Barima for Registrar, Kwame Nkrumah University of Science and Technology to the Secretary, National Council for Higher Education, Accra, December 4, 1962 in PRAAD RG 11/1/224 Technical Assistance from Union of Soviet Socialist Republic, 1962.

63 Letter from Executive Secretary, National Research Council to the Secretary, National Council for Higher Education, Office of the President, Accra, November 30, 1962 in PRAAD RG 11/1/224.

64 R.P. Baffour, Vice-Chairman Atomic Energy Commission, Kwame Nkrumah University of Science and Technology, Kumasi to Osagyefo, President, Flagstaff House, Accra, February 5, 1962 in RG 17/1/88.

65 Quoted in Report of the Ghana Delegation to the International Atomic Energy Conference held in Vienna from September 26 to October 10, 1961, in PRAAD RG 11/1/315 Confidential: National Research Council-Conferences.

66 B.W. Garbrah and J.E. Whitley, "Assessment of Neutron Capture Γ-Ray Analysis," *The International Journal of Applied Radiation and Isotopes* 19, no. 8 (1968): 605–614; "Determination of Boron by Thermal Neutron Capture Gamma-Ray Analysis," *Analytical Chemistry* 39, no. 3 (1967): 345–349.

67 Interview with Benjamin Woarabae Garbrah, Garbrah residence, Nyanyiba Estates, January 18, 2006.

68 *Ghana Atomic Energy Commission Status Report 1962–1973*, 13–16.

69 Letter from J.A. Boateng, for Principal Secretary, Ministry of External Affairs, Accra to the Chairman of the Management Committee, Ghana Atomic Energy Commission, Chemistry Department, University of Ghana, Legon, November 14, 1967 in PRAAD RG 3/6/1165 Ghana Atomic Energy Commission-Conferences, 1968.

70 "International Atomic Energy Agency: Third Conference on Plasma Physics and Controlled Nuclear Fusion Research, Novosibirsk, USSR, August 1–7, 1968, Information Sheet," in PRAAD RG 3/6/1165.

71 Interview with Isaac N. Acquah, Professor, School of Nuclear and Allied Sciences, August 3, 2015.

72 Interview, Benjamin Nyarko, GAEC Director General, Ghana Atomic Energy Commission, Kwabenya, Ghana, July 27, 2015.

73 Interview with Victoria Appiah, Professor, School of Nuclear and Allied Sciences, July 29, 2015.

74 John Justice Fletcher, Professor, School of Nuclear and Allied Sciences, August 4, 2015.

75 Donald MacKenzie and Graham Spinardi, "Tacit Knowledge, Weapons Design, and the Uninvention of Nuclear Weapons," *American Journal of Sociology* 101, no. 1 (1995): 44–99.

76 R.G. Abrefah et al., "Design of Serpentine Cask for Ghana Research Reactor-1 Spent Nuclear Fuel," *Progress in Nuclear Energy* 77 (2014): 84–91.

77 J.H. Amuasi et al., "Medical Physics Practice and Training in Ghana," *Physica Medica-European Journal of Medical Physics* 32, no. 6 (2016): 826–830; G. Chinangwa, J.K. Amoako, and J.J. Fletcher, "Radiation Dose Assessment for Occupationally Exposed Workers in Malawi," *Malawi Medical Journal* 29, no. 3 (2017): 254–258; "Investigation of the Status of Occupational Radiation Protection in Malawian Hospitals," *Malawi Medical Journal* 30, no. 1 (2018): 22–24; S. Osei, J. K. Amoako, and J. J. Fletcher, "Assessment of Levels of Occupational Exposure to Workers in Radiofrequency Fields of Two Television Stations in Accra, Ghana," *Radiation Protection Dosimetry* 168, no. 3 (2016): 419–426; C. Subaar et al., "Numerical Studies of Radiofrequency of the Electromagnetic Radiation Power Absorption in Paediatrics Undergoing Brain Magnetic Resonance Imaging," *Journal of Radiation Research and Applied Sciences* 10, no. 3 (2017): 188–193.

78 Interview with Mungubariki Nyaki, physicist, Tanzania Atomic Energy Commission during visit to GAEC, July 25, 2008.

79 Gordin, *Scientific Babel*.

4 Atomic Reactors

1 Author interview with John Humphrey Amuasi, Graduate School of Nuclear and Allied Sciences, Kwabenya, Ghana, July 2015.

2 PRO DO 35/8330.

3 Amuasi, *The History*, pp. iii, 82.

4 Professor H.E. Huntley, "Strictly Confidential: The Introduction of Nuclear Power into the Gold Coast, Report of Enquiries made in the United Kingdom April and May 1965," in PRO CO 554/1421 Erection of an Experimental Nuclear Reactor in the Gold Coast, 1956.

5 Strictly confidential letter from G.E. Mercer, Development Secretariat, Accra, Gold Coast to A. Emanuel, Colonial Office, London, June 22, 1956 in PRO CO 554/1421.

6 Secretary of State for the Colonies to the Officer Administering the Government of Gold Coast, September 10, 1956 in PRO DO 35/8330; PRO CO 554/1421 Feasibility of Establishing an Experimental Reactor in the Gold Coast, 1956–1957.

7 Letter from Professor H.E. Huntley, Physics Department, University College, Achimota to Mr. A. Emmanuel, Colonial Office, London, May 19, 1956 in PRO CO 554/1421.

8 Agbodeka, *A History of the University of Ghana*, pp. 66–68.

9 Luc Gillon, *Servir: En Actes Et En Vérité* (Kinshasa: Éditions Centre de Recherches Pédagogiques, 1995), 126–127. Chris McGreal, "Missing Keys, Holes in Fence and a Single Padlock: Welcome to Congo's Nuclear Plant," *Guardian*, November 23, 2006.

10 Gillon, *Servir*, 127, translation mine.

11 John Krige, "Atoms for Peace, Scientific Internationalism, and Scientific Intelligence," *Osiris* 21 (2006): 161–181.

12 "Nuclear 1955 for D.D.E., '15: He Would Share Atomic Benefits," *Life Magazine* 38, no. 25 (1955): 33; "First U. S. Reactor Goes Critical in Europe," *The Science News-Letter* 71, no. 22 (1957): 341.

13 Angela N.H. Creager, "Nuclear Energy in the Service of Biomedicine: The U.S. Atomic Energy Commission's Radioisotope Program, 1946–1950," *Journal of the History of Biology* 39, no. 4 (2006): 649–684; Angela N.H. Creager, *Life Atomic: A History of Radioisotopes in Science and Medicine* (Chicago: University of Chicago Press, 2013).

14 "More Uranium, More Reactors and More Power: More Atomic Progress: A Report," *Life Magazine* 42, no. 7 (1957): 23–31.

15 Paul R. Josephson, *Red Atom: Russia's Nuclear Power Program from Stalin to Today* (Pittsburgh, PA: University of Pittsburgh Press, 2005), 2, 28.

16 "Reactor Unit Is Removed from Plant," *The New York Times*, December 15, 1988; Angela N.H. Creager, *Life Atomic: A History of Radioisotopes in Science and Medicine* (Chicago: University of Chicago Press, 2015), 196; D.T. Ingersoll, "Deliberately Small Reactors and the Second Nuclear Era," *Progress in Nuclear Energy* 51, no. 4–5 (2009): 589–603.

17 "Deliberately Small Reactors and the Second Nuclear Era"; "One Sure Bet for U.S. Of Tomorrow: Twice as Much Power, New Sources Will Satisfy Immense Appetite for Energy," *Life Magazine* 36, no. 1 (1954): 79–91.

18 Letter from Kwame Nkrumah to Chairman Mao Zedong, October 26, 1964 in CFMA 108/00546/01 Recent Report of China's Explosion of a Nuclear Device, 1964.

19 Abraham, *The Making*.

20 My gratitude to Titas Chakraborty for highlighting this comparison.

21 Letter from R.P. Baffour, Vice-Chairman, Atomic Energy Committee, Kwame Nkrumah University of Science and Technology, Kumasi to M.F. Dei-Anang, African Affairs Secretariat, Flagstaff House, Accra, March

13, 1962 in PRAAD RG 17/1/259 Ghana Atomic Energy Committee, 1961–1964.

22 "Ghanaian Times Editorial: World without the Bomb," *The Ghanaian Times*, 1962.

23 Department of State, Central Files, 745J.11/10–760, reprinted in *Priority in Foreign Relations of the United States*, 1958–1960, Volume XIV, Africa, Document 303 Telegram from the Embassy in Ghana to the Department of State, Confidential, 1960.

24 *Ibid.*

25 Paraphrased and translated by Yuxi Wang, CFMA [no number] 外交部同我驻加纳使馆就加纳总统恩克鲁玛建议召开世界非核国家会议事的来往电报 [Back-and-Forth Telegrams between Chinese Foreign Ministry and the Embassy of China in Ghana Regarding the International Nuclear-Free Conference], 1960.

26 Joe S. Annan, Ministry of Defence, Ghana, January 25, 1960.

27 CFMA [no number].

28 "Nuclear Centre Will Train Our Scientists," *The Ghanaian Times*, November 9, 1964.

29 "Atomic Reactor – Correction," *The Ghanaian Times*, November 10, 1964.

30 "Ghana to Refine Gold in 1966," *The Ghanaian Times*, January 5, 1965.

31 Itty Abraham, "The Ambivalence of Nuclear Histories," *Osiris* 21, no. 1 (2006): 49–65.

32 Letter from Kwame Nkrumah to Chairman Mao Zedong, October 26, 1964 in CFMA 108/00546/01.

33 Morton H. Halperin, "Chinese Nuclear Strategy: The Early Post-Detonation Period," *Asian Survey* 5, no. 6 (1965): 271–279.

34 CFMA 108/00546/01.

35 "Chinese Praised for Atom Test," *The Ghanaian Times*, October 19, 1964.

36 Frank Gerits, "'When the Bull Elephants Fight': Kwame Nkrumah, Non-Alignment, and Pan-Africanism as an Interventionist Ideology in the Global Cold War (1957–66)," *The International History Review* 37, no. 5 (2015): 951–969.

37 Noer, "The New Frontier and African Neutralism: Kennedy, Nkrumah, and the Volta River Project." "U.S. Lends £10m for Big Volta Project, They Make Conditions."

38 "Kwame Visits Dam Site–as Work Begins on Final Phase," *The Ghanaian Times*, February 26, 1963.

39 Department of State, Central Files, 745J.11/10–760, reprinted in *Priority in Foreign Relations of the United States*, 1958–1960, Volume XIV, Africa, Document 303.

40 Ali A. Mazrui, "Nkrumah, Obote and Vietnam," *Transition*, no. 43 (1973): 36–39. Ernest W. Lefever, "Nehru, Nasser and Nkrumah on Neutralism," *Neutralism and Nonalignment* (1962): 544–609.
41 "Our Friendship Is Unbreakable!," *Pravda*, February 20, 1961.
42 "National Research Council: Minutes of the Fourth Meeting," November 19, 1960 in PRAAD RG 17/1/82 National Research Council, 1960–1961.
43 "Our Friendship."
44 "Soviet Exposition Opens in Ghana," *Pravda*, July 12, 1962, No. 193, p. 5.
45 "No Place in the World for Colonialism Now – Khrushchev," *Evening News*, February 22, 1960.
46 Adu Gyamfi, "Russia's Khrushchev Thinks Highly of Nkrumah: Exclusive Interview with the New Ghana Ambassador to USSR," *ibid.*, January 13.
47 *Ghana Atomic Energy Commission Status Report 1962–1973*, p. 5.
48 Press Release: The Development of Economic, Cultural and Technical Co-operation and Trade Relations between the Soviet Union and the Republic of Ghana.
49 "Supply by Russia of Nuclear Reactor to Ghana," in PRO DO 195/45 Ghana Desire for a Nuclear Reactor, 1960–1961. PRAAD RG 3/6/977 Report of the Commission of Enquiry into the Ghana Atomic Energy Commission, 1970.
50 Kwame Nkrumah to R.P. Baffour, February 22, 1961 in PRAAD RG 17/1/60 USSR, 1960–1961.
51 CMFA 108/00252/04 Trade Protocol to the Trade and Payments Agreement between the Government of the People's Republic of China and the Government of the Republic of Ghana, 1961.
52 Letter, H.C. Hainsworth to G.W. St. J. Chadwick, Esq., Commonwealth Relations Office, February 13, 1961 in PRO DO 195/45.
53 It took from around June 1961 to November 1961 to obtain a translation of the agreement. Note from V.E. Davies to B.D. MacLean, United Kingdom Atomic Energy Authority, Overseas Relation II, London, November 13, 1961 in PRO DO 195/45.
54 PRO DO 195/45.
55 Note from S.W.F. Martin to Mr. Hampshire, October 19, 1960 in PRO DO 195/45.
56 Confidential letter from A.W. Redpath, Commonwealth Relations Office to B.A. Flack, Accra, August 14, 1961 in PRO DO 195/45.
57 Letter, H.C. Hainsworth to G.W. St. J. Chadwick, Esq., Commonwealth Relations Office, February 13, 1961 in PRO DO 195/45.

58 Letter from G.P. Hampshire to Mr. Pritchard, February 2, 1961 in PRO DO 195/45.
59 Osseo-Asare, "Scientific Equity." This theory of scientific equity is discussed in the introduction and throughout the book.
60 Kwame Nkrumah, "Nuclear War is an Economic and Political Suicide – Kwame," *The Ghanaian Times*, June 23, 1962.
61 Adrian Seligman, "Nuclear Research and Irradiation Centres for Universities," The Engineering, Marine, Welding & Nuclear Energy Exhibition, London, April 20 to May 4, 1961 in PRO DO 195/45.
62 Nkrumah's position quoted in letter from G.P. Hampshire to Mr. Pritchard, February 2, 1961 in PRO DO 195/45.
63 Letter from G.P. Hampshire to Mr. Pritchard, February 2, 1961 in PRO DO 195/45.
64 Letter from S.T. Quansah, Executive Secretary, National Research Council to E.K. Okoh, Acting Secretary to the Cabinet, Office of the President, Flagstaff House and R.P. Baffour, Principal, Kumasi College of Science and Technology, April 28, 1961 in PRAAD RG 17/1/259.
65 Letter from R.P. Baffour, Vice-Chairman, Atomic Energy Committee to Osagyefo, the President, February 5, 1962 in PRAAD RG 17/1/259.
66 PRAAD RG 3/6/977.
67 J.E.O. Lindsay, *The Ghana Atomic Energy Project: A Scientific Review* (Accra, 1966) in PRAAD RG 3/6/1166.
68 *Ibid.*
69 *Ibid.*
70 J.E.O. Lindsay, *The Ghana Atomic Energy Project: A Scientific Review* (Accra, 1966), 4 in PRAAD RG 3/6/1166.
71 IAEA, *Research Reactors in Africa* (2011), 12, 22.
72 Lindsay, *The Ghana*, 11.
73 "Nuclear Reactor for Ghana," *The Ghanaian Times*, June 30, 1962, p. 1.
74 PRAAD Act 204 Act 204: Atomic Energy Commission, 1963.
75 PRAAD RG 3/6/977.
76 PRAAD RG 3/6/977.
77 Letter from Ward to Dr. Wilson, January 29, 1963 in PRAAD GAEC 8.
78 Aerogram from Dr. R.P. Baffour, Chevron-Hilton Hotel, Sydney, Australia to Dr. Yanney-Wilson, Secretary Academy of Sciences, Accra, May 4, 1963 in PRAAD GAEC 8.
79 Copy of letter from Personal Secretary to the President to J. Yanney Ewusie, Esq., Secretary, Ghana Atomic Energy Commission, June 16, 1964 in PRAAD RG 17/1/259.
80 Kwame Nkrumah, "Science Academy Must Be Part of National Life– Osagyefo," *The Ghanaian Times*, November 16, 1964.

81 PRAAD RG 3/6/977.

82 Confidential letter from D. Hopson, Office of the British Chargé d'Affaires, Peking to Michael Stewart, M.P., March 2, 1966 in PRO FO 371/187903 Dr. Nkrumah's visit to Peking, 1966. From China, Nkrumah returned to West Africa. He lived in exile in Sekou Touré's Guinea until traveling to Romania in late 1971 to treat cancer, where he died in 1972. Mazrui, "Nkrumah, Obote," 37; D. Chau, *Exploiting Africa: The Influence of Maoist China in Algeria, Ghana, and Tanzania* (Annapolis, MD: Naval Institute Press, 2014).

83 *Foreign Relations of the United States, 1964–1968*, Volume XXIV, Africa, Document 253, p. 447.

84 David H. Shin and Joshua Eisenman, *China and Africa: A Century of Engagement* (Philadelphia, PA: University of Pennsylvania Press, 2012), 288.

85 PRO FO 371/189505 Nuclear Programmes: Ghana, 1966.

86 Letter from M.I. Michaels, Ministry of Technology, London to H.J. Millen, United Kingdom Atomic Energy Authority, July 1, 1966 in PRO FO 371/189505.

87 Memorandum from Sir John Cockcroft to the Chairman, National Liberation Council of Ghana, November 29, 1966 in PRAAD RG 3/6/1167 Ghana Atomic Energy Commission.

88 Letter from R.P. Baffour, Chairman, Ghana Atomic Energy Commission, University of Science and Technology, Kumasi, Ghana to Mr. S. Addo, Secretary Education Review Committee, Parliament House, Accra, July 16, 1966 in PRAAD RG 3/6/1167.

89 PRAAD ADM 5/3/145 Report of the Commission of Enquiry, University of Science and Technology, Kumasi, 1966.

90 Lindsay, *The Ghana*.

91 "Confidential: Management Committee of the Ghana Atomic Energy Reactor," January 30, 1967 in SCR. 148 SF.2 Atomic Energy Commission: Recommendations by Sir John Cockroft, 1966–1967.

92 PRAAD RG 3/6/1167 White Paper on the Report of the Atomic Reactor Review Committee, 1973.

93 Letter from U.L. Goswami, Deputy Director General, Department of Technical Assistance, IAEA to Prof. J.A.K. Quartey, Ghana Atomic Energy Commission, March 12, 1968 in "Reactor Report Appendix 2: Assistance from the International Atomic Energy Agency: Part of a Report Submitted by Professor J.A.K. Quartey to the Chairman of the Education Review Committee."

94 IAEA General Conference, "Delegations, Information Received by Noon on September 18, 1967," in PRAAD RG 3/5/1165 Ghana Atomic Energy Commission – Conferences, 1967.

95 *Kwabenya Nuclear Research Establishment Handbook* (Kwabenya, Accra: GAEC, 1977), 77.

96 Ghana Atomic Energy Commission: The Objectives and Assessments of the Atomic Reactor Project and the Programme of the Atomic Energy Commission, Prepared at the Request of the Commissioner for Education by J.A.K. Quartey, Chairman, Management Committee of GAEC, and B.W. Garbrah, Officer-in-Charge, March 17, 1972 in PRAAD RG 3/6/1167.

97 Quartey, J.A.K. *Reactor Report* 1966, p. 6.

98 "White Paper on the Report of the Atomic Reactor Review Committee, May 1973," in PRAAD RG 3/6/1167 Ghana Atomic Energy Commission. On the politics behind Baffour's departure from the University of Science and Technology, see Laura J. McGough, "Civil Society in Post-Colonial Ghana: A Case Study of the Ghana Institution of Engineers," *Transactions of the Historical Society of Ghana*, no. 3 (1999): 1–26.

99 "White Paper on the Report of the Atomic Reactor Review Committee, May 1973," in PRAAD RG 3/6/1167 Ghana Atomic Energy Commission.

100 McGreal, "Missing Keys."

101 IAEA, *Research Reactors in Africa.*

102 Report of T. Ayeh, assistant economic officer, Supreme Military Council, June 1, 1979 in PRAAD RG 6/6/323 Research Reactor (Kwabenya), 1977–1979.

103 Memorandum from Francis Allotey, chairman, Management Committee, Ghana Atomic Energy Commission to the Supreme Military Council, on November 2, 1978, "Completion of the Ghana Nuclear Reactor Project – Contract for the Installation of the Research Reactor Facility at Kwabenya," 4 in PRAAD RG 6/6/323.

104 Handwritten comments, June 1, 1979, financial advisors to Supreme Miltary Council in PRAAD RG 6/6/323.

105 McGough, "Civil Society in Post-Colonial Ghana: A Case Study of the Ghana Institution of Engineers," 3.

106 Minister of Environment, Science & Technology Christine Amoako-Nuamah speaking at the opening of the GHARR-1, full speech quoted in Amuasi, *The History*, 34.

107 Ingersoll, "Deliberately Small Reactors and the Second Nuclear Era," 590.

108 "Deliberately Small Reactors and the Second Nuclear Era," 590.

109 Shin and Eisenman, *China and Africa*, 288.

110 Amuasi, *The History*, 31.

111 Hans Blix, "Inauguration of Ghana Research Reactor," *IAEA Newscenter*, March 8, 1995.

112 Minister of Environment, Science, and Technology Christine Amoako-Nuamah speaking at the opening of the GHARR-1; full speech quoted in Amuasi, *The History*, 34–35.
113 Interview with John Humphrey Amuasi, Graduate School of Nuclear and Allied Sciences, Kwabenya, Ghana, July 2015.

5 Radiation Within

1 PRAAD Act 204 Atomic Energy Commission, 1963.
2 "Information to Assist the Agency in Expediting Action on Requests from Member States for Small Quantities of Special Fissionable or Source Materials," in PRAAD GAEC 4/SF1.
3 R.P. Baffour, Vice-Chancellor, Kwame Nkrumah University of Science and Technology to J. Yanny-Wilson, Secretary, Ghana Atomic Energy Commission, February 13, 1964 in PRAAD GAEC 4/SF1.
4 PRAAD GAEC AG/SF22 Vol. IV IAEA Nuclear Safety, Accident Radiation Protection, 1988–1989.
5 Letter from A. Buckner, Radiographer to the Resident Medical Officer, Gold Coast Hospital, Korle Bu, September 25, 1933 in PRAAD CSO 11/1/329 X-Ray Apparatus at the Gold Coast Hospital, 1933.
6 Buckner to Resident Medical Officer in PRAAD CSO 11/1/329.
7 PRAAD CSO 11/1/283 British Red Cross, Gold Coast Branch, Ashanti – X-Ray Apparatus, 1933.
8 Letter from D. Duff, Director of Medical Services to G.J. Christian, Sekondi, May 19, 1938, in PRAAD CSO 11/1/431 X-Ray Apparatus for Sekondi African Hospital.
9 Letter from H.C. Thornton, London to the Colonial Secretary, Gold Coast, August 11, 1933 in PRAAD CSO 11/1/335 X-Ray & Electro-Medical Apparatus, Circulation and Interchange of Information Regarding Operation and Maintenance of, 1933.
10 Salome Francois, retired radiographer, Korle Bu Teaching Hospital, Accra, August 10, 2017.
11 Amelia Djabanor, "Salome's Story," *Obra Pa: Righteous Living* 1, no. 1 (1991): 6–10.
12 Letter from S.R.A. Dodu to Ag. Principal Secretary, Ministry of Health, Medical Public Relations Division, cc. Secretary, GAEC, February 28, 1972 in PRAAD GAEC AG 16 Vol II Radiation Protection Board, 1970–1978.
13 Interview with Dorothy Mills, retired radiographer, Korle Bu Teaching Hospital, Mills residence, Korle Bu, July 3, 2017.
14 J. Sekiguchi and S.R. Collens, "Radiological Services in Rural Mission Hospitals in Ghana," *Bulletin of the World Health Organization* 73, no. 1 (1995): 65–69.

15 24th World Health Assembly: "The Development of the Medical Use of Ionizing Radiation," May 18, 1971 and Letter from E.G. Beusoleil, Director of Medical Services, Ministry of Health to L.K. Derban, Ghana Medical School, Director, GAEC, Nunn May, Department of Physics, University of Ghana, Legon etc. September 5, 1972 in PRAAD GAEC AG 16 Vol II Radiation Protection Board, 1970–1978.

16 Curriculum Vitae: Mr. J.K.E. Amusah, and letters from S. Amankrah, Account, GAEC to the Resident Representative, United Nations Development Programme, Accra, December 23, 1975, February 13, 1976, September 15, 1976 in PRAAD GAEC AG 16 Vol II Radiation Protection Board, 1970–1978.

17 J.J. Fletcher, Health Physics Unit, GAEC to The Secretary, GAEC, December 2, 1976 in PRAAD GAEC AG 16 Vol II Radiation Protection Board, 1970–1978.

18 B.W. Garbrah, Head, Physics Department, GAEC to the Secretary G.A.R.C., Kwabenya, February 4, 1977 in PRAAD GAEC AG 16 Vol II Radiation Protection Board, 1970–1978.

19 "Radiation Protection Law Coming Soon – Schandorf," *People's Daily Graphic*, November 15, 1991.

20 C. Schandorf and G.K. Tetteh, "Analysis of Dose and Dose Distribution for Patients Undergoing Selected X-Ray Diagnostic Procedures in Ghana," *Radiation Protection Dosimetry* 76, no. 4 (1998): 249–256.

21 Osseo-Asare, "Scientific Equity."

22 "Nuclear System Used for Plant Production," *The Ghanaian Times*, April 21, 1967.

23 Dr. B. Amoako-Atta, Acting Head, Department of Biology, Food and Agriculture, GAEC, "Research Activities in GAEC in relation to Cereal Production in Ghana," in PRAAD GAEC AG 34 Agricultural Research 1978–1980.

24 PRAAD GAEC AG 34.

25 Alfred Coffie-Johnson, "Radioisotopes, Ionizing Radiation Centres Set Up," *The Ghanaian Times*, July 16, 1993.

26 Samuel Sarpong and Albert K. Salia, "Insect Sterilisation Technique Developed," *Daily Graphic*, March 11, 1998.

27 Charles Emmanuel Annoh, research scientist, Animal Science Department, Ghana Atomic Energy Commission, July 21, 2008.

28 Nehemia Owusu Achiaw, "Scientific Renaissance Day for Africa Marked in Kumasi," *Daily Graphic*, June 29, 1991. Interview with Francis K.A. Allotey, mathematical physicist, former GAEC director, Allotey residence, Accra, July 30, 2008.

29 "Radiation Protection Law."

30 "Ghana Atomic Energy Commission, Vacant Positions," *The Ghanaian Times*, July 29, 1994.

31 *National Nuclear Research Institute (Nnri) at a Glance* (Accra: Ghana Atomic Energy Commission, c. 2000), 1.

32 Interview with Emmauel O. Darko, Head, Radiation Protection Institute, Ghana Atomic Energy Commission, July 21, 2008.

33 Interview with Emmauel O. Darko.

34 Obeng kindly allowed us to film him on his rounds and during a tour of the Radiation Protection Institute. Michael Kojo Asare Obeng, Chief Technologist, Radiation Protection Institute, Ghana Atomic Energy Commission, July 23, 2008.

35 Carl Christian Lokko, mechanical engineer, Tema Port, July 23, 2008.

36 Samuel Opoku, Head of Radiotherapy, National Center for Radiotherapy and Nuclear Medicine, Korle Bu Teaching Hospital/Head of Department of Radiography, College of Health Sciences, University of Ghana, August 1, 2017.

37 Interview with Samuel Opoku.

38 Interview with Steven Boateng, Chief Radiographer, Korle Bu Teaching Hospital, July 7, 2017.

39 In Gabon in the 1970s, dosimeter badges were sent to France for testing; see Hecht, *Being Nuclear*, 202.

40 Carl Mutt, "Nuke Energy for Whose Belly?," *The Mirror*, October 30, 1993.

41 Golda Idan, "G.A.E.C., IAEA To Help H.I.V./A.I.D.S. Patients," *Daily Graphic*, 2002.

42 I.K. Mac Arthur, "Nuke Energy for Food Storage," *Daily Graphic*, October 21, 1993.

43 Mutt, "Nuke Energy for Whose Belly?"

44 "Nuke Energy for Whose Belly?"

45 Charles M. Gbedemah, "Uncle Carl, Irradiation Is Harmless," *The Mirror* December 4.

46 "Irradiation."

47 Carl Mutt, "Nuke Energy for Whose Belly?," *Daily Graphic*, October 30.

48 "Nuke Energy for Whose Belly?"

49 Charles M. Gbedemah, "Uncle Carl, Irradiation Is Harmless," *Daily Graphic*, December 4.

50 József Farkas and Csilla Mohácsi-Farkas, "History and Future of Food Irradiation," *Trends in Food Science & Technology* 22, no. 2 (2011): 121–126.

51 Memorandum from Dr. B. Amoako-Atta, Ag. Head, Department of Biology, Food and Agriculture, GAEC to Agricultural Research Advisory

Committee, Ministry of Agriculture, "Research Activities in GAEC of Relevance to Cereal Production in Ghana," in PRAAD GAEC AG 34.

52 Ato Aidoo and I.K. Max Arthur, "Work on Irradiation Centre Progresses," *Daily Graphic*, December 3, 1993.

53 "Lack of Funds Stalls Irradiation Project," *Daily Graphic*, 2007.

54 "Ghana Inaugurates Radioactive Waste Storage Facility," *Ghana News Agency*, September 13, 2011.

55 "Radioactive Waste Centre Set Up," *The Ghanaian Times*, August 10, 1994.

56 Gustav Gbeddy, "Radioactive Waste Management in Ghana; a Country Currently without Nuclear Power Plant," Powerpoint presentation, 2015.

57 *Ibid.*

58 The above-ground facility is projected to house waste from across West Africa and is the first of its kind on the continent. "Ghana Inaugurates Radioactive Waste Storage Facility"; E.O. Darko and J.J. Fletcher, "National Waste Management Infrastructure in Ghana," *Journal of Radiological Protection* 18 (1998): 293–299. GAEC has also begun exploratory borehole disposal of radioactive waste in the Kwabenya area; see G. Emi-Reynolds et al., "Safe and Secure Management."

59 A.M.A. Dawood et al., "Borehole Disposal Concept for Radioactive Waste Disposal-the Gaec Project," *Pollution* 47 (2012): 8752–8756.

60 Kofi Thompson, "Ghana Incapable of Storing Dangerous Radioactive Waste Safely!" *Ghana Web*, March 7, 2013.

61 Francis K.A. Allotey, "African Physicist, World Citizen," in *One Hundred Reasons to Be a Scientist* (Trieste: The Abdus Salam International Centre for Theoretical Physics, 2005).

6 Atomic Lands

1 Charles Takyi-Boadu, "Shock and Chaos," *The Ghanaian Chronicle*, October 15, 2009.

2 "G.A.E.C. Demolishes "Illegal" Structures on Its Property at Dome-Kwabenya," *Ghana News Agency*, January 24, 2012.

3 "Atomic Land Owners Speak," *Daily Guide*, January 31, 2012; "Encroachment of Ghana Atomic Lands," *The Enquirer*, December 30, 2011; Bernice Bessey, "Ghana: Estate Developers Take over Atomic Lands," *The Ghanaian Chronicle*, March 10, 2014.

4 Joseph Masco, *The Nuclear Borderlands: The Manhattan Project in Post-Cold War New Mexico* (Princeton, NJ: Princeton University Press, 2006), 39. On frontiers in Ghana, see also B. Chalfin, *Neoliberal Frontiers: An*

Ethnography of Sovereignty in West Africa (Chicago: University of Chicago Press, 2010).

5 Masco, *Nuclear Borderlands*, 30. See also David Hecht and A.M. Simone, *Invisible Governance: The Art of African Micro-Politics* (Brooklyn, NY: Autonomedia, 1994).

6 Danesi et al., "Residual Radionuclide Concentrations and Estimated Radiation Doses at the Former French Nuclear Weapons Test Sites in Algeria."

7 Adriana Petryna, *Life Exposed: Biological Citizens after Chernobyl* (Princeton, NJ: Princeton University Press, 2002), 4; Olga Kuchinskaya, *The Politics of Invisibility: Public Knowledge About Radiation Health Effects after Chernobyl* (Cambridge: MIT Press, 2014).

8 Shoji Hashimoto et al., "The Total Amounts of Radioactively Contaminated Materials in Forests in Fukushima, Japan," *Scientific Reports* 2 (2012); see www.nature.com/articles/srep00416.pdf; Teppei J. Yasunari et al., "Cesium-137 Deposition and Contamination of Japanese Soils Due to the Fukushima Nuclear Accident," *Proceedings of the National Academy of Sciences* 108, no. 49 (2011): 19530–19534; Naohiro Yoshida and Yoshio Takahashi, "Land-Surface Contamination by Radionuclides from the Fukushima Daiichi Nuclear Power Plant Accident," *Elements* 8, no. 3 (2012): 201–206.

9 Peter Galison and Robb Moss, directors, *Containment* (documentary film), 2015, 81 mins; Galison, "Nuclear Wastelands, Nuclear Wilderness" (Physical Science Forum Distinguished Lecture, Annual Meeting of the History of Science Society, Boston, MA, November 23, 2013); Corydon Ireland, "Wasteland and Wilderness: Galison uses a Radcliffe Year to Ponder 'Zones of Exclusion'," *Harvard Gazette* (2009). See also: Allison MacFarlane, "Underlying Yucca Mountain: The Interplay of Geology and Policy in Nuclear Waste Disposal," *Social Studies of Science* 33, no. 5 (2003): 783–807.

10 Gavin Hilson and Frank Nyame, "Gold Mining in Ghana's Forest Reserves: A Report on the Current Debate," *Area* 38, no. 2 (2006): 175–185; Gavin Hilson and Natalia Yakovleva, "Strained Relations: A Critical Analysis of the Mining Conflict in Prestea, Ghana," *Political Geography* 26, no. 1 (2007): 98–119; R. Kasim Kasanga, "Land Tenure and Regional Investment Prospects: The Case of the Tenurial Systems of Northern Ghana," *Property Management* 13, no. 2 (1995): 21–31.

11 Abraham, *The Making*; Holly M. Barker, *Bravo for the Marshallese: Regaining Control in a Post-Nuclear, Post-Colonial World*, Case Studies on Contemporary Social Issues (Belmont, CA: Wadsworth/Thomson, 2004); Hugh Gusterson, *People of the Bomb: Portraits of America's*

Nuclear Complex (Minneapolis, MN: University of Minnesota Press, 2004); Hugh Guterson, *Nuclear Rites: A Weapons Laboratory at the End of the Cold War* (Berkeley, CA: University of California Press, 1998); Gabrielle Hecht, *The Radiance of France: Nuclear Power and National Identity after World War II*, ed. Wiebe E. Bijker, W. Bernard Carlson, and Trevor Pinch, *Inside Technology* (Cambridge, MA: MIT Press, 1998); George Perkovich, *India's Nuclear Bomb* (Berkeley, CA; London: University of California Press, 1999).

12 On debates over nuclear waste in Ghana, see G. Emi-Reynolds et al., "Safe and Secure Management of Sealed Radioactive Sources in Ghana," in *Safety and Security of Radioactive Sources: Maintaining Continuous Global Control of Sources Throughout Their Life Cycle: Proceedings of an International Conference, Abu Dhabi, United Arab Emirates, 27–31 October 2013* (Vienna: International Atomic Energy Agency, 2015); Kofi Thompson, "Ghana Incapable of Storing Dangerous Radioactive Waste Safely!" *Ghana Web*, March 7, 2013.

13 Naaborko Sackeyfio, "The Politics of Land and Urban Space in Colonial Accra," *History in Africa* 39 (2012): 293–329.

14 "K. Bosumpim & Anor. v Martei & Ors." December 12, 1901 in PRAAD RG 15/1/2161 Supreme Court: In the Matter of the Public Lands (Leasehold) Ordinance (Cap. 138) and in the Matter of Land Acquired for the Service of the Colony and Ashanti Situate at Mile Post 9 on the Accra-Dodowa Road for Presbyterian Secondary School, 1901.

15 Sara Berry, *No Condition Is Permanent: The Social Dynamics of Agrarian Change in Sub-Saharan Africa* (Madison, WI: University of Wisconsin Press, 1993), 101.

16 Chief Bosumpim speaking in the Supreme Court of the Gold Coast Colony held at Victoriasborg, Accra, April 28, 1904 before Sir W. Brandford Griffith, Knight, Chief Justice in PRAAD RG 15/1/2161.

17 Akyeampong, *Between the Sea & the Lagoon: An Eco-Social History of the Anlo of Southeastern Ghana C. 1850 to Recent Times*; Sean Hawkins, *Writing and Colonialism in Northern Ghana: The Encounter between the Lodagaa and 'the World on Paper'*, Anthropological Horizons (Toronto: University of Toronto Press, 2002); Naaborko Sackeyfio-Lenoch, *The Politics of Chieftaincy: Authority and Property in Colonial Ghana, 1920–1950*, Rochester Studies in African History and the Diaspora (Rochester, NY: University of Rochester Press, 2014).

18 Osabu speaking at Supreme Court, April 28, 1904 in PRAAD RG 15/1/2161.

19 PRAAD RG 15/1/2161.

20 On Africa's "Innumerable local frontiers": John Iliffe, *Africans: The History of a Continent* (Cambridge; New York: Cambridge University

Press, 2007), 2, 62, 63; Carola Lentz, "Decentralization, the State and Conflicts over Local Boundaries in Northern Ghana," *Development and Change* 37, no. 4 (2006): 901–919; "'This Is Ghanaian Territory!': Land Conflicts on a West African Border," *American Ethnologist* 30, no. 2 (2003): 273–289.

21 S. Quartey, *Missionary Practices on the Gold Coast, 1832–1895* (Youngstown, NY: Cambria Press), 119; Kathryn Firmin-Sellers, *The Transformation of Property Rights in the Gold Coast: An Empirical Study Applying Rational Choice Theory* (Cambridge: Cambridge University Press, 2007); C.C. Reindorf, *History of the Gold Coast and Asante* (Accra: Ghana Universities Press, 2007). Nii Akrade Annan Oti II, the acting chief of Kwabenya, read passages from Reindorf to me to bolster his land claims in 2008.

22 W. Brandforth Griffith, Chief Justice, Supreme Court of the Gold Coast, Victoriaborg, May 3, 1904 in PRAAD RG 15/1/2161.

23 R. Addo-Fening, "Customary Land-Tenure System in Akyem-Abuakwa," *Universitas* 9 (1987): 95–107. Also: Robert Addo-Fening, *Akyem Abuakwa and the Politics of the Inter-War Period in Ghana* (Basel: Basler Afrika-Bibliographien, 1975); Kojo Sebastian Amanor, *Land, Labour and the Family in Southern Ghana: A Critique of Land Policy under Neo-Liberalisation* (Uppsala: Nordiska Afrikainstitutet, 2001), 25–44; Emmanuel Ababio Ofosu-Mensah, "Mining and Conflict in the Akyem Abuakwa Kingdom in the Eastern Region of Ghana, 1919–1938," *The Extractive Industries and Society* 2 (2015): 480–490; Firmin-Sellers, *The Transformation*.

24 On later boundary disputes between Akuapem and Ga lands: "The Fate of Collections: Social Justice and the Annexation of Plant Genetic Resources," in *People, Plants and Justice: The Politics of Nature Conservation*, ed. Charles Zerner (New York: Columbia University Press).

25 Interview with Nii Tetteh Kwao I, kingmaker, Haatso Palace, August 4, 2015.

26 Interview with Lawrence Nii Noi, elder, Haatso Palace, August 4, 2015.

27 *Ibid.*

28 Emphasis mine, PRAAD Act 204. "Act 204: Atomic Energy Commission." Previously, there was a Ghana Atomic Energy Committee established in 1961.

29 PRAAD RG 3/6/1167.

30 PRAAD RG 3/6/1163 Memorandum to the National Liberation Council: Ghana Atomic Energy Commission – (a) Staff and (B) Vacant Bungalows and Flats, 1967; Amuasi, *The History*, 5.

31 Kwame Nkrumah, *The World without the Bomb [Sound Recording]* (Berkeley, CA: Bancroft Library Phonotape 3667A, 1962).

32 Interview, Reverend B.W. Garbrah, Nyaniba Estates, Accra, Ghana, January 18, 2006.

33 T.F. Gieryn, "Boundary-Work and the Demarcation of Science from Non-Science: Strains and Interests in Professional Ideologies of Scientists," *American Sociological Review* 48, no. 6 (1983): 781–795.

34 Hugh Gusterson, *Nuclear Rites: A Weapons Laboratory at the End of the Cold War* (Berkeley, CA: University of California Press, 1996), 68.

35 Benjamin Sims and Christopher R. Henke, "Repairing Credibility: Repositioning Nuclear Weapons Knowledge after the Cold War," *Social Studies of Science* 42, no. 3 (2012): 324–347.

36 PRAAD RG 3/6/1167.

37 Adjoa Van-Ess, "Help Improve Gamma Irradiation Facility- Prof Allotey Tells Industrialists," *Daily Graphic*, August 3, 1999.

38 "Code on the Safety of Nuclear Research Reactors: Design, The International Atomic Energy Agency: Vienna 1991," in PRAAD GAEC AG/SF22 Vol VI IAEA Nuclear Safety Accident Radiation Protection, 1991–1992.

39 Interview, E.O. Darko, Radiation Protection Institute, Ghana Atomic Energy Commission, Kwabenya, Ghana, July 21, 2008.

40 Joseph Martin, "The Peaceful Atom Comes to Campus," *Physics Today* 69, no. 2 (2016): 40–46.

41 Nuruddeen M. Abdallah, "Inside Nigeria's Only Nuclear Research Centre," *Sunday Trust*, July 12, 2009.

42 *Safety of Research Reactors: Safety Requirements*, Vol. NS-R-4, Safety Standards Series (Vienna: IAEA, 2005), 62.

43 Interview, Benjamin Nyarko, GAEC Director General, Ghana Atomic Energy Commission, Kwabenya, Ghana, July 27, 2015.

44 IAEA CN-82/05 Safety of Ghana Research Reactor (GHARR-1).

45 Measures are under way to convert the reactor to low-enriched uranium; see H.C. Odoi et al., *Implementation of Reactor Core Conversion Program of GHARR-1*, 36th International Meeting on Reduced Enrichment for Research and Test Reactors (2015).

46 Nii Tettey Commey II, chief's advisor, Kwabenya Palace, July 26, 2008.

47 Naa Yaboley II, Queen of the Youth, sister of the chief, Kwabenya Palace, July 26, 2008.

48 PRAAD RG 3/6/1167.

49 Amuasi, *The History*, 4, 19.

50 Interview, Francis K.A. Allotey, Allotey residence, Accra, Ghana, July 30, 2008.

51 On "suburbanization" in physics in the United States, see David Kaiser, "The Postwar Suburbanization of American Physics," *American Studies* 56, no. 4 (2004): 851–888.
52 PRAAD SCT 2/6/63 High Court of Justice, Accra, July 1979–June 1980.
53 Interview, Nii Akrade Annan Oti II, acting chief of Kwabenya Palace, Kwabenya, Ghana, July 26, 2008.
54 Interview, Nii Tettey Commey II, chief's advisor, Kwabenya Palace, Kwabenya, Ghana, July 26, 2008.
55 Interview, Nii Tetteh Kwao I and Lawrence Nii Noi, August 4, 2015.
56 Interview, Nii Akrade Annan Oti II, acting chief of Kwabenya Palace, Kwabenya, Ghana, July 26, 2008.
57 Zuoyi Zhang and Yuliang Sun, "Economic Potential of Modular Reactor Nuclear Power Plants Based on the Chinese HTR-PM Project," *Nuclear Engineering and Design* 237, no. 23 (2007): 2265–2274.
58 "Encroachment."
59 Interview, Uriel Andoh, Atomic Road Pharmacy, Haatso-Atomic Road, Ghana, July 29, 2008.
60 "Advertiser's Announcement: Encroachment on Ghana Atomic Energy Commission (G.A.E.C.) Lands," *Daily Graphic*, September 22, 2005. Italics mine.
61 Abraham, "Geopolitics and Biopolitics in India's High Natural Background Radiation Zone."
62 Petryna, *Life Exposed*.
63 Interview, Nii Tetteh Kwao I and Lawrence Nii Noi, chief's palace, Haatso, Ghana, August 4, 2015. Local leaders were especially disturbed after GAEC's successive attempts to partner with Taysec, the British government, and the waste management company Zoomlion to build a recycling facility on part of Atomic Lands. See "Encroachment of Ghana Atomic Lands," *The Enquirer*, December 30, 2011. www.ghanaweb.com/GhanaHomePage/NewsArchive/artikel.php?ID=226700 (September 20, 2013). Also: "Kwabenya Landfill Project Suffers Setback," *Daily Graphic*, March 18, 2002, p. 23.
64 Stephen Sah, "School for Nuclear, Allied Sciences Takes Off Sept," *Daily Graphic*, January 24, 2005.
65 Interview, Charles A. Ocran, Haatso-Atomic Road, Ghana, July 29, 2008.
66 Interview, Benjamin Nyarko, GAEC Director General, Ghana Atomic Energy Commission, Kwabenya, Ghana, July 27, 2015.
67 Kasim Kasanga and Nii Ashie Kotey, *Land Management in Ghana: Building on Tradition and Modernity* (London: International Institute for Environment and Development, 2001), 4–6. See also

Catherine Boone, *Property and Political Order in Africa: Land Rights and the Structure of Politics* (New York: Cambridge University Press, 2014), 36–37.

68 "Article 20: Fundamental Human Rights and Freedoms," *The Constitution of the Republic of Ghana 1992* (Accra: Government Printers, 1992).

69 Takyi-Boadu, "Shock and Chaos."

70 Interview, G.K.A. Ofosu-Amaah, videochat, September 22, 2013.

71 Naa Korkoi Ashalley, "Kwabenya Lands," *Daily Graphic*, March 11, 1998.

72 Kasanga and Kotey, *Land Management*, iii. For a summary of customary and state land law, see Katherine V. Gough and Paul W.K. Yankson, "Land Markets in African Cities: The Case of Peri-Urban Accra, Ghana," *Urban Studies* 37, no. 13 (2000): 2485–2500.

73 Nii Ayikai Aryee, "The Land Crisis in Ghana," *Daily Graphic*, September 4, 2000; Gough and Yankson, "Land Markets in African Cities: The Case of Peri-Urban Accra, Ghana."

74 The above-ground facility is projected to house waste from across West Africa and is the first of its kind on the continent. "Ghana Inaugurates Radioactive Waste Storage Facility"; Darko and Fletcher, "National Waste Management Infrastructure in Ghana." GAEC has also begun exploratory borehole disposal of radioactive waste in the Kwabenya area; see G. Emi-Reynolds et al., "Safe and Secure Management."

75 Callistus Mahama and Martin Dixon, "Acquisition and Affordability of Land for Housing in Urban Ghana: A Study in the Formal Land Market Dynamics," *RCIS Research Paper Series* 10 (2006).

76 "Arson & Demolition: Atomic Energy Boss, 30 Others in Police Custody," *Peace FM Online*, January 24, 2012. http://news.peacefmonline.com/pages/news/201201/90495.php. See also Isaac Essel, "National Security Stalls Construction of Multi-Million Project," *Myjoyonline.com*, June 4, 2012; Charles Takyi-Boadu, "Anaina Takes Off," *Daily Guide*, January 4, 2012; Eunice Asante, "Ultra Modern Business Centre Commissioned," *citifmonline.com*, June 4, 2012; Takyi-Boadu, "Anaina Takes Off"; Essel, "National Security Stalls Construction of Multi-Million Project"; Asante, "Ultra Modern Business Centre Commissioned."

77 "Arson & Demolition: Atomic Energy Boss."

78 "Greater Accra P.S.W.U. Supports Demolition of Illegal Structures on Atomic Energy Land," *VibeGhana*, February 15, 2012.

79 Godwin Allotey Akweiteh, "G.A.E.C. Wins Court Case over Atomic Land," June 4, 2012.

80 "Gas Station Explosion Shakes Ghana's Capital: Unknown Number Killed after Blast at Natural Gas Station Sends Giant Fireball into

Sky over City." *The Guardian*, October 7, 2017. www.theguardian
.com/world/2017/oct/07/petrol-station-explosion-ghana-accra-fireball
(October 10, 2017).

81 Olga Kuchinskaya, *The Politics of Invisibility: Public Knowledge About
Radiation Health Effects after Chernobyl*; "Twice Invisible: Formal
Representations of Radiation Danger," *Social Studies of Science* 43,
no. 1 (2013): 78–96.

Epilogue

1 Masco, *Nuclear Borderlands*.
2 For an important overview, see Pauline E. Peters, "Conflicts over Land
and Threats to Customary Tenure in Africa," *African Affairs* 112,
no. 449 (2013): 543–562. For recent comparative work across countries, see Boone, *Property and Political Order*.
3 For instance, Rivo Andrianirina-Ratsialonana et al., *After Daewoo?
Current Status and Perspectives of Large-Scale Land Acquisition in
Madagascar* (Rome: International Land Coalition (ILC), 2011).
4 Mahama and Dixon, "Acquisition," 32.
5 Amuasi, *The History*, pp. 90–91; S.A. Jonah et al., "Neutron Spectrum
Parameters in Irradiation Channels of the Nigeria Research Reactor-1
(NIRR-1) for the K0-NAA Standardization," *Journal of Radioanalytical
and Nuclear Chemistry* 266, no. 1 (2005): 83–88; *African Regional
Cooperative Agreement for Research, Development and Training
Related to Nuclear Science and Technology: Profile of the Regional
Strategic Cooperative Framework (2008–2013)* (Vienna: IAEA, 2010);
Mark-Anthony Vinorkor, "Boost Energy Supply with Nuclear Power –
Akaho," *Daily Graphic*, November 25, 2006.
6 Michael Donkor, "Ghana Will Harness Peaceful Use of Nuclear Energy,"
ibid., January 18, 2011; "Ghana to Export Nuclear Energy?," *Safari
Radio (via Ghana News Agency)*, June 4, 2012; George Amexo, "Nation
Targets Nuclear Power by 2018," *Public Agenda*, April 4, 2011; "No
Fears About Country's Nuclear Program," *Public Agenda*, March 21,
2011; "Ghana Nuclear Regulatory Authority Board Inaugurated,"
Ghana Business News, January 15, 2016.

Persons Cited and Consulted

Aboh, Kwame. Research scientist, Ghana Atomic Energy Commission, July 21, 2008.

Acheampong, Franklin Agyare. Research scientist, Biotechnology and Nuclear Agriculture Research Institute, Ghana Atomic Energy Commission, July 21, 2008.

Acquah, Issac N. Professor, School of Nuclear and Allied Sciences, August 3, 2015.

Adukpo, Oscar Kwaku. Research scientist, Radiation Protection Institute, Ghana Atomic Energy Commission, August 2, 2017.

Affum, Hannah Asamoah. Research scientist, Ghana Atomic Energy Commission, August 2, 2017.

Agyewaa, Akosua. GAEC market, Kwabenya, July 29, 2008.

Ahiamadjie, Hyacinthe. Research scientist, Ghana Atomic Energy Commission, August 2, 2017.

Akiti, Tetteh. Research scientist, Ghana Atomic Energy Commission, 2015.

Akoto, G.E. Rev. Chief Technologist, Radiation Protection Institute, Ghana Atomic Energy Commission, July 23, 2008.

Akoto-Bamford, Samuel. Reverend, professor, School of Nuclear and Allied Sciences, August 3, 2015.

Allotey, Francis K.A. Mathematical physicist, former Director of GAEC, Allotey residence, Accra, July 30, 2008.

Ameertey, Nii. Member of family, Kwabenya Palace, July 26, 2008.

Amoako, Joseph. Research scientist, Ghana Atomic Energy Commission, August 2, 2017.

Ampim II, Asafoatse Nii Ayitey. Member of family, Kwabenya Palace, July 26, 2008.

Amuasi, John Humphrey. GAEC residences, Kwabenya, Ghana, January 15, 2006; professor, School of Nuclear and Allied Sciences, July 29, 2015.

Andoh, Uriel. Manager, Atomic Road Pharmacy, July 29, 2008.

Annkah, James Kwame. Radiation physicist, Ghana Atomic Energy Commission, July 23, 2008.

Annoh, Charles Emmanuel. Research scientist, Animal Science Department, Ghana Atomic Energy Commission, July 21, 2008.

Appiah, Victoria. Professor, School of Nuclear and Allied Sciences, July 29, 2015.

Arthur, Lawrence. Retired radiographer, Korle Bu Teaching Hospital, July 31, 2017.

Aryee, Joseph. Student, Sam Bell Academy, Kwabenya Village, July 26, 2008.

Aryeetey, Jonathan. Member of family, Kwabenya Palace, July 26, 2008.

Asante, Johnson. Haatso-Atomic Road, July 29, 2008.

Asare, Daniel Kwasi. Scientist, Biotechnology and Nuclear Agriculture Research Institute, Ghana Atomic Energy Commission, July 22, 2008.

Bekoe, Samuel. Haatso Transport Station, July 30, 2008.

Boateng, Steven. Chief Radiographer, Korle Bu Teaching Hospital, July 7, 2017.

Bortei-Doku, Sam. Retired educationist, Accra, November 11, 2010.

Commey II, Nii Tettey. Chief's advisor, Kwabenya Palace, July 26, 2008.

Darko, Emmauel O. Head, Radiation Protection Institute, Ghana Atomic Energy Commission, July 21, 2008.

Debrah, Esther. GAEC market, Kwabenya, July 7, 2008.

Dokyi, Emmanuel. Haatso Transport Station, July 30, 2008.

Fletcher, John Justice. Professor, School of Nuclear and Allied Sciences, August 4, 2015.

Forson, Amos. Research scientist, Ghana Atomic Energy Commission, August 2, 2017.

Francois, Salome. Retired radiographer, Korle Bu Teaching Hospital, Accra, August 10, 2017.

Franklin, Agyare Acheampong. Attendee, National Training Course on Radiation Protection, School of Nuclear and Allied Sciences, July 21, 2008.

Fry-Ammam, John. Kwabenya, July 29, 2008.

Garbrah, Benjamin Woarabae. Very Reverend Professor, former Director, Ghana Atomic Energy Commission, Garbrah residence, Nyanyiba Estates, January 18, 2006; July 30, 2015.

Kwao I, Nii Tetteh. Kingmaker, Haatso Palace, August 4, 2015.

Larbi, Florence, Utta Alifo Larbi, and Emmanuel Larbi. Staff daycare managers and GAEC employee (relations of the author), GAEC staff housing, July 29, 2008.

Lawrence, Korblah. Secretary, Haatso Transport Yard, July 30, 2008.

Lokko, Carl Christian. Mechanical engineer, Tema Port, July 23, 2008.

Mangena, Simbarashe. Student (Zimbabwe), School of Nuclear and Allied Sciences, July 29, 2015.

Mensah, Ben Kwamena. Member of family, Kwabenya Palace, July 23, 2008.

Mensah II, Nii Okine. Stool father, Kwabenya Palace, July 26, 2008.

Mensah, Okyeame Tettey. Member of family, Kwabenya Palace, July 26, 2008.

Mills, Dorothy. Retired radiographer, Korle Bu Teaching Hospital, Mills residence, Korle Bu, July 3, 2017.

Nani, Emmanuel Kwaku. Research scientist, Ghana Atomic Energy Commission, July 21, 2008.

Nii Tetteh, Patrick. Member of family, Kwabenya Palace, July 23, 2008.

Noi, Lawrence Nii. Elder, Haatso Palace, August 4, 2015.

Nuviadenu, Christian Kwasi. Research scientist, Ghana Atomic Energy Commission, August 2, 2017.

Nyaki, Mungubariki. Physicist, Tanzania Atomic Energy Commission during visit to GAEC, July 25, 2008.

Obeng, Letitia. Biologist, launch of her autobiography, Ghana Academy of Arts and Sciences, Accra, July 7, 2008.

Obeng, Michael Kojo Asare. Chief Technologist, Radiation Protection Institute, Ghana Atomic Energy Commission, July 23, 2008.

Ocran, Charles Abaidoo. Haatso-Atomic Road, July 29, 2008.

Oduraa, Obayaa Gladys. GAEC market, July 29, 2008.

Ofosu-Amaah, G.K.A. Videochat to Accra, September 22, 2013.

Oka-Ayitey, Nii Okai. Member of family, Kwabenya Palace, July 26, 2008.

Okai, Lawrence. Student, Sower's Academy, Kwabenya Village, July 26, 2008.

Opoku, Samuel. Head of Radiotherapy, National Center for Radiotherapy and Nuclear Medicine, Korle Bu Teaching Hospital/Head of Department of Radiography, College of Health Sciences, University of Ghana, August 1, 2017.

Osae, Michael. Manager, Radiation Entomology and Pest Management Centre, Biotechnology and Nuclear Agriculture Research Institute, Ghana Atomic Energy Commission, 2017.

Osei, Rexford. Director of Science, Ghana Ministry of Education, Science and Sports, July 4, 2008; July 14, 2008.

Oti II, Nii Akrade Annan. Head of family, Acting Chief of Kwabenya, Kwabenya Palace, July 26, 2008.

Otoo, Francis. Research scientist, Ghana Atomic Energy Commission, August 2, 2017.

Schandorf, Cyril. Professor, School of Nuclear and Allied Sciences, August 2, 2017.

Tandoh, Joseph. Research scientist, Ghana Atomic Energy Commission, August 2, 2017.

Tettey, Isaac. Haatso-Atomic Road, July 29, 2008.

Vealle, Irene. Participant, training course in radiation protection, School of Nuclear and Allied Sciences, July 21, 2008.

Vincent, Agbodemegbe. Research scientist, Nuclear Power Institute, Ghana
    Atomic Energy Commission, 2017.
Ware, Naa Opoku Adashi. Chief Priestess, Kwabenya Palace, July 26, 2008.
Wisdom, Obideah. Haatso Transport Station, July 30, 2008.
Yaboley II, Naa. Queen of the Youth, sister of the chief, Kwabenya Palace,
    July 26, 2008.
Yemofio, Erasmus. Community member and liaison, Haatso Palace, August
    4, 2015.

Works Cited and Consulted

Archival Collections

Ghana Public Records and Archives Administration Department (PRAAD), Accra

PRAAD Act 204 Act 204: Atomic Energy Commission, 1963.

PRAAD ADM 5/4/18 Kitson, A.E. The Possible Sources of Power for Industrial Purposes in the Gold Coast, British West Africa, 1928.

PRAAD CSO 11/1/283 British Red Cross, Gold Coast Branch, Ashanti – X-Ray Apparatus, 1933.

PRAAD CSO 11/1/329 X-Ray Apparatus at the Gold Coast Hospital, 1933.

PRAAD CSO 11/1/431 X-Ray Apparatus for Sekondi African Hospital, 1938.

PRAAD CSO 11/1/335 X-Ray & Electro-Medical Apparatus, Circulation and Interchange of Information Regarding Operation and Maintenance of, 1933.

PRAAD GAEC 1/Vol. 8 Ghana Atomic Energy Commission, 1965–1966.

PRAAD GAEC 4/SF1 International Atomic Energy Technical Aid (Equipment), 1963–1964.

PRAAD GAEC 8 Finances: Ghana Atomic Energy Commission, 1963–1964.

PRAAD GAEC AG 16 Vol II Radiation Protection Board, 1970–1978.

PRAAD GAEC AG 34 Agricultural Research 1978–1980.

PRAAD GAEC AG/SF22 Vol. IV IAEA Nuclear Safety, Accident Radiation Protection, 1988–1989.

PRAAD GAEC AG/SF22 Vol VI IAEA Nuclear Safety Accident Radiation Protection, 1991–1992.

PRAAD GAEC AG/SF22 Vol. VII IAEA Nuclear Safety Accident Radiation Protection, 1992–1993.

PRAAD GAEC PA NNR1/1 Passage Arrangements, 1990–1993.

PRAAD GAEC 23 Research Centre – Correspondence on, 1965.

PRAAD RG 3/1/496 Science Centres: Curricula, Syllabuses, Teachers Notes, 1964.

PRAAD RG 3/1/499 Kumasi Science Centre, 1964–1969.

PRAAD RG 3/1/500 Sekondi Science Centre, 1964.

PRAAD RG 3/1/501 Science Centres Policy, 1964–1966.

PRAAD RG 3/1/133 Ghana National Anthem, 1955–1959.

PRAAD RG 3/6/184 Ghana Police Docket, 1966–1968.

PRAAD RG 3/6/977 Report of the Commission of Enquiry into the Ghana Atomic Energy Commission, 1970.

PRAAD RG 3/6/1163 Memorandum to the National Liberation Council: Ghana Atomic Energy Commission – (a) Staff and (B) Vacant Bungalows and Flats, 1967.

PRAAD RG 3/6/1165 Ghana Atomic Energy Commission – Conferences, 1968.

PRAAD RG 3/6/1166 The Ghana Atomic Energy Project: A Scientific Review by J.E.O. Lindsay, Ghana Atomic Energy Commission, Accra, 19th July 1966, 1966.

PRAAD RG 3/6/1167 White Paper on the Report of the Atomic Reactor Review Committee, 1973.

PRAAD RG 5/1/389 Ministry of Works: Electricity Organisation, 1957.

PRAAD RG 6/6/323 Research Reactor (Kwabenya), 1977–1979.

PRAAD RG 11/1/115 Ghana Atomic Energy Commission School, 1972.

PRAAD RG 11/1/201 The Academy of Sciences of the USSR, 1961–1962.

PRAAD RG 11/1/224 Technical Assistance from Union of Soviet Socialist Republic, 1962.

PRAAD RG 11/1/298 Radio Isotope Research Project, 1961.

PRAAD RG 11/1/286 Ghana Academy of Learning – Agenda and Minutes of General Meetings (Interim National Council for Higher Education and Research), 1959.

PRAAD RG 11/1/315 Confidential: National Research Council – Conferences, 1961.

PRAAD RG 11/1/345 Ghana Academy of Sciences Educational Research Committee, 1961.

PRAAD RG 11/2/35 Special Appointment: Dr. A.N. May, 1961–1965.

PRAAD RG 14/4/210 Nuclear Weapons Test, 1959–1961.

PRAAD RG 14/4/211 Peaceful Uses of Atomic Energy, 1959–.

PRAAD RG 15/1/2161 Supreme Court: In the Matter of the Public Lands (Leasehold) Ordinance (Cap. 138) and in the Matter of Land Acquired for the Service of the Colony and Ashanti Situate at Mile Post 9 on the Accra-Dodowa Road for Presbyterian Secondary School, 1901.

PRAAD RG 17/1/60 USSR, 1960–1961.

PRAAD RG 17/1/82 National Research Council, 1960–1961.

PRAAD RG 17/1/259 Ghana Atomic Energy Committee, 1961–1964.

PRAAD SCR 148/SF 2 Atomic Energy Commission: Recommendations by Sir John Cockcroft, 1966–1972.

PRAAD SCT 2/6/63 High Court of Justice, Accra, July 1979–June 1980, 1979.

PRAAD SLBS 33/40 Transcript Copy of Notes: Tema, Nungua, Teshie and Labadi Order, 1956 (L.N. 247) and Akwapim State Boundary Enquiry Order, 1955 (L.N. 241).

Archives of the University of Ghana, Legon (UG)

UG 1/3/2/3/61A Organisation and Establishment Department of Physics, 1965–2000.

UG 1/3/2/3/10 Radioactive Fallout Unit – Organisation and Establishment, 1959–1963.

UG 1/3/3/2/73 Design and Construction – Department of Physics Non-Magnetic Research Laboratory, 1956–1961.

UG 1/3/8/4/74 Ghana Atomic Energy Commission: Relations with the University, 1972–1975.

UG 1/3/8/5/6 Visits of Russian Scientists and Exchange of Professors, 1958.

Archives of the International Atomic Energy Agency (IAEA)

IAEA CN-82/05 Safety of Ghana Research Reactor (GHARR-1), 2000.

IAEA GC (II)/INF/10/Rev.5 Members of the Agency: List of 20 September 1958, 1958.

IAEA GC(VI)/OR.72 Official Record of the Seventy-Second Plenary Meeting Held at the Neue Hofburg, Vienna, on Wednesday, 26 September 1962, at 3.20 P.M. President: Mr. Baffour (Ghana), 1962.

IAEA GC(III)/83 Scale of Members' Contributions: Revised Scale for 1959, 1959.

IAEA GC.1/INF/3 Agreement between the Government of Austria and the Prepatory Commission of the International Atomic Energy Agency Concerning Arrangements in Vienna for the Preparatory Commission and the First General Conference of the Agency, 1957.

IAEA GC.1/INF/6 International Atomic Energy Agency General Conference First Session List of Delegates, 1957.

Chinese Foreign Ministry Archives, Beijing (CFMA)

CMFA 108/00252/04 Trade Protocol to the Trade and Payments Agreement between the Government of the People's Republic of China and the Government of the Republic of Ghana, 1961.

CFAA 108/00546/01 Nkrumah's Letters to Mao Zeodong and Zhou Enlai Regarding China's Successful Explosion of a Nuclear Device, 1964.

CFMA 108/00546/01 Recent Report of China's Explosion of a Nuclear Device, 1964.

CFMA [no number] 外交部同我驻加纳使馆就加纳总统恩克鲁玛建议召开世界非核国家会议事的来往电报 [Back-and-Forth Telegrams between Chinese Foreign Ministry and the Embassy of China in Ghana Regarding the International Nuclear-Free Conference], 1960.

Faculty of Pharmacy Administrative Records, Kwame Nkrumah University of Science and Technology (KNUST)

KNUST FP/R1/199 E.A. Allman correspondence, Faculty of Pharmacy, 1961–1962.
KNUST FP/R1/199 Research – General, 1960–1971.

Public Record Office, United Kingdom (PRO)

PRO CO 554/1421 Feasibility of Establishing an Experimental Reactor in the Gold Coast, 1956–1957.
PRO CO 937/474 Possible Diversion of Aircraft Due to Atomic Tests, 1959.
PRO DO 35/8330 Atomic Energy Development in Ghana, 1956–1960.
PRO DO 35/9340 Ghana Protest at Proposed French Atomic Explosion in the Sahara, 1959.
PRO DO 35/9341 Ghana Protest at Proposed French Bomb Test, 1959.
PRO DO 35/9342 Reappraisal of United Kingdom Policy in Regard to French Atomic Tests, 1960.
PRO DO 182/13 Ghanaian Proposal for an Atom and Base Free Africa, 1960.
PRO DO 195/45 Ghana Desire for a Nuclear Reactor, 1960–1961.
PRO EG 1/685 Military Research and Production: French Atomic Tests in the Sahara, 1959–1961.
PRO FO 94/2142 Country: Ghana Treaty: Nuclear Weapons Tests Ban. Place and Date of Signature: Moscow, 5 August, 1963.
PRO FO 94/2569 Country: Ghana Non-Proliferation of Nuclear Weapons Treaty Place and Date of Signature: London, 1 July 1970.
PRO FO 371/138609 France's Atom Bomb Tests in the Sahara, 1959.
PRO FO 371/149448 Introduction of a Resolution by Ghana to Remove All Foreign Military Bases and Nuclear Weapons, 1960.
PRO FO 371/149450 UN General Assembly Ghana's Proposal on an Atom and Base Free Africa, 1960.
PRO FO 371/157294 Ghana's Efforts to Get a Nuclear Reactor Reactor, Asks If There Are Any Indicators That the Russians Intend to Supply One, 1961.
PRO FO 371/187903 Dr. Nkrumah's visit to Peking, 1966.
PRO FO 371/189505 Nuclear Programmes: Ghana, 1966.
PRO OD 11/149 Visits of Sir John Cockcroft to Ghana to Advise the Ghana Academy of Sciences, 1964.

PRO OD 30/457 Technical Assistance to the Ghana Atomic Energy Commission; Reactivation of Atomic Reactor Project, 1973–1975.

Russian State Archives of the Economy (RGAE)

RGAE 265/2/846 Соглашение Между Ссср И Ганой От 4 Августа 1960 Г. Об Экономическом И Техническом Сотрудничестве И Ноты Правительства Ганы Относительно Соглашения [Agreement between USSR and Ghana from August 4, 1960 About Economic and Technical Assistance and Notes of the Government of Ghana Relating to This Agreement], 1960.

RGAE 365/2/277 Аписи Бесед С Представителями Ганы, Гвинеи, Гдр, Индии, Индонезии, Ирака, Йемена [Notes from Meetings with Representatives], 1961.

RGAE 365/2/466 Материалы Об Оказании Экономического И Технического Содействия Гане, Гвинее, Дагомее, Индонезии, Ираку, Йемену, Камбодже, Кении, Корее, Кубе, Кувейту (Просьбы, Ноты, Памятные Записки, Справки, Переписка) [Materials About Rendering Economic and Technical Co-operation (Questions, Notes, Correspondence) for Ghana], 1964.

RGAE 365/2/3369 Обращения И Заявки Правительств Афганистана, Болгарии, Венгрии, Ганы, Гвинеи, Гдр, Индонезии, Монголии, Оар, Польши, Румынии, Сомали, Сирии, Чехословакии, Эфиопии, Югославии О Командировании Советских Специалистов За Границу И Приеме На Обучение В Ссср Иностранных Специалистов [Address and Requests from the Government ... of Ghana for Sending Soviet Specialists Abroad and Receiving for Education in the USSR, Foreign Specialists], 1963.

RGAE 365/3/975 Соглашения, Протоколы, Письма Между Ссср И Ганой И Проекты Указанных Документов [Protocol Letters between USSR And Ghana], 1964.

United States Department of State

Department of State, Central Files, 745J.11/10–760, reprinted in *Priority in Foreign Relations of the United States, 1958–1960 Volume XIV, Africa*, Document 303 Telegram from the Embassy in Ghana to the Department of State, Confidential, 1960.

Egypt and US, *Agreement for Cooperation between the Government of the United States of America and the Government of the Arab Republic of Egypt Concerning Peaceful Uses of Nuclear Energy: Message from the President of the United States Transmitting the Text of a*

Proposed Agreement between the United States Government and the Arab Republic of Egypt Concerning Peaceful Uses of Nuclear Power, Pursuant to Section 123d of the Atomic Energy Act of 1954, as Amended. Washington, DC: US Government Printing Office, 1981.

Atomic Energy, Peaceful Uses of Nuclear Energy: Agreement between the United States of America and Egypt Signed at Washington June 29, 1981 with Agreed Minute. Washington, DC: Deptartment of State: For sale by the Supt. of Docs, US GPO, 1982.

Atomic Energy, Technical Information Exchange and Cooperation in Nuclear Safety Matter: Arrangement between the United States of America and Egypt Signed at Bethesda and Cairo April 27 and June 8, 1981. Washington, DC: Deptartment of State: For sale by the Supt. of Docs, US GPO, 1982.

News Reports

"The Atomic Bomb Entirely Sweeps Another City into River." *Gold Coast Independent*, August 25, 1945.

"The Defeat of Japan." *Gold Coast Independent*, August 18, 1945.

"One Atom Bomb Smashes Four Square Miles of Hiroshima." *Gold Coast Independent*, August 11, 1945.

"Mcmahon Bars Soviet Atom Plan; Sees War If World Accord Fails." *The New York Times*, May 22, 1947.

"Atom Weapon Is Seen as Power by-Product." *The New York Times*, November 23, 1951.

"Radio Today: Wednesday December 24, 1952." *The Daily Echo*, December 24, 1952.

"Total Ban on Atomic Weapons: "Matter of Principle with India," Tests Must End First." *The Times of India*, October 7, 1957.

"A French Bomb – Not Only for France?" *Manchester Guardian*, July 10, 1959.

"British Imperialists Again Misfire! Fresh Attack on Nkrumah, Africa! Africa!! Africa!!! Be Warned." *Evening News*, January 5, 1960.

"We Can't Help but Embrace the United States of Africa: British Press Reaction to Nkrumah's Revolutionary Stand." *Evening News*, January 13, 1960, 3.

"Graham Mum on French Atom Test." *Evening News*, January 25, 1960.

"France: Stop This Hell Bomb Test." *Evening News*, February 10, 1960.

"France: Atomic Club Member." *West African Pilot*, February 15, 1960.

"Poison Cloud Hangs over Africa." *Evening News*, February 16, 1960.

"No Place in the World for Colonialism Now – Khrushchev." *Evening News*, February 22, 1960.

"Bomb Explosion Can't Intimidate Africa." *Evening News*, February 26, 1960.

"Reporter: A Doctor of Science: Death Dust: There Is Danger Ahead!" *Evening News*, February 26, 1960.

"USSR To Set up Friendship of Nations University." *Evening News*, March 12, 1960.

"Ghana Envoy on His Recall." *The Times*, April 5, 1960.

"U.S. Lends £10m for Big Volta Project, They Make Conditions." *Daily Graphic*, August 20, 1960.

"A Book for Baido-Ansah." *Daily Graphic*, January 3, 1961.

"French Atom Test in Sahara: Nigera Will Take 'Strong Action' If…" *Daily Graphic*, January 3, 1961.

"Nigeria Breaks with France." *Daily Graphic*, January 7, 1961.

"Our Friendship Is Unbreakable!" *Pravda*, February 20, 1961.

"Meeting Dear Guests: The Arrival in Moscow of President and Head of State of the Republic of Ghana, Dr. Kwame Nkrumah." *Pravda*, July 11, 1961.

"Joint Soviet-Ghanaian Address." *Pravda*, July 26, 1961.

"Dinner for Spaceman Gagarin." *The Ghanaian Times*, February 7, 1962.

"Soviets to Build a Railway Line from Kumasi to Upper Volta." *The Ghanaian Times*, February 2, 1962.

"Pushkin, the Great Afro-Russian Poet." *The Ghanaian Times*, February 19, 1962.

"Hausa-Russian Dictionary to Be Published Soon." *The Ghanaian Times*, April 3, 1962.

"Ghanaian Poetry Gets Big Audition in Moscow." *The Ghanaian Times*, April 16, 1962.

"'Auntie Mansa': The Wonders of Science." *The Ghanaian Times*, June 1, 1962.

"Ghanaian Times Editorial: The Path to 'World without the Bomb'." *The Ghanaian Times*, June 22, 1962.

"'The World without the Bomb,' Accra Assembly: Nuclear War Is an Economic and Political Suicide–Kwame." *The Ghanaian Times*, June 23, 1962.

"Emphasis on Science Is Praised." *The Ghanaian Times*, December 1, 1962.

"Ghanaian Times Editorial: World without the Bomb." *The Ghanaian Times*, June 23, 1962.

"Kwame Visits Dam Site–as Work Begins on Final Phase." *The Ghanaian Times*, February 26, 1963.

"Ghanaian Scientists Visit USSR" *The Ghanaian Times*, August 30, 1963.

"Soviet Science Equipment for Ghana Schools." *The Ghanaian Times*, August 30, 1963.

"We Can't Fan the Embers of Tribalism." *The Ghanaian Times*, August 31, 1963.

"Large Vote Margin Asked for Nkrumah." *The New York Times*, January 24, 1964. www.nytimes.com/1964/01/24/large-vote-margin-asked-for-nkrumah.html (April 10, 2016).

"Chinese Praised for Atom Test." *The Ghanaian Times*, October 19, 1964.

"Atomic Reactor–Correction." *The Ghanaian Times*, November 10, 1964.

"A Woman's Height of Scientific Achievement." *The Ghanaian Times*, November 24, 1964.

"In All Things Scientific and Technological, Ghanaians Are on the Run." *The Ghanaian Times*, November 30, 1964.

"Ghana to Refine Gold in 1966." *The Ghanaian Times*, January 5, 1965.

"Our Country Can Step up Export of Bauxite." *The Ghanaian Times*, November 24, 1965.

"Science, Technology – Vital Basis of Our Development." *The Ghanaian Times*, November 24, 1965.

"Our Science Correspondent: Focus on Ghana Atomic Reactor Project: Nuclear Research in Ghana." *The Ghanaian Times*, November 14, 1966.

"Nuclear System Used for Plant Production." *The Ghanaian Times*, April 21, 1967.

"Reactor Unit Is Removed from Plant." *The New York Times*, December 15, 1988.

"Radiation Protection Law Coming Soon – Schandorf." *People's Daily Graphic*, November 15, 1991.

"Ghana Atomic Energy Commission, Vacant Positions." *The Ghanaian Times*, July 29, 1994.

"Radioactive Waste Centre Set Up." *The Ghanaian Times*, August 10, 1994.

"Kwabenya Landfill Project Suffers Setback." *Daily Graphic*, March 18, 2002.

"Advertiser's Announcement: Encroachment on Ghana Atomic Energy Commission (G.A.E.C.) Lands." *Daily Graphic*, September 22, 2005.

"Lack of Funds Stalls Irradiation Project." *Daily Graphic*, August 16, 2007.

"Un Urges Stronger, Effective Nuclear Safety Standards." *Public Agenda*, June 24, 2011 http://allafrica.com/stories/201106290566.html.

"Encroachment of Ghana Atomic Lands." *The Enquirer*, December 30, 2011. www.ghanaweb.com/GhanaHomePage/NewsArchive/artikel.php?ID=226700 (September 23, 2013).

"Ghana Inaugurates Radioactive Waste Storage Facility." *Ghana News Agency*, September 13, 2011. www.ghananewsagency.org/science/ghana-inaugurates-radioactive-waste-storage-facility-33398 (March 17, 2016).

"Arson & Demolition: Atomic Energy Boss, 30 Others in Police Custody." *Peace FM Online*, January 24, 2012. http://news.peacefmonline.com/pages/news/201201/90495.php (September 24, 2013).

"G.A.E.C. Demolishes 'Illegal' Structures on Its Property at Dome-Kwabenya." *Ghana News Agency*, January 24, 2012. www.ghananewsagency.org/social/gaec-demolishes-illegal-structures-on-its-property-at-dome-kwabenya-38357 (March 3, 2014).

"Greater Accra P.S.W.U. Supports Demolition of Illegal Structures on Atomic Energy Land." *VibeGhana*, February 15, 2012. http://vibeghana.com/2012/02/15/greater-accra-pswu-supports-demolition-of-illegal-structures-on-atomic-energy-land/ (September 24, 2013).

"25th January, 2012." *Ghana Broadcasting Corporation*, June 4, 2012. http://gbcghana.com/index.php?id=1.748700> (June 4, 2012).

"Ghana to Export Nuclear Energy?" *Safari Radio (via Ghana News Agency)*, June 4, 2012. www.safariradio.net/?p=2459 (June 4, 2014).

"Ghana's Progresses [Sic] with Nuclear Power Project." *Ghana News Agency*, July 16, 2014. www.ghananewsagency.org/science/ghana-s-progresses-with-nuclear-power-project-77296 (May 6, 2016).

"Ghana Nuclear Regulatory Authority Board Inaugurated." *Ghana Business News*, January 15, 2016. www.ghanabusinessnews.com/2016/01/15/ghana-nuclear-regulatory-authority-board-inaugurated/ (February 14, 2016).

"Gas Station Explosion Shakes Ghana's Capital: Unknown Number Killed after Blast at Natural Gas Station Sends Giant Fireball into Sky over City." *The Guardian*, October 7, 2017 www.theguardian.com/world/2017/oct/07/petrol-station-explosion-ghana-accra-fireball (October 10, 2017).

"Profile of the late Prof Atukwei Okai." *Ghana Web*, July 14, 2018. www.ghanaweb.com/GhanaHomePage/NewsArchive/Profile-of-the-late-Prof-Atukwei-Okai-668610 (June 8, 2019).

Abdallah, Nuruddeen M. "Inside Nigeria's Only Nuclear Research Centre." *Sunday Trust*, July 12, 2009. www.dailytrust.com.ng/sunday/index.php/63-sunday-trust-magazine/motoring/2874-inside-nigerias-only-nuclear-research-centreinside-nigerias-only-nuclear-research-centre (June 26, 2018).

Achiaw, Nehemia Owusu. "Scientific Renaissance Day for Africa Marked in Kumasi." *People's Daily Graphic*, June 29, 1991.

Aidoo, Ato and I.K. Max Arthur. "Work on Irradiation Centre Progresses." *People's Daily Graphic*, December 3, 1993.

Akweiteh, Godwin Allotey. "G.A.E.C. Wins Court Case over Atomic Land." June 4, 2012. www.ghanadistricts.com/news/?read=45668 (June 23, 2013).

Amexo, George. "Nation Targets Nuclear Power by 2018." *Public Agenda*,
    April 4, 2011. http://allafrica.com/stories/201104050606.html (August
    28, 2013).
    "No Fears About Country's Nuclear Program." *Public Agenda*, March
    21, 2011. http://allafrica.com/stories/201103211808.html (September
    23, 2013).
Armah, Pearl. "Nadmo Prepares Feverishly for Any Disaster." *Accra
    Daily Mail*, 2004. http://allafrica.com/stories/200408260913.html
    (November 24, 2018).
Aryee, Nii Ayikai. "The Land Crisis in Ghana." *Daily Graphic*, September
    4, 2000.
Asante, Eunice. "Ultra Modern Business Centre Commissioned."
    citifmonline.com, June 4, 2012. www.ghanaweb.com/GhanaHomePage/
    NewsArchive/artikel.php?ID=227571 (September 24, 2013).
Ashalley, Naa Korkoi. "Kwabenya Lands." *Daily Graphic*, March 11, 1998.
Awodipe, Tobi. "Nigeria: Crossing the T's Ahead of Nigeria's Power Plant."
    The Guardian (Lagos), May 28, 2018. http://allafrica.com/stories/
    201805280291.html (June 26, 2018).
Bady, Aaron. "Things to Come." *The New Inquiry*, March 6, 2015. https://
    thenewinquiry.com/things-to-come/ (June 26, 2018).
Bessey, Bernice. "Ghana: Estate Developers Take over Atomic Lands." *The
    Ghanaian Chronicle*, March 10, 2014. http://allafrica.com/stories/
    201403102278.html (Feburary 15, 2016).
Blix, Hans. "Inauguration of Ghana Research Reactor." *IAEA Newscenter*,
    March 8, 1995. www.iaea.org/newscenter/statements/inauguration-
    ghana-research-reactor-1 (April 9, 2016).
Boateng, Caroline and Abigail Rockson. "Ghana Needs More Nuclear
    Scientists – Says Prof. Adzei Bekoe." *Daily Graphic*, September
    12, 2007.
Braestrup, Peter. "France Will End Tests in Sahara: Nuclear Facilities in
    Desert Are Being Dismantled." *The New York Times*, March 16, 1964.
    www.nytimes.com/1964/03/16/france-will-end-tests-in-sahara.html
    (April 11, 2016).
Burke, Timothy. "District 9." *Easily Distracted*, September 2, 2009. https://
    blogs.swarthmore.edu/burke/blog/2009/09/02/district-9/.
Coffie-Johnson, Alfred. "Radioisotopes, Ionizing Radiation Centres Set Up."
    The Ghanaian Times, July 16, 1993.
Donkor, Michael. "Ghana Will Harness Peaceful Use of Nuclear Energy."
    Daily Graphic, January 18, 2011.
Essegbey, George O. "Irradiation Use in Ghana." *Daily Graphic*, September
    1, 1998.

Essel, Isaac. "National Security Stalls Construction of Multi-Million Project." *Myjoyonline.com*, June 4, 2012. http://edition.myjoyonline .com/pages/news/201201/79717.php (24 September 2013).

Feeman, Koryekpor Awlesu. "You'll Die … Atomic Landowners Warn G.A.E.C. Boss." *Todaygh.com*, June 4, 2012. www.todaygh.com/youll-die/ (24 September 2013).

Frankels, Max. "Khruschchev Suggests Trip to Soviet [Union] by Eisenhower." *The New York Times*, February 6, 1959.

Frempong, Beatrice Adepa. "Pratt: I Feel So Embarrassed and Ashamed … Is This the Same N.D.C.?" *Peacefmonline.com*, June 4, 2012. http://elections.peacefmonline.com/politics/201201/90649.php (June 26, 2018).

Frimpong-Manso, K. "Sahara Protest Team Send Message to Ghana: An Appeal to the Youth of Africa." *Evening News*, January 4, 1960.

Gbedemah, Charles M. "Uncle Carl, Irradiation Is Harmless." *The Mirror*, December 4, 1993.

Gyamfi, Adu. "Russia's Khrushchev Thinks Highly of Nkrumah: Exclusive Interview with the New Ghana Ambassador to USSR" *Evening News*, January 13, 1960.

Idan, Golda. "G.A.E.C., IAEA To Help H.I.V./A.I.D.S. Patients." *Daily Graphic*, 2002.

Love, Kennett. "African Nations Ask Nuclear Ban." *The New York Times*, April 23, 1958. http://search.proquest.com/hnpnewyorktimes/docview/ 114596379/abstract/1379526CDAD4553A801/20? (June 26, 2018).

Mac Arthur, I.K. "Nuke Energy for Food Storage." *Daily Graphic*, October 21, 1993.

Magomba, Leonard. "Gold, Coal to Help Tanzania to Grow Mining by 7.7 Percent." *The East African*, May 2, 2011. http://allafrica.com/stories/ 201105030448.html (June 26, 2018).

McGreal, Chris. "Missing Keys, Holes in Fence and a Single Padlock: Welcome to Congo's Nuclear Plant." *Guardian*, November 23, 2006. www .theguardian.com/world/2006/nov/23/congo.chrismcgreal.

Mutt, Carl. "Nuke Energy for Whose Belly?" *The Mirror*, October 30, 1993.

Nkrumah, Kwame. "'The World without the Bomb' Accra Assembly: A New Thinking on the Issue of Man's Preservation Is Demanded, Full Text of the Osagyefo's Speech at the Opening of the Accra Assembly." *The Ghanaian Times*, June 22, 1962.

"Osagyefo Dedicates Atomic Reactor: Science City for Ghana." *The Ghanaian Times*, November 16, 1964.

"Science Academy Must Be Part of National Life–Osagyefo." *The Ghanaian Times*, November 16, 1964.

Okorafor, Nnedi. "My Response to District 419… I Mean District 9.:-)." *Facebook*, August 23, 2009. www.facebook.com/notes/nnedi-okorafor/my-response-to-district-419i-mean-district-9-/119750833778/ (June 27, 2018).

Reddy, G.K. "Astounding Success of Bandung Meet: New Pattern Set for Co-Existence." *The Times of India*, April 26, 1955.

Reed, Fred. "China May Set High-Tech Standard." *The Washington Times*, June 23, 2006.

Sah, Stephen. "School for Nuclear, Allied Sciences Takes Off Sept." *Daily Graphic*, January 24, 2005.

Sarpong, Samuel and Albert K. Salia. "Insect Sterilisation Technique Developed." *Daily Graphic*, March 11, 1998.

Singh, Naunihal. "What 'Black Panther's' Wakanda Can Teach Us About Africa's History – and Its Future." *Washington Post*, February 28, 2018. www.washingtonpost.com/news/monkey-cage/wp/2018/02/28/what-black-panthers-wakanda-can-teach-us-about-africas-history-and-its-future/ (February 29, 2018).

Takyi-Boadu, Charles. "Shock and Chaos." *The Ghanaian Chronicle*, October 15, 2009. http://allafrica.com/stories/200910160931.html (September 22, 2013).

"Anaina Takes Off." *Daily Guide*, January 4, 2012. www.dailyguideghana.com/?p=35874 (June 4, 2012).

"Atomic Land Owners Speak." *Daily Guide*, January 31, 2012. www.modernghana.com/news/375419/atomic-land-owners-speak.html (February 12, 2012).

Thompson, Kofi. "Ghana Incapable of Storing Dangerous Radioactive Waste Safely!" *Ghana Web*, March 7, 2013. www.ghanaweb.com/GhanaHomePage/NewsArchive/Ghana-Incapable-Of-Storing-Dangerous-Radioactive-Waste-Safely-266972 (March 17, 2016).

Tully, John. "London Letter: Atom Bomb." *Daily Graphic*, October 14, 1952. http://dds.crl.edu/issue.asp?tid=17824&pubdate=10/14/1952(June 26, 2018).

Twum, Chris. "Nuclear Power Generation Ripe in Ghana." *The Ghanaian Chronicle*, April 4, 2006. http://allafrica.com/stories/200604040723.html (June 26, 2018).

Van-Ess, Adjoa. "Help Improve Gamma Irradiation Facility – Prof Allotey Tells Industrialists." *Daily Graphic*, August 3, 1999.

Vinorkor, Mark-Anthony. "Boost Energy Supply with Nuclear Power – Akaho." *Daily Graphic*, November 25, 2006.

"Boost Energy Supply with Nuclear Power – Akaho." *Daily Graphic*, November 25, 2006.

Whitney, Craig R. "France Ending Nuclear Tests That Caused Broad Protests." *The New York Times*, January 30, 1996. www.nytimes.com/1996/01/30/world/france-ending-nuclear-tests-that-caused-broad-protests.html (April 11, 2016).

Journal Articles

"Soviet Statements on Atom Energy and U.S. Answers." *Bulletin Of The Atomic Scientists* 3, no. 7 (July 1947): 187–192.

"One Sure Bet for U.S. Of Tomorrow: Twice as Much Power, New Sources Will Satisfy Immense Appetite for Energy." *Life Magazine* 36, no. 1 (January 4, 1954): 79–91.

"Nuclear 1955 for D.D.E., '15: He Would Share Atomic Benefits." *Life Magazine* 38, no. 25 (June 20, 1955): 33.

"First U.S. Reactor Goes Critical in Europe." *The Science News-Letter* 71, no. 22 (1957): 341.

"More Uranium, More Reactors and More Power: More Atomic Progress: A Report." *Life Magazine* 42, no. 7 (February 18, 1957): 23–31.

"Energy Research and Development Administration." *Issue: A Journal of Opinion* 8, no. 2/3, United States Federal Government Activities in or concerning Africa, FY 1976-FY 1978 (summer–autumn 1978): 106–107.

"Adoption of the African Nuclear-Weapon-Free Zone Treaty." *Journal of African Law* 41, no. 1 (1997): 152.

"Review of the Radioactive Waste Management System in Nigeria." *Journal of Radiological Protection* 23, no. 1 (March 10, 2003).

"Stopping Africa's Medical Brain Drain." *BMJ: British Medical Journal* 331, no. 7507 (2005): 2–3.

"Congratulations on the 90th Anniversary of Pyotr Ivanovich Kupriyanov." *Institute for African Studies of the Russian Academy of Sciences Newsletter* 5, no. 1 (March 2015): 1.

Aboh, I.J.K., D. Henriksson, J. Laursen, M. Lundin, F.G. Ofosu, N. Pind, E.S. Lindgren, and T. Wahnstrom. "Identification of Aerosol Particle Sources in Semi-Rural Area of Kwabenya, near Accra, Ghana, by Edxrf Techniques." *X-Ray Spectrometry* 38, no. 4 (July–August 2009): 348–353.

Abraham, Itty. "The Ambivalence of Nuclear Histories." *Osiris* 21, no. 1 (2006): 49–65.

"Geopolitics and Biopolitics in India's High Natural Background Radiation Zone." *Science Technology & Society* 17, no. 1 (March 1, 2012): 105–122.

Abrefah, R.G., S.A. Birikorang, B.J.B. Nyarko, J.J. Fletcher, and E.H.K. Akaho. "Design of Serpentine Cask for Ghana Research Reactor-1 Spent Nuclear Fuel." *Progress in Nuclear Energy* 77 (November 2014): 84–91.

Adamson, Matthew. "Peut-on Faire Une Histoire Nucléaire Du Maroc: Le Maroc, L'afrique et L'énergie Nucléaire/ Is There a History of Nuclear Power in Morocco? Morocco, Africa and Nuclear Energy." *Afrique contemporaine* 261–262, no. 1 (2017): 85–102.

"The Secret Search for Uranium in Cold War Morocco." *Physics Today* 70, no. 6 (2017): 54–60.

Addo-Fening, R. "Customary Land-Tenure System in Akyem-Abuakwa." *Universitas* 9 (1987): 95–107.

Adeniran, Tunde. "Nuclear Proliferation and Black Africa: The Coming Crisis of Choice." *Third World Quarterly* 3, no. 4 (1981/10/01 1981): 673–683.

Adu, S., G. Emi-Reynolds, C. Schandorf, E.O. Darko, and P.K. Gyekye. "Radiological Assessment of the Structural Shielding Adequacy of the Radiotherapy Facility at Korle-Bu Teaching Hospital, Accra, Ghana." *Radiation Protection Dosimetry* 149, no. 2 (April 2012): 216–221.

Agrawal, Arun. "Dismantling the Divide between Indigenous and Scientific Knowledge." *Development and Change* 26, no. 3 (1995): 413–439.

Agrawal, Arun, Ashwini Chhatre, and Rebecca Hardin. "Changing Governance of the World's Forests." *Science* 320, no. 5882 (2008): 1460.

Ahlman, Jeffrey S. "The Algerian Question in Nkrumah's Ghana, 1958–1960." *Africa Today* 57, no. 12 (2010): 67–84.

"The Algerian Question in Nkrumah's Ghana, 1958–1960: Debating "Violence" and "Nonviolence" in African Decolonization." *African Today* 57, no. 2 (Winter 2010): 66–84.

Ahmadu Bello University, CERT. "Annual Report of the Centre for Energy Research and Training, Ahmadu Belo University, Zaria, Nigeria." *Annual report of the Centre for Energy Research and Training, Ahmadu Belo University, Zaria, Nigeria* (serial).

Ahmed, Y.A., G.I. Balogun, S.A. Jonah, and Funtua, I.I. "The Behavior of Reactor Power and Flux Resulting from Changes in Core-Coolant Temperature for a Miniature Neutron Source Reactor." *Annals of Nuclear Energy* 35, no. 12 (December 2008): 2417–2419.

Ahmed, Y.A., I.B. Mansir, I. Yusuf, G.I. Balogun, and S.A. Jonah. "Effects of Core Excess Reactivity and Coolant Average Temperature on Maximum Operable Time of Nirr-1 Miniature Neutron Source Reactor." *Nuclear Engineering and Design* 241, no. 5 (May 2011): 1559–1564.

Akaho, E.H.K., J.D.K. Intsiful, B.T. Maakuu, S. Anim-Sampong, and B.J.B. Nyarko. "Feynman-Alpha Technique for Measurement of Detector Dead Time Using a 30 Kw Tank-in-Pool Research Reactor." *Nuclear Instruments & Methods in Physics Research Section A: Accelerators Spectrometers Detectors and Associated Equipment* 479, no. 2–3 (March 2002): 585–590.

Akaho, E.H.K. and B.T. Maakuu. "Nuclear Safety-Related Calculations for Ghana Research Reactor -1 Core." *Journal of Applied Science and Technology* 5, no. 1 & 2 (2000): 32–38.

Akaho, E.H.K., B.T. Maakuu, and M.K. Qazi. "Comparision for Some Measured and Calculated Nuclear Parameters for Ghana Resesarch Reactor -1 Core." *Journal of Applied Science and Technology* 5, no. 1 (2000): 25–31.

Akaho, E.H.K. and B.J.B. Nyarko. "Characterization of Neutron Flux Spectra in Irradiation Sites of MNSR Reactor Using the Westcott-Formalism for the K(0) Neutron Activation Analysis Method." *Applied Radiation and Isotopes* 57, no. 2 (August 2002): 265–273.

Albright, D. and M. Hibbs. "South Africa: The A.N.C. And the Atom Bomb." *Bulletin of the Atomic Scientists* 49, no. 3 (1993): 32–37.

Aliyu, A.S., A.T. Ramli, and M.A. Saleh. "Environmental Impact Assessment of a New Nuclear Power Plant (NPP) Based on Atmospheric Dispersion Modeling." *Stochastic Environmental Research and Risk Assessment* 28, no. 7 (October 2014): 1897–1911.

Allman, Jean. "Nuclear Imperialism and Pan-African Struggle for Peace and Freedom: Ghana, 1959–1962." *Souls: A Critical Journal of Black Politics, Culture, and Society* 10, no. 2 (2008): 83–102.

Allotey, F.K. "Effect of Electron-Hole Scattering Resonance on X-Ray Emission Spectrum." *Physical Review* 157, no. 3 (1967): 467–479.

"Effect of Threshold Behaviour on Calculations of Soft X-Ray Spectra of Lithium." *Solid State Communications* 9, no. 2 (1971): 91–94.

Alvarez, Robert R. "The Mexican-US Border: The Making of an Anthropology of Borderlands." *Annual Review of Anthropology* 24, no. 1 (1995): 447–470.

Amamoo, Joseph G. "Ghana and the Western Democracies." *African Affairs* 58, no. 230 (January 1959): 54–60.

Amoah, A.G.B. "Spectrum of Cardiovascular Disorders in a National Referral Centre, Ghana." *East African Medical Journal* 77, no. 12 (December 2000): 648–653.

Ampofo, D.A., D.D. Nicholas, M.B. Amonooacquah, S. Ofosuamaah, and A.K. Neumann. "Training of Traditional Birth Attendants in Ghana-Experience of Danfa Rural Health Project." *Tropical and Geographical Medicine* 29, no. 2 (1977): 197–203.

Ampomah-Amoako, E., E.H.K. Akaho, S. Anim-Sampong, and B.J.B. Nyarko. "Transient Analysis of Ghana Research Reactor-1 Using PARET/ANL Thermal–Hydraulic Code." *Nuclear Engineering and Design* 239, no. 11 (November 2009): 2479–2483.

Amuasi, J.H., A.K. Kyere, C. Schandorf, J.J. Fletcher, M. Boadu, E.K. Addison, F. Hasford, et al. "Medical Physics Practice and Training in Ghana." *Physica Medica-European Journal of Medical Physics* 32, no. 6 (June 2016): 826–830.

Anderson, Warwick. "From Subjugated Knowledge to Conjugated Subjects: Science and Globalisation, or Postcolonial Studies of Science?" *Postcolonial Studies* 12, no. 4 (2009): 389–400.

Andersson, Kjell. "Copper Corrosion in Nuclear Waste Disposal: A Swedish Case Study on Stakeholder Insight." *Bulletin of Science, Technology & Society* 33, no. 3–4 (June 1, 2013): 85–95.

Appiah, Kwame Anthony. "Is the Post – in Postmodernism the Post – in Postcolonial?" *Critical Inquiry* 17, no. 2 (Winter, 1991): 336–357.

Ashmore, Malcolm and Darren Reed. "Innocence and Nostalgia in Conversation Analysis: The Dynamic Relations of Tape and Transcript." *Historical Social Research* 30, no. 1 (2005): 73–94.

Astin, A.V. "Scientists and Public Responsibility". *Physics Today* 10, no. 11 (1957): 23–27.

Awudu, A.R., E.O. Darko, C. Schandorf, E.K. Hayford, M.K. Abekoe, and P.K. Ofori-Danson. "Determination of Activity Concentration Levels of 238u, 232th, and 40k in Drinking Water in a Gold Mine in Ghana". *Health Physics* 99(2) suppl. 2, Operational Radiation, no. Safety (2010): S149–S153.

Ayivor, J.E., L.K.N. Okine, S.B. Dampare, B.J.B. Nyarko, and S.K. Debrah. "The Application of Westcott Formalism K(0) Naa Method to Estimate Short and Medium Lived Elements in Some Ghanaian Herbal Medicines Complemented by Aas". *Radiation Physics and Chemistry* 81, no. 4 (April 2012): 403–409.

Baggoura, B., A. Noureddine, and M. Benkrid. "Level of Natural and Artificial Radioactivity in Algeria." *Applied Radiation and Isotopes* 49, no. 7 (1998): 867–873.

Barkaoui, Miloud. "Managing the Colonial Status Quo: Eisenhower's Cold War and the Algerian War of Independence." *The Journal of North African Studies* 17, no. 1 (2012): 125–141.

Basalla, George. "The Spread of Western Science." *Science* 156 (1967): 612–619.

Bates, David. "Survey of Science Teaching in Ghanaian Secondary Schools." *Ghana Association of Science Teachers* 12, no. 1 (1971): 1–5.

Berry, Sara. "Property, Authority and Citizenship: Land Claims, Politics and the Dynamics of Social Division in West Africa." *Development and Change* 40, no. 1 (2009): 23–45.

"Questions of Ownership: Proprietorship and Control in a Changing Rural Terrain – a Case Study from Ghana." *Africa* 83, no. 1 (2013): 36–56.

Bhabha, Homi. "Of Mimicry and Man: The Ambivalence of Colonial Discourse." *October* 28 (1984): 125–133.

Biney, Ama. "The Intellectual and Political Legacies of Kwame Nkrumah." *The Journal of Pan African Studies* 4, no. 10 (January 2012): 127–142.

Boadu, Mary, Cyril Schandorf, Geoffrey Emi-Reynolds, Augustine Faanu, Stephen Inkoom, Prince Kwabena Gyekye, and Cynthia Kaikor Mensah. "Systematic Approach to Training Occupationally Exposed Workers in Ghana and the Rest of Africa". *Health Physics* 101(2) Supplement 2, Operational Radiation, no. Safety (2011): S116–S120.

Borst, L.B., M. Fox, D.H. Gurinsky, I. Kaplan, R.W. Powell, C. Williams, and W.E. Winsche. "Nuclear Reactor at Brookhaven National Laboratory." *Physical Review* 74, no. 12 (1948): 1883–1884.

Briggs, John and Davis Mwamfupe. "Peri-Urban Development in an Era of Structural Adjustment in Africa: The City of Dar Es Salaam, Tanzania." *Urban Studies* 37, no. 4 (2000): 797–809.

Brown, A.A., L. Derkyi-Kwarteng, and H.S. Amonoo-Kuofi. "Study on the Time Frame for Ossification of the Medial Clavicular Epiphyseal Cartilage by X-Ray in Ghanaian Students." *International Journal of Morphology* 31, no. 2 (June 2013): 491–496.

Burkhardt, G. "Science Education in Africa." *Bulletin of The Atomic Scientists* 22, no. 2 (1966): 46–48.

Chakrabarty, Dipesh. "Postcoloniality and the Artifice of History: Who Speaks for 'Indian' Pasts?" *Representations* 37 (1992): 1–26.

Chau, Donovan C. "Assistance of a Different Kind: Chinese Political Warfare in Ghana, 1958–1966." *Comparative Strategy* 26, no. 2 (2007): 141–161.

Cherry, Michael. "Science in Africa: All Eyes on Addis." *Nature* 445 (January 25, 2007): 356–358.

Chinangwa, G., J.K. Amoako, and J.J. Fletcher. "Radiation Dose Assessment for Occupationally Exposed Workers in Malawi." *Malawi Medical Journal* 29, no. 3 (September 2017): 254–258.

"Investigation of the Status of Occupational Radiation Protection in Malawian Hospitals." *Malawi Medical Journal* 30, no. 1 (March 2018): 22–24.

Cirincione, Joseph. "The Asian Nuclear Reaction Chain." *Foreign Policy*, no. 118 (Spring 2000): 120–136.

Clignet, Remi P. and Philip Foster. "Potential Elites in Ghana and the Ivory Coast a Preliminary Comparison." *American Journal of Sociology* 70, no. 3 (November 1964): 349–362.

Collins, Kevin, Chris Blackmore, Dick Morris, and Drennan Watson. "A Systemic Approach to Managing Multiple Perspectives and Stakeholding in Water Catchments: Some Findings from Three UK Case Studies." *Environmental Science & Policy* 10, no. 6 (2007): 564–574.

Conde, Marta and Giorgos Kallis. "The Global Uranium Rush and Its Africa Frontier. Effects, Reactions and Social Movements in Namibia." *Global Environmental Change* 22, no. 3 (2012): 596–610.

Cowan, Robin. "Nuclear Power Reactors: A Study in Technological Lock-In." *The Journal of Economic History* 50, no. 3 (1990): 541–567.

Creager, Angela N.H. "Tracing the Politics of Changing Postwar Research Practices: The Export of 'American' Radioisotopes to European Biologists." *Studies in History and Philosophy of Science Part C: Studies in History and Philosophy of Biological and Biomedical Sciences* 33, no. 3 (2002): 367–388.

"Nuclear Energy in the Service of Biomedicine: The U.S. Atomic Energy Commission's Radioisotope Program, 1946–1950." *Journal of the History of Biology* 39, no. 4 (2006): 649–684.

Creager, Angela N.H. and María Jesús Santesmases. "Radiobiology in the Atomic Age: Changing Research Practices and Policies in Comparative Perspective." *Journal of the History of Biology* 39, no. 4 (2006): 637–647.

Crumley, Bruce. "France Votes to Pay Nuclear-Testing Victims." *Time* (30 June 2009). http://content.time.com/time/world/article/0,8599,1907887,00.html (August 20, 2010).

Curtin, Phillip. "Field Techniques for Collecting and Processing Oral Data." *Journal of African History* 9, no. 3 (1968): 367–385.

Danesi, P.R., J. Moreno, M. Makarewicz, and D. Louvat. "Residual Radionuclide Concentrations and Estimated Radiation Doses at the Former French Nuclear Weapons Test Sites in Algeria." *Applied Radiation and Isotopes* 66, no. 11 (2008): 1671–1674.

Darko, E.O. and J.J. Fletcher. "National Waste Management Infrastructure in Ghana." *Journal of Radiological Protection* 18 (December 1998): 293–299.

Darko, E.O., D.O. Kpeglo, E.H.K. Akaho, C. Schandorf, P.A.S. Adu, A. Faanu, E. Abankwah, H. Lawluvi, and A.R. Awudu. "Radiation Doses and Hazards from Processing of Crude Oil at the Tema Oil Refinery in Ghana." *Radiation Protection Dosimetry* 148, no. 3 (February 2012): 318–328.

Davis, Jeffrey Sasha. "Representing Place: "Deserted Isles" and the Reproduction of Bikini Atoll." *Annals of the Association of American Geographers* 95, no. 3 (2005): 607–625.

Dawood, A.M.A., E.T. Glover, P. Essel, Y. Adjei-Kyereme, G.S. Asumadu-Sakyi, E. Akortia, and M. Nyarku. "Borehole Disposal Concept for Radioactive Waste Disposal-the Gaec Project." *Pollution* 47 (2012): 8752–8756.

de Villiers, J.W., Roger Jardin, and Mitchell Reiss. "Why South Africa Gave up the Bomb." *Foreign Affairs* 72, no. 5 (November–December 1993): 98–109.

Debrah, E.M. "Will Most Uncommitted Nations Remain Uncommitted?" *The Annals of the American Academy of Political and Social Science* 336, Is International Communism Winning? (July 1961): 83–97.

Djabanor, Amelia. "Salome's Story." *Obra Pa: Righteous Living* 1, no. 1 (1991): 6–10.

Draganić, I.G., Z.D. Draganić, and D. Altiparmakov. "Natural Nuclear Reactors and Ionizing Radiation in the Precambrian." *Precambrian Research* 20, no. 2–4 (1983): 283–298.

Edington, G.M., A.H. Ward, J.M. Judd, and R.H. Mole. "The Acute Lethal Effects of Monkeys of Radiostrontium." *Journal of Pathology and Bacteriology* 71 (1956): 277–293.

Ehrlich, Thomas. "The Nonproliferation Treaty and Peaceful Uses of Nuclear Explosives." *Virginia Law Review* 56, no. 4 (May 1970): 587–601.

Eisenbud, Merril and John H. Harley. "Radioactive Dust from Nuclear Detonations." *Science* 117, no. 3033 (1953): 141–147.

Ellis, Stephen. "Writing Histories of Contemporary Africa." *Journal of African History* 43, no. 1 (2002): 1–26.

Elshakry, Marwa S. "Knowledge in Motion: The Cultural Politics of Modern Science Translations in Arabic." *Isis* 99, no. 4 (2008): 701–730.

Elwood, Sarah and Helga Leitner. "Gis and Spatial Knowledge Production for Neighborhood Revitalization: Negotiating State Priorities and Neighborhood Visions." *Journal of Urban Affairs* 25, no. 2 (2003): 139–157.

Emi-Reynolds, Geoffrey, Cynthia Kaikor Mensah, Prince Kwabena Gyekye, and Ann Etornam Amekudzie. "Status of Radiation Protection of Medical X-Ray Facilities in Greater Accra Region, Ghana". *Health Physics* 102(5S) Supplement no. 2 (2012): S63–S66.

Emi-Reynolds, G., C.K. Mensah, P.K. Gyekye, and A.E. Amekudzie. "Status of Radiation Protection of Medical X-Ray Facilities in Greater Accra Region, Ghana." *Health Physics* 102, no. 5 (May 2012): S63–S66.

Epstein, William. "A Nuclear-Weapon-Free Zone in Africa?" *The Stanley Foundation Occasional Papers* 14 (1977): 5–26.

Faanu, A., E.O. Darko, A.R. Awudu, C. Schandorf, G. Emi-Reynolds, J. Yeboah, E.T. Glover, and V.K. Kattah. "Radiation Exposure Control from the Application of Nuclear Gauges in the Mining Industry in Ghana". *Health Physics* 98(2) suppl. 2, Operational Radiation, no. Safety (2010): S33–S38.

Fage, J.D. "Some Notes on a Scheme for the Investigation of Oral Tradition in the Northern Territories of the Gold Coast." *Journal of the Historical Society of Nigeria* 1 (December 1956): 15–19.

Farkas, József and Csilla Mohácsi-Farkas. "History and Future of Food Irradiation." *Trends in Food Science & Technology* 22, no. 2 (2011): 121–126.

Fasasi, M.K., P. Tchokossa, J.O. Ojo, and F.A. Balogun. "Occurrence of Natural Radionuclides and Fallout Cesium-137 in Dry-Season Agricultural Land of South Western Nigeria." *Journal of Radioanalytical and Nuclear Chemistry* 240, no. 3 (June 1999): 949–952.

Finkelstein, A., J. Kramer, B. Nuseibeh, L. Finkelstein, and M. Goedicke. "Viewpoints: A Framework for Integrating Multiple Perspectives in System Development." *International Journal of Software Engineering and Knowledge Engineering* 2, no. 1 (1992): 31–57.

Fitzpatrick, Daniel. "Disputes and Pluralism in Modern Indonesian Land Law." *Yale Journal of International Law* 22 (1997): 171–212.

Frame, J. Davidson, Francis Narin, and Mark P. Carpenter. "The Distribution of World Science." *Social Studies of Science* 7, no. 4 (1977): 501–516.

Fukai, Y. "A History of Studies on Neutron Chain-Reaction in Japan and the Other Countries During the World War II." *Journal of the Atomic Energy Society of Japan* 39, no. 7 (July 1997): 546–557.

Gaillard, Jacques. "Overcoming the Scientific Generation Gap in Africa: An Urgent Priority." *Interdisciplinary Science Reviews* 28, no. 1 (March 2003): 15–25.

Garbrah, B.W. and J.E. Whitley. "Determination of Boron by Thermal Neutron Capture Gamma-Ray Analysis." *Analytical Chemistry* 39, no. 3 (1967): 345–349.

"Assessment of Neutron Capture γ-Ray Analysis." *The International Journal of Applied Radiation and Isotopes* 19, no. 8 (1968): 605–614.

Gerits, Frank. "'When the Bull Elephants Fight': Kwame Nkrumah, Non-Alignment, and Pan-Africanism as an Interventionist Ideology in the Global Cold War (1957–66)." *The International History Review* 37, no. 5 (2015): 951–969.

Gieryn, Thomas F. "Boundary-Work and the Demarcation of Science from Non-Science: Strains and Interests in Professional Ideologies of Scientists." *American Sociological Review* 48, no. 6 (1983): 781–795.

Gorman, M. "Introduction of Western Science into Colonial India, Role of the Calcutta-Medical-College." *Proceedings of the American Philosophical Society* 132, no. 3 (September 1988): 276–298.

Gough, Katherine V. and Paul W.K. Yankson. "Land Markets in African Cities: The Case of Peri-Urban Accra, Ghana." *Urban Studies* 37, no. 13 (December 1, 2000): 2485–2500.

"Land Markets in African Cities: The Case of Peri-Urban Accra, Ghana." *Urban Studies* 37, no. 13 (December 1, 2000): 2485–2500.

Graham, Loren and Jean-Michel Kantor. "A Comparison of Two Cultural Approaches to Mathematics: France and Russia, 1890–1930." *Isis* 97, no. 1 (2006): 56–74.

Green, Toby. "Africa and the Price Revolution: Currency Imports and Socioeconomic Change in West and West-Central Africa During the Seventeenth Century." *The Journal of African History* 57, no. 1 (2016): 1–24.

Gupta, A. and S. Seshasai. "24-Hour Knowledge Factory: Using Internet Technology to Leverage Spatial and Temporal Separations." *ACM Transactions on Internet Technology* 7, no. 3, Article 14 (2007) 22 pages.

Gusterson, Hugh. "The Assault on Los Alamos National Laboratory: A Drama in Three Acts." *Bulletin of the Atomic Scientists* 67, no. 6 (November 1, 2011): 9–18.

Gutteridge, William F. "The Political Role of African Armed Forces: The Impact of Foreign Military Assistance." *African Affairs* 66, no. 263 (1967): 93–103.

Ha, Young-sun. "Nuclearization of Small States and World Order: The Case of Korea." *Asian Survey* 18, no. 11 (1978): 1134–1151.

Hafstad, L.R. "Science, Technology and Society". *American Scientist* 45, no. 2 (1957): 157–168.

Hall, John A. "Atoms for Peace, or War." *Foreign Affairs* 43, no. 4 (1965): 602–615.

Halperin, Morton H. "Chinese Nuclear Strategy: The Early Post-Detonation Period." *Asian Survey* 5, no. 6 (June 1965): 271–279.

Hamblin, Jacob Darwin. "Let There Be Light... and Bread: The United Nations, the Developing World, and Atomic Energy's Green Revolution." *History and Technology* 25, no. 1 (2009): 25–48.

Harms, A.A. "The Dynamic Pattern of Nuclear Synergetics." *Atomkernenergie-Kerntechnik* 43, no. 3 (1983): 146–150.

Harrison, Mark. "Science and the British Empire." *Isis* 96, no. 1 (2005): 56–63.

Harrison, Michael M. "French Nuclear Testing: Acquitted by Politics." *SAIS Review* 18, no. 2 (1974): 10.

Hart, David. "Dhirenda Sharma, India's Nuclear Estate." *Social Studies of Science* 13, no. 4 (November 1, 1983): 627–629.

Hart, Jennifer. "'Nifa Nifa': Technopolitics, Mobile Workers, and the Ambivalence of Decline in Acheampong's Ghana." *African Economic History* 44, no. 1 (2016): 181–201.

Hashimoto, Shoji, Shin Ugawa, Kazuki Nanko, and Koji Shichi. "The Total Amounts of Radioactively Contaminated Materials in Forests in Fukushima, Japan." *Scientific Reports* 2 (2012): 416.

Hecht, Gabrielle. "Rebels and Pioneers: Technocratic Ideologies and Social Identities in the French Nuclear Workplace, 1955–69." *Social Studies of Science* 26, no. 3 (August 1, 1996): 483–530.

"Rupture-Talk in the Nuclear Age: Conjugating Colonial Power in Africa." *Social Studies of Science* 32, no. 5–6 (October–December 2002): 691–727.

Hessler, Julie. "Death of an African Student in Moscow: Race, Politics, and the Cold War." *Cahiers du Monde Russe* 47, no. 1–2 (2006): 33–63.

Hilson, Gavin and Frank Nyame. "Gold Mining in Ghana's Forest Reserves: A Report on the Current Debate." *Area* 38, no. 2 (2006): 175–185.

Hilson, Gavin and Natalia Yakovleva. "Strained Relations: A Critical Analysis of the Mining Conflict in Prestea, Ghana." *Political Geography* 26, no. 1 (2007): 98–119.

Holl, Jack M. and Sheila C. Convis. "Teaching Nuclear History." *History Teacher* 24, no. 2 (February 1991): 175–190.

Ingersoll, D.T. "Deliberately Small Reactors and the Second Nuclear Era." *Progress in Nuclear Energy* 51, no. 4–5 (2009): 589–603.

Inkoom, Stephen, James Togobo, Geoffrey Emi-Reynolds, Adrian Oddoye, Theophilus Ofosu Ntiri, and Prince Kwabena Gyekye. "Retrospective Patient Dose Analysis of Ghana's First Direct Digital Radiography System". *Health Physics* 103, no. 2 (2012): 133–137.

Ireland, Corydon. "Wasteland and Wilderness: Galison Uses a Radcliffe Year to Ponder 'Zones of Exclusion'." *Harvard Gazette* (October 8, 2009).

Itai, T., M. Otsuka, K.A. Asante, M. Muto, Y. Opoku-Ankomah, O.D. Ansa-Asare, and S. Tanabe. "Variation and Distribution of Metals and Metalloids in Soil/Ash Mixtures from Agbogbloshie E-Waste Recycling Site in Accra, Ghana." *Science of the Total Environment* 470 (February 2014): 707–716.

Jack, Homer A. "Nonalignment and a Test Ban Agreement: The Role of the Nonaligned States." *Journal of Conflict Resolution* 7, no. 3, Weapons Management in World Politics: Proceedings of the International Arms Control Symposium, December, 1962 (September 1963): 542–552.

Jacobs, Nancy Joy. "The Intimate Politics of Ornithology in Colonial Africa." *Comparative Studies in Society and History* 48, no. 3 (2006): 564–603.

Jacobs, Robert. "Nuclear Conquistadors: Military Colonialism in Nuclear Test Site Selection During the Cold War." *Asian Journal of Peacebuilding* 1, no. 2 (2013): 157.

Jibiri, N.N. and A.A. Okusanya. "Radionuclide Contents in Food Products from Domestic and Imported Sources in Nigeria." *Journal of Radiological Protection* 28, no. 3 (September 2008): 405–413.

Jonah, S.A. "Measured and Simulated Reactivity Insertion Transients Characteristics of Nirr-1." *Annals of Nuclear Energy* 38, no. 2–3 (February–March 2011): 295–297.

Jonah, S.A., G.I. Balogun, I.M. Umar, and M.C. Mayaki. "Neutron Spectrum Parameters in Irradiation Channels of the Nigeria Research Reactor-1 (NIRR-1) for the K0-NAA Standardization." *Journal of Radioanalytical and Nuclear Chemistry* 266, no. 1: 83–88.

Jonah, S.A., Y.V. Ibrahim, and E.H.K. Akaho. "The Determination of Reactor Neutron Spectrum-Averaged Cross-Sections in Miniature Neutron Source Reactor Facility." *Applied Radiation and Isotopes* 66, no. 10 (October 2008): 1377–1380.

Jonah, S.A., J.R. Liaw, and J.E. Matos. "Monte Carlo Simulation of Core Physics Parameters of the Nigeria Research Reactor-1 (NIRR-1)." *Annals of Nuclear Energy* 34, no. 12 (December 2007): 953–957.

Jonah, S.A., I.M. Umar, M.O.A. Adipo, G.I. Balogun, and D.J. Adeyemo. "Standardization of NIRR-1 Irradiation and Counting Facilities for Instrumental Neutron Activation Analysis." *Applied Radiation and Isotopes* 64, no. 7 (July 2006): 818–822.

Jue, Melody. "Intimate Objectivity: On Nnedi Okorafor's Oceanic Afrofuturism." *Women's Studies Quarterly* 45, no. 1 & 2 (2017): 171–188.

Kadidal, Shayana. "Plants, Poverty, and Pharmaceutical Patents." *The Yale Law Journal* 103, no. 1 (1993): 223.

Kaiser, David. "The Postwar Suburbanization of American Physics." *American Studies* 56, no. 4 (December 2004): 851–888.

Kasanga, R. Kasim. "Land Tenure and Regional Investment Prospects: The Case of the Tenurial Systems of Northern Ghana." *Property Management* 13, no. 2 (1995): 21–31.

King, Nicholas B. "Security, Disease, Commerce: Ideologies of Postcolonial Global Health." *Social Studies of Science* 32, no. 5–6 (2002): 763–789.

Klaeger, Gabriel. "Dwelling on the Road: Routines, Rituals and Roadblocks in Southern Ghana." *Africa: Journal of the International African Institute/ Revue de l'Institut Africain International* 83, no. 3 (2013): 446–469.

"Introduction: The Perils and Possibilities of African Roads." *Africa* 83, no. 3 (2013): 359–366.

Klu, G.Y.P. and A.M. van Harten. "Optimization of Mutant Recovery from Plants Obtained from Gamma-Radiated Seeds of Winged Bean (*Psophocarpus Tetragonolobus* (L) Dc)." *Journal of Applied Science and Technology* 5, no. 1 (2000): 56–62.

Kopp, Carolyn. "The Origins of the American Scientific Debate over Fallout Hazards." *Social Studies of Science* 9, no. 4 (November 1, 1979): 403–422.

Krige, John. "Atoms for Peace, Scientific Internationalism, and Scientific Intelligence." *Osiris* 21 (2006): 161–181.

Kuchinskaya, Olga. "Twice Invisible: Formal Representations of Radiation Danger." *Social Studies of Science* 43, no. 1 (February 1, 2013): 78–96.

Laveaga, Gabriela Soto. "Uncommon Trajectories: Steroid Hormones, Mexican Peasants, and the Search for a Wild Yam." *Studies in History and Philosophy of Biological and Biomedical Sciences, University of Cambridge* 36, no. 4 (December 2005): 743–760.

Lefever, Ernest W. "Nehru, Nasser and Nkrumah on Neutralism." *Neutralism and Nonalignment* (1962): 544–609.

Lentz, Carola. "'This Is Ghanaian Territory!': Land Conflicts on a West African Border." *American Ethnologist* 30, no. 2 (2003): 273–289.

"Decentralization, the State and Conflicts over Local Boundaries in Northern Ghana." *Development and Change* 37, no. 4 (2006): 901–919.

Lomax, H. and N. Casey. "Recording Social Life: Reflexivity and Video Methodology." *Sociological Research Online* 3, no. 2 (1998): 1–26.

Low, M.F. "Japan's Secret War – Instant Scientific Manpower and Japan World-War-II Atomic-Bomb Project." *Annals of Science* 47, no. 4 (July 1990): 347–360.

MacFarlane, Allison. "Underlying Yucca Mountain: The Interplay of Geology and Policy in Nuclear Waste Disposal." *Social Studies of Science* 33, no. 5 (October 1, 2003): 783–807.

MacKenzie, Donald and Graham Spinardi. "Tacit Knowledge, Weapons Design, and the Uninvention of Nuclear Weapons." *American Journal of Sociology* 101, no. 1 (1995): 44–99.

Mahama, Callistus and Martin Dixon. "Acquisition and Affordability of Land for Housing in Urban Ghana: A Study in the Formal Land Market Dynamics." *RCIS Research Paper Series* 10 (October 2006).

Makhubu, Lydia. "Bioprospecting in an African Context." *Science* 282, no. 5386 (October 2, 1998): 41–42.

Mancia, Joel Rolim and Denise Gastaldo. "Editorial: Production and Consumption of Science in a Global Context." *Nursing Inquiry* 11, no. 2 (2004): 65–66.

Martin, Joseph. "The Peaceful Atom Comes to Campus." *Physics Today* 69, no. 2 (2016): 40–46.

Mazrui, Ali A. "Nkrumah, Obote and Vietnam." *Transition*, no. 43 (1973): 36–39.

"Changing the Guards from Hindus to Muslims: Collective Third World Security in a Cultural Perspective." *International Affairs (Royal Institute of International Affairs 1944-)* 57, no. 1 (Winter 1980): 1–20.

Mazur, Allan and Beverlie Conant. "Controversy over a Local Nuclear Waste Repository." *Social Studies of Science* 8, no. 2 (May 1, 1978): 235–243.

Mbiti, John S. "Theological Impotence and the Universality of the Church." *Mission Trends* 3: Third World Theologies (1976): 6–18.

McGough, Laura J. "Civil Society in Post-Colonial Ghana: A Case Study of the Ghana Institution of Engineers." *Transactions of the Historical Society of Ghana*, no. 3 (1999): 1–26.

McGowan, Patrick J. "African Military Coups d'État, 1956–2001: Frequency, Trends and Distribution." *The Journal of Modern African Studies* 41, no. 3 (2003): 339–370.

Mensah, S.Y., F.K. Allotey, S.K. Adjepong, and N.G. Mensah. "Photostimulated Attenuation of Hypersound in Superlattices." *Superlattices and Microstructures* 22, no. 4 (1997): 453–457.

Miescher, Stephan F. "Building the City of the Future: Visions and Experiences of Modernity in Ghana's Akosombo Township." *Journal of African History* 53, no. 3 (2012): 367–390.

"'Nkrumah's Baby': The Akosombo Dam and the Dream of Development in Ghana." *Water History* 6, no. 4 (2014): 341–366.

Miescher, Stephan F. and Dzozi Tsikata. "Hydro-Power and the Promise of Modernity and Development in Ghana: Comparing the Akosombo and Bui Dam Projects." *Ghana Studies* 12/13 (2009/2010): 55–75.

Migot-Adholla, Shem, Peter Hazell, Benoît Blarel, and Frank Place. "Indigenous Land Rights Systems in Sub-Saharan Africa: A Constraint on Productivity?" *The World Bank Economic Review* 5, no. 1 (January 1, 1991): 155–175.

Miller, Manjari Chatterjee. "India's Global Ambition and the Nuclear Deal." *Christian Science Monitor* 100, no. 169 (July 25, 2008): 9.

Mokobia, C.E., F.O. Ogundare, E.P. Inyang, F.A. Balogun, and S.A. Jonah. "Determination of the Elemental Constituents of a Natural Dolerite Using NIRR-1." *Applied Radiation and Isotopes* 66, no. 12 (December 2008): 1916–1919.

Mondada, Lorenza. "Working with Video: How Surgeons Produce Video Records of Their Actions." *Visual Studies* 18, no. 1 (2003): 58–73.

Moore, Samuel K. and Alan Gardner. "Megacities by the Numbers." *IEEE Spectrum* 44, no. 6 (June 2007): 24–25.

Moote, Margaret A. and Mitchel P. McClaran. "Viewpoint: Implications of Participatory Democracy for Public Land Planning." *Journal of Range Management* 50, no. 5 (1997): 473–481.

Musa, Y., Y.A. Ahmed, Y.A. Yamusa, and I.O.B. Ewa. "Determination of Radial and Axial Neutron Flux Distribution in Irradiation Channel of NIRR-1 Using Foil Activation Technique." *Annals of Nuclear Energy* 50 (December 2012): 50–55.

Nehring, Holger. "Cold War, Apocalypse and Peaceful Atoms. Interpretations of Nuclear Energy in the British and West German Anti-Nuclear Weapons Movements, 1955–1964." *Historical Social Research/ Historische Sozialforschung* 29, no. 3 (109) (2004): 150–170.

Nelson, Alondra. "Introduction: Future Texts." *Social Text (Special Issue on Afrofuturism)* 20, no. 2 (2002): 1–15.

Nemetz, Patricia L. and Sandra L. Christensen. "The Challenge of Cultural Diversity: Harnessing a Diversity of Views to Understand Multiculturalism." *The Academy of Management Review* 21, no. 2 (April 1996): 434–462.

Noer, Thomas J. "The New Frontier and African Neutralism: Kennedy, Nkrumah, and the Volta River Project." *Diplomatic History* 8, no. 1 (1984): 61–79.

Nwosu, E.J. "Some Problems of Appropriate Technology and Technology Transfer." *Developing Economies* 13, no. 1 (1975): 82–93.

Nyaki, Mungubariki. "Powerpoint: UNFC-2009 for Evaluation of Uranium and Thorium Resources." *UNECE: Regional Training Course* (October 2015).

Nyarko, B.J.B., E.H.K. Akaho, J.J. Fletcher, and A. Chatt. "Neutron Activation Analysis for Dy, Hf, Rb, Sc and Se in Some Ghanaian Cereals and Vegetables Using Short-Lived Nuclides and Compton Suppression Spectrometry." *Applied Radiation and Isotopes* 66, no. 8 (2008): 1067–1072.

Nyarko, B.J.B., E.H.K. Akaho, and Y. Serfor-Armah. "Application of NAA Standardization Methods Using a Low Power Research Reactor." *Journal of Radioanalytical and Nuclear Chemistry* 257, no. 2 (2003): 361–366.

Nyarko, B.J.B., Y. Serfor-Armah, S. Osae, E.H.K. Akaho, S. Anim-Sampong, and B.T. Maakuu. "Epiboron Instrumental Neutron Activation Analysis for the Determination of Iodine in Various Salt Samples." *Journal of Radioanalytical and Nuclear Chemistry* 251, no. 2 (February 2002): 281–284.

Obafemi Awolowo University, CERD. "Cerd News." (serial).

Obeng, Letitia. "Should Dams Be Built? The Volta Lake Example." *Ambio* 6, no. 1 (1977): 46–50.

O'Driscoll, Mervyn. "Explosive Challenge: Diplomatic Triangles, the United Nations, and the Problem of French Nuclear Testing, 1959–1960." *Journal of Cold War Studies* 11, no. 1 (Winter 2009): 28–56.

Ofori, E.K., W.K. Antwi, L. Arthur, and H. Duah. "Comparison of Patient Radiation Dose from Chest and Lumbar Spine X-Ray Examinations in 10 Hospitals in Ghana." *Radiation Protection Dosimetry* 149, no. 4 (May 2012): 424–430.

Ofosu, F.G., P.K. Hopke, I.J.K. Aboh, and S.A. Bamford. "Biomass Burning Contribution to Ambient Air Particulate Levels at Navrongo in the Savannah Zone of Ghana." *Journal of the Air & Waste Management Association* 63, no. 9 (September 2013): 1036–1045.

Ofosu-Mensah, Emmanuel Ababio. "Mining and Conflict in the Akyem Abuakwa Kingdom in the Eastern Region of Ghana, 1919–1938." *The Extractive Industries and Society* 2, no. 3 (2015): 480–490.

Ogunbadejo, Oye. "Africa's Nuclear Capability." *Journal of Modern African Studies* 22, no. 1 (March 1984): 19–43.

Ogunniyi, M.B. "Two Decades of Science Education in Africa." *Science Education* 70, no. 2 (April 1986): 111–122.

Olick, Jeffery K. and Joyce Robbins. "Social Memory Studies: From 'Collective Memory' to the Historical Sociological of Mnemonic Practices." *Annual Review of Sociology* 24 (1998): 105–140.

Omosewo, Esther O. "Historical Development of Senior Secondary School Physics Teaching in Nigeria." *African Journal of Historical Sciences in Education* 4, no. 1 & 2 (2008): 93–101.

Osibote, O.A., J.B. Olomo, P. Tchokossa, and F.A. Balogun. "Radioactivity in Milk Consumed in Nigeria 10 Years after Chernobyl Reactor Accident." *Nuclear Instruments & Methods in Physics Research Section A: Accelerators Spectrometers Detectors and Associated Equipment* 422, no. 1–3 (February 1999): 778–783.

Osei, S., J.K. Amoako, and J.J. Fletcher. "Assessment of Levels of Occupational Exposure to Workers in Radiofrequency Fields of Two Television Stations in Accra, Ghana." *Radiation Protection Dosimetry* 168, no. 3 (March 2016): 419–426.

Osseo-Asare, Abena Dove. "Bioprospecting and Resistance: Transforming Poisoned Arrows into Strophanthin Pills in Colonial Gold Coast, 1885–1922." *Social History of Medicine* 21, no. 2 (August 2008): 269–290.

"Scientific Equity: Experiments in Laboratory Education in Ghana." *Isis* 104, no. 4 (2013): 713–741.

Pabian, Frank V. "South Africa's Nuclear Weapon Program: Lessons for U.S. Nonproliferation Policy." *The Nonproliferation Review* 3, no. 1 (1995): 1–19.

Paterson, Barbara L., Joan L. Bottorff, and Roberta Hewat. "Blending Observational Methods: Possibilities, Strategies, and Challenges." *International Journal of Qualitative Methods* 2, no. 1 (2003): 29–38.

Peil, Margaret. "Ghanaians Abroad." *African Affairs* 94, no. 376 (July 1995): 345–367.

Peters, Pauline E. "Conflicts over Land and Threats to Customary Tenure in Africa." *African Affairs* 112, no. 449 (October 1, 2013): 543–562.

Quarcoopome, C.O. "Epidemic Haemorrhagic Conjunctivitis in Ghana. Further Observations." *British Journal of Ophthalmology* 57, no. 9 (September 1, 1973): 692–693.

Ramana, M.V. "The Forgotten History of Small Nuclear Reactors." *IEEE Spectrum* 52, no. 5 (2015): 44–58.

Ramsay, W.B. "The Use of Numerical Weather Forecasts for Radioactive-Fallout Predictions." *Journal of Geophysical Research* 64, no. 8 (1959): 1120–1121.

Richards, Zoe T., Maria Beger, Silvia Pinca, and Carden C. Wallace. "Bikini Atoll Coral Biodiversity Resilience Five Decades after Nuclear Testing." *Marine Pollution Bulletin* 56, no. 3 (2008): 503–515.

Roberts, Nancy C. and Raymond Trevor Bradley. "Stakeholder Collaboration and Innovation: A Study of Public Policy Initiation at the State Level." *The Journal of Applied Behavioral Science* 27, no. 2 (June 1, 1991): 209–227.

Sackeyfio, Naaborko. "The Politics of Land and Urban Space in Colonial Accra." *History in Africa* 39 (2012): 293–329.

Sagan, Scott D. "Why Do States Build Nuclear Weapons?: Three Models in Search of a Bomb." *International Security* 21, no. 3 (Winter 1996): 54–86.

Schandorf, C. and G. K. Tetteh. "Analysis of Dose and Dose Distribution for Patients Undergoing Selected X Ray Diagnostic Procedures in Ghana." *Radiation Protection Dosimetry* 76, no. 4 (1998): 249–256.

"Analysis of the Status of X-Ray Diagnosis in Ghana." *British Journal of Radiology* 71, no. 850 (October 1998): 1040–1048.

Schenck, Lisa M. and Robert A. Youmans. "From Start to Finish: A Historical Review of Nuclear Arms Control Treaties and Starting over with the New Start." *Cardozo Journal of International and Comparative Law* 20, no. 2 (Winter 2012): 299–435.

Seaborg, Glenn T. "A Scientific Safari to Africa." *Science* 169, no. 3945 (August 7, 1970): 554–561.

"Scientific Development in Africa." *Science* 172, no. 3987 (June 4, 1971): 987.

Sekiguchi, J. and S.R. Collens. "Radiological Services in Rural Mission Hospitals in Ghana." *Bulletin of the World Health Organization* 73, no. 1 (1995): 65–69.

Serfor-Armah, Y., B.J.B. Nyarko, D.K. Adotey, S.B. Dampare, and D. Adomako. "Levels of Arsenic and Antimony in Water and Sediment from Prestea, a Gold Mining Town in Ghana and Its Environs." *Water, Air and Soil Pollution* 175, no. 1–4 (September 2006): 181–192.

Seth, Suman. "Putting Knowledge in Its Place: Science, Colonialism, and the Postcolonial." *Postcolonial Studies* 12, no. 4 (2009): 373–388.

Simon, Steven L. and André Bouville. "Radiation Doses to Local Populations near Nuclear Weapons Test Sites Worldwide." *Health Physics* 82, no. 5 (2002): 706–725.

Sims, B. and C. Henke. "Maintenance and Transformation in the US Nuclear Weapons Complex." *IEEE Technology and Society Magazine* 27, no. 3 (fall 2008): 32–38.

Sims, Benjamin and Christopher R. Henke. "Repairing Credibility: Repositioning Nuclear Weapons Knowledge after the Cold War." *Social Studies of Science* 42, no. 3 (2012): 324–347.

Skinner, Rob. "Bombs and Border Crossings: Peace Activist Networks and the Post-Colonial State in Africa, 1959–62." *Journal of Contemporary History* (November 17, 2014): 418–438.

Solodovnikov, Vasily. "The Soviet Union and the African Nations." *Political Affairs* 47, no. 7 (1968): 41–53.

Spence, J.E. "South Africa: The Nuclear Option." *African Affairs* 80, no. 321 (October 1981): 441–452.

Steelman, Toddi A. and Lynn A. Maguire. "Understanding Participant Perspectives: Q-Methodology in National Forest Management." *Journal of Policy Analysis and Management* 18, no. 3 (1998): 361–388.

Subaar, C., J.K. Amoako, A. Owusu, J.J. Fletcher, and J. Suurbaar. "Numerical Studies of Radiofrequency of the Electromagnetic Radiation Power Absorption in Paediatrics Undergoing Brain Magnetic Resonance Imaging." *Journal of Radiation Research and Applied Sciences* 10, no. 3 (July 2017): 188–193.

Sutton, John R. "Organizational Autonomy and Professional Norms in Science: A Case Study of the Lawrence Livermore Laboratory." *Social Studies of Science* 14, no. 2 (May 1, 1984): 197–224.

Sur, Abha. "Aesthetics, Authority, and Control in an Indian Laboratory: The Raman-Born Controversy on Lattice Dynamics." *Isis* 90, no. 1 (1999): 25–49.

Teitel, S. "Concept of Appropriate Technology for Less Industrialized Countries." *Trimestre Economico* 43, no. 171 (1976): 775–804.

Teng-Zeng, Frank K. "The Same Story or New Directions? Science and Technology within the Framework of the African Union and New Partnership for Africa's Development." *Science and Public Policy* 32, no. 3 (June 2005): 231–246.

Tonkin, Elizabeth. "Investigating Oral Tradition." *Journal of African History* 27 (1986): 203–213.

Townsend, Leslie H. "Out of the Silence: Writing Interactive Women's Life Histories in Africa." *History in Africa* 17 (1990): 351–358.

Tshuma, Lawrence. "Colonial and Post-Colonial Reconstructions of Customary Land Tenure in Zimbabwe." *Social & Legal Studies* 7, no. 1 (March 1, 1998): 77–95.

Uba, Sam. "Nigeria Takes the Plunge into the Nuclear Age: It Can Be Argued That Nigeria Has No Immediate Need for Nuclear Energy; yet It Has Begun Negotiations with West Germany to Purchase Nuclear Reactors." *African Development* 10 (November 1, 1976): 993.

Ugbor, K.O. "Science, Education and Development in Sub-Saharan Africa – Zymelman, M." *Canadian Journal Of African Studies-Revue Canadienne Des Etudes Africaines* 26, no. 3 (1992): 563–565.

Ward, A.H. and J.D. Marr. "Radioactive Fall-out in Ghana." *Nature* 187, no. 4734 (July 23, 1960): 299–300.

Weart, Spencer. "Secrecy, Simultaneous Discovery, and the Theory of Nuclear Reactors." *American Journal of Physics* 45, no. 11 (1977): 1049–1060.

Wellerstein, A. "Patenting the Bomb – Nuclear Weapons, Intellectual Property, and Technological Control." *Isis* 99, no. 1 (March 2008): 57–87.

Wellerstein, Alex. "Patenting the Bomb: Nuclear Weapons, Intellectual Property, and Technological Control." *Isis* 99, no. 1 (2008): 57–87.

Wharton, C.R. "Green Revolution – Cornucopia or Pandaora's Box." *Foreign Affairs* 47, no. 3 (1969): 464–476.

Williams, M.M.R. "The Development of Nuclear Reactor Theory in the Montreal Laboratory of the National Research Council of Canada (Division of Atomic Energy) 1943–1946." *Progress in Nuclear Energy* 36, no. 3 (2000): 239–322.

Williams, Paul. "Going Critical: On the Historic Preservation of the World's First Nuclear Reactor." *Future Anterior: Journal of Historic Preservation, History, Theory, and Criticism* 5, no. 2 (2008): vi–18.

Wright, R.W.H. "University Physics in Developing Countries." *Physics Education* 2 (1967): 35–39.

Yamamoto, M., T. Takada, S. Nagao, T. Koike, K. Shimada, M. Hoshi, K. Zhumadilov, et al. "An Early Survey of the Radioactive Contamination of Soil Due to the Fukushima Dai-Ichi Nuclear Power Plant Accident, with Emphasis on Plutonium Analysis." *Geochemical Journal* 46, no. 4 (2012): 341–353.

Yarrow, Thomas. "Remains of the Future: Rethinking the Space and Time of Ruination through the Volta Resettlement Project, Ghana." *Cultural Anthropology* 32, no. 4 (2017): 566–591.

Yasunari, Teppei J., Andreas Stohl, Ryugo S. Hayano, John F. Burkhart, Sabine Eckhardt, and Tetsuzo Yasunari. "Cesium-137 Deposition and Contamination of Japanese Soils Due to the Fukushima Nuclear Accident." *Proceedings of the National Academy of Sciences* 108, no. 49 (December 6, 2011): 19530–19534.

Yaszek, Lisa. "Afrofuturism, Science Fiction, and the History of the Future." *Socialism and Democracy* 20, no. 3 (November 2010): 41–60.

Yoshida, Naohiro and Yoshio Takahashi. "Land-Surface Contamination by Radionuclides from the Fukushima Daiichi Nuclear Power Plant Accident." *Elements* 8, no. 3 (2012): 201–206.

Young, Oran R. "Chinese Views on the Spread of Nuclear Weapons." *China Quarterly*, no. 26 (April–June 1966): 136–170.

Young, Wayland. "Mosquitoes in Accra." *Bulletin of the Atomic Scientists* 18, no. 7 (September 1962): 45–47.

Zhang, Zuoyi and Yuliang Sun. "Economic Potential of Modular Reactor Nuclear Power Plants Based on the Chinese HTR-PM Project." *Nuclear Engineering and Design* 237, no. 23 (2007): 2265–2274.

Zimmerman, Jonathan. "'Money, Materials, and Manpower': In-Service Teacher Education and the Economy of Failure, 1961–1971." *History of Education Quarterly* 51, no. 1 (2011): 1–27.

Zoppo, Ciro. "Nuclear Technology, Weapons, and the Third World." *The Annals of the American Academy of Political and Social Science* 386, no. Protagonists, Power, and the Third World: Essays on the Changing International System (November 1969): 113–125.

Book Chapters

Allotey, Francis K.A. "African Physicist, World Citizen." In *One Hundred Reasons to Be a Scientist*, 38–40. Trieste: The Abdus Salam International Centre for Theoretical Physics, 2005.

Amuzu, Josef K.A. "The Nuclear Option for Ghana." In *Ghana: Changing Values/ Changing Technologies (Ghanaian Philosophical Studies, II)*, edited by Helen Lauer. Cultural Heritage and Contemporary Change. Washington, DC: Council for Research in Values and Philosophy, 2000.

Benjamin, Ruha. "Black Afterlives Matter." In *Making Kin Not Population*, edited by Adele Clarke and Donna Haraway. Chicago: Prickly Paradigm Press, 2018.

Emi-Reynolds, G., E.T. Glover, M. Nyarku, P. Essel, and Y. Adjei-Kyereme. "Safe and Secure Management of Sealed Radioactive Sources in Ghana." In *Safety and Security of Radioactive Sources: Maintaining Continuous Global Control of Sources Throughout Their Life Cycle: Proceedings of an International Conference, Abu Dhabi, United Arab Emirates,*

27–31 October 2013, 465–476. Vienna: International Atomic Energy Agency, 2015.

Jolly, Richard. "Planning Education for African Development: Economic and Manpower Perspectives." Nairobi: Published for the Makerere Institute of Social Research by East African Publishing House, 1969.

Joly, Vincent. "The French Army and Malian Independence (1956–1961)." In *Francophone Africa at Fifty*, edited by Tony Chafer and Alexander Keese, 75–89. New York: Manchester University Press, 2013.

Justice, Christopher O., David Wilkie, Francis E. Putz, and Jake Brunner. "Climate Change in Sub-Saharan Africa: Assumptions, Realities and Future Investments." In *Climate Change and Africa*, edited by Pak Sum Low, 172–181. Cambridge; New York: Cambridge University Press, 2005.

Lee, Christopher J. "Between a Moment and an Era: The Origins and Afterlives of Bandung." In *Making a World after Empire: The Bandung Moment and Its Political Afterlives*, edited by Christopher J. Lee. Athens, OH: Ohio University Press, 2010.

——— ed. *Making a World after Empire: The Bandung Moment and Its Political Afterlives*, Ohio University Research in International Studies: Global and Comparative Studies Series No. 11. Athens, OH: Ohio University Press, 2010.

Mavhunga, Clapperton Chakanetsa. "Energy, Industry, and Transport in South-Central Africa's History." In *Energy (and) Colonialism, Energy (in)Dependence Africa, Europe, Greenland, North America*, edited by Clapperton Chakanetsa Mavhunga and Helmuth Trischler, 9–17. Munich: Rachel Carson Center Perspectives, 2014.

Miescher, Stephan F. "'No One Should Be Worse Off': The Akosombo Dam, Modernization, and the Experience of Resettlement in Ghana." In *Modernization as Spectacle in Africa*, edited by Peter Jason Bloom, Stephan F. Miescher, and Takyiwaa Manuh, 317–342. Bloomington, IN: Indiana University Press, 2014.

Nkrumah, Kwame. "Speech by the Hon. Dr. Kwame Nkrumah, Prime Minister of Ghana." In *Conference of Independent African States: Speeches Delivered at the Inaugural Session, 15th April, 1958*, 1–8. Accra: Government Printer, n.d.

Samatar, Sofia. "Ogres of East Africa." In *Tender*. Easthampton, MA: Small Beer Press, 2017.

Vinciguerra, Venusia. "How the Daewoo Attempted Land Acquisition Contributed to Madagascar's Political Crisis in 2009." In *Contest for Land in Madagascar: Environment, Ancestors and Development*, edited by Sandra Evers, Gwyn Campbell, and Michael Lambek, 221–246. Leiden, the Netherlands: Brill, 2013.

Ward, A.H. "Ghana's Contribution to World Science." In *Ghana, One Year Old: A First Independence Anniversary Review*, edited by Moses Danquah, Chapter 14. Accra: Publicity Promotions, 1958.

Ward, M.A., E.K. Ofori, D. Scutt, and B.M. Moores. "Experiences of in-Field and Remote Monitoring of Diagnostic Radiological Quality in Ghana Using an Equipment and Patient Dosimetry Database." In *World Congress on Medical Physics and Biomedical Engineering, Vol. 25, Pt 13*, edited by O. Dossel and W.C. Schlegel. IFMBE Proceedings, 36–39, 2009.

Books and Reports

The Consolidation Development Plan. 2 vols. Accra: Government Printer, 1958.

Second Development Plan, 1959–64. Accra: Government Printer, 1959.

Seven-Year Development Plan: A Brief Outline. Accra: Office of the Planning Commission, 1963.

Seven-Year Plan for National Reconstruction and Development: Financial Years, 1963/64–1969/70. Accra: Office of the Planning Commission, 1964.

Ethiopia: A Study of Manpower Needs, Educational Capabilities, and Overseas Study. New York: Education and World Affairs, 1965.

International Atomic Energy Agency, General Conference, Ninth Regular Session: Delegations. IAEA, 1965.

Seven-Year Development Plan: Annual Plan for the Second Plan Year, 1965 Financial Year. Accra: Office of the Planning Commission, 1965.

Volta Resettlement Symposium Papers. Translated by Accra Volta River Authority and Kwame Nkrumah University of Science and Technology Faculty of Architecture, Kumasi, Ghana. Volta Resettlement Symposium. Edited by Robert Chambers. Kumasi: University of Science and Technology, 1965.

Directory of British Scientists, 1966–1967. London: Ernest Benn Limited, 1966.

International Atomic Energy Agency: General Conference, Eleventh Regular Session: Delegations, Information Received by Noon on 18 September 1967. Vienna: IAEA, 1967.

Ghana Atomic Energy Commission Status Report 1962–1973. Accra: Crown Press Limited, 1973.

Korle Bu Hospital 1923–1973: Golden Jubilee Souvenir. Christianborg: The Advent Publishing House, 1973.

International Atomic Energy Agency: General Conference, Nineteenth Regular Session, Vienna, 22–26 September 1975: Delegations. Vienna: IAEA, 1975.

Kwabenya Nuclear Research Establishment Handbook. Kwabenya, Accra: GAEC, 1977.

International Atomic Energy Agency: General Conference, Twenty-Second Regular Session: List of Participants, Information Received by Noon on 14 September 1978. Vienna: IAEA, 1978.

The Constitution of the Republic of Ghana 1992. Accra: Government Printer, 1992.

Safety of Research Reactors: Safety Requirements. Safety Standards Series. Vol. NS-R-4, Vienna: IAEA, 2005.

African Regional Cooperative Agreement for Research, Development and Training Related to Nuclear Science and Technology: Profile of the Regional Strategic Cooperative Framework (2008–2013). Vienna: IAEA, 2010.

Biotechnology and Nuclear Agriculture Research Institute (BNARI) Annual Report, January–December 2015. Accra: Ghana Atomic Energy Commission, 2016.

National Nuclear Research Institute (NNRI) at a Glance. Accra: Ghana Atomic Energy Commission, c. 2000.

Abraham, Itty. *The Making of the Indian Atomic Bomb: Science, Secrecy and the Postcolonial State.* London; New York: Zed Books, 1998.

Adamafio, Tawia. *French Nuclear Tests in the Sahara.* Accra: C.P.P. National Headquarters, Bureau of Information & Publicity, 1960.

   By Nkrumah's Side: The Labour and the Wounds. Accra: Westcoast Publishing House, 1982.

Addo-Fening, R. *Akyem Abuakwa and the Politics of the Inter-War Period in Ghana.* Basel: Basler Afrika-Bibliographien, 1975.

Agbodeka, Francis. *Achimota in the National Setting: A Unique Educational Experiment in West Africa.* Accra: Afram Publications, 1977.

   A History of University of Ghana: Half a Century of Higher Education (1948–1998). Accra: Woeli Publishing Services, 1998.

Ahlman, Jeffrey S. *Living with Nkrumahism: Nation, State, and Pan-Africanism in Ghana.* Athens, OH: Ohio University Press, 2017.

Akyeampong, Emmanuel Kwaku. *Between the Sea & the Lagoon: An Eco-Social History of the Anlo of Southeastern Ghana C. 1850 to Recent Times.* Oxford: James Currey, 2001.

Aldrich, Daniel P. *Site Fights: Divisive Facilities and Civil Society in Japan and the West.* Ithaca, NY: Cornell University Press, 2008.

Algeria, Argentina, Bangladesh, Egypt, Ethiopia, Ghana, Iraq, et al. *Peaceful Use of Nuclear Energy for Economic and Social Development: Draft Resolution.* New York: UN, 1979.

Alley, Roderic. *A Nuclear-Weapon-Free Zone in Africa?* Occasional Paper. Vol. 14, Muscatine, IA: The Stanley Foundation, 1977.

Allotey, Asie Mirekuwa and Francis Kofi Ampenyin Allotey. *The Saga of Professor F.K.A. Allotey "the African Scientist."* Accra: Institute for Scientific and Technological Information, 2002.

Amanor, Kojo Sebastian. *Land, Labour and the Family in Southern Ghana: A Critique of Land Policy under Neo-Liberalisation.* Uppsala: Nordiska Afrikainstitutet, 2001.

Amuasi, J.H. *The History of Ghana Atomic Energy Commission 1963– 2003: Forty Years of Nuclear Science and Technology Applications in Ghana.* Accra: AGOL Gh. Ltd, 2003.

Anderson, Robert S. *Nucleus and Nation: Scientists, International Networks, and Power in India.* Chicago; London: The University of Chicago Press, 2010.

Andrianirina-Ratsialonana, Rivo, Landry Ramarojohn, Perrine Burnod, and André Teyssier. *After Daewoo? Current Status and Perspectives of Large-Scale Land Acquisition in Madagascar.* Rome: International Land Coalition (ILC), 2011.

Anti-Taylor, William. *Moscow Diary.* London: Robert Hale, 1967.

Appiah, Kwame Anthony. *Cosmopolitanism: Ethics in a World of Strangers.* New York: W.W. Norton & Co., 2006.

  In My Father's House: Africa in the Philosophy of Culture. New York: Oxford University Press, 1993.

Appiah-Denkyira, E., C.H. Herbst, A. Soucat, C. Lemiere, and K. Saleh. *Toward Interventions in Human Resources for Health in Ghana: Evidence for Health Workforce Planning and Results.* Washington, DC: World Bank Publications, 2013.

Barker, Holly M. *Bravo for the Marshallese: Regaining Control in a Post-Nuclear, Post-Colonial World.* Case Studies on Contemporary Social Issues. Belmont, CA: Wadsworth/Thomson, 2004.

Beck, K., G. Klaeger, and M. Stasik. *The Making of the African Road.* Leiden, the Netherlands: Brill, 2017.

Bediako, Kwame. *Christianity in Africa: The Renewal of Non-Western Religion.* Studies in World Christianity. Edinburgh: Edinburgh University Press, 1995.

Berry, Daina Ramey. *The Price for Their Pound of Flesh: The Value of the Enslaved, from Womb to Grave, in the Building of a Nation.* Boston, MA: Beacon Press, 2017.

Berry, Sara. *No Condition Is Permanent: The Social Dynamics of Agrarian Change in Sub-Saharan Africa.* Madison, WI: University of Wisconsin Press, 1993.

Biney, Ama. *The Political and Social Thought of Kwame Nkrumah.* New York: Palgrave Macmillan US, 2011.

Boahen, A. Adu. *African Perspectives on Colonialism*. The Johns Hopkins Symposia in Comparative History. Baltimore, MD: Johns Hopkins University Press, 1987.

Boone, Catherine. *Property and Political Order in Africa: Land Rights and the Structure of Politics*. New York: Cambridge, 2014.

Braut-Hegghammer, Malfrid. *Unclear Physics: Why Iraq and Libya Failed to Build Nuclear Weapons*. Ithaca, NY: Cornell Press, 2016.

Brown, Kate. *Plutopia: Nuclear Families, Atomic Cities, and the Great Soviet and American Plutonium Disasters*. New York: Oxford University Press, 2013.

Burrell, Jenna. *Invisible Users: Youth in the Internet Cafés of Urban Ghana*. Cambridge, MA: MIT Press Books, 2012.

Chakrabarty, Dipesh. *Provincializing Europe: Postcolonial Thought and Historical Difference*. Princeton, NJ: Princeton University Press, 2000.

Chalfin, B. *Neoliberal Frontiers: An Ethnography of Sovereignty in West Africa*. Chicago: University of Chicago Press, 2010.

Chau, D. *Exploiting Africa: The Influence of Maoist China in Algeria, Ghana, and Tanzania*. Annapolis, MD: Naval Institute Press, 2014.

Choy, T. *Ecologies of Comparison: An Ethnography of Endangerment in Hong Kong*. Durham, NC: Duke University Press, 2011.

Coe, Cati. *Dilemmas of Culture in African Schools: Youth, Nationalism, and the Transformation of Knowledge*. Chicago: University of Chicago Press, 2005.

Cohn, Avner and Terence McNamee. *Why Do States Want Nuclear Weapons?: The Cases of Israel and South Africa*. Oslo: Institutt for forsvarsstudier, 2005.

Cole, Teju. *Everyday Is for the Thief*. New York: Random House, 2014.

Comaroff, Jean and John Comaraoff. *Of Revelation and Revolution*. Chicago: University of Chicago Press, 1991.

Conway, Gordon R. and Edward B. Barbier. *After the Green Revolution: Sustainable Agriculture for Development*. London: Earthscan, 1990.

Cooper, W.G.G. *The Bauxite Deposits of the Gold Coast, with Maps and Sections*. Gold Coast Geological Survey. London: Waterlow & Sons Ltd, 1936.

Coquery-Vidrovitch, Catherine. *The History of African Cities South of the Sahara: From the Origins to Colonization*. Princeton, NJ: Markus Wiener Publishers, 2005.

Creager, Angela N.H. *Life Atomic: A History of Radioisotopes in Science and Medicine*. Chicago: University of Chicago Press, 2013.

Diop, Cheik Anta. *Nations Negres Et Culture*. Paris: Présence africaine, 1955.
    Physique Nucléaire Et Chronologie Absolue. Dakar: Institut Fondamental d'Afrique Noire (IFAN), 1974.

Diop, Cheik Anta, E. Curtis Alexander, and Mwalimu Imara Mwadilifu. *Cheikh Anta Diop: An African Scientist: An Axiomatic Overview of His Teachings and Thoughts*. Pan African Internationalist Handbook. New York: ECA Associates, 1984.

Divine, Robert A. *Blowing on the Wind: The Nuclear Test Ban Debate, 1954–1960*. New York: Oxford University Press, 1978.

Dwarko, D.A. *A History of University of Cape Coast: Forty Years of Resilience, 1962–2002*. Accra: Woeli Publishing Services, 2003.

A History of University of Cape Coast: Forty Years of Resilience, 1962–2002. Accra: Woeli Publishing Services, 2003.

Edgerton, David. *The Shock of the Old: Technology and Global History since 1900*. Oxford; New York: Oxford University Press, 2007.

Escobar, A. *Encountering Development: The Making and Unmaking of the Third World*. Princeton, NJ: Princeton University Press, 2011.

Ewusi, Kodwo. *Economic Development Planning in Ghana*. New York: Exposition Press, 1973.

Fairhead, James and Melissa Leach. *Misreading the African Landscape: Society and Ecology in a Forest-Savanna Mosaic*. African Stuides Series. Cambridge: Cambridge University Press, 1996.

Science, Society and Power: Environmental Knowledge and Policy in West Africa and the Caribbean. Cambridge; New York: Cambridge University Press, 2003.

Faola, Toyin and Steven J. Salm. *African Urban Spaces in Historical Perspective*. Rochester, NY: University of Rochester Press, 2005.

Ferguson, James. *Global Shadows: Africa in the Neoliberal World Order*. Durham, NC: Duke University Press, 2006.

Findlay, John M. and Bruce W. Hevly. *Atomic Frontier Days: Hanford and the American West*. Seattle, WA: University of Washington Press, 2015.

Firmin-Sellers, Kathryn. *The Transformation of Property Rights in the Gold Coast: An Empirical Study Applying Rational Choice Theory*. Cambridge: Cambridge University Press, 2007.

Freund, Bill. *The African City: A History*. Cambridge; New York: Cambridge University Press, 2007.

Fuller, Harcourt. *Building the Ghanaian Nation-State: Kwame Nkrumah's Symbolic Nationalism*. New York: Palgrave Macmillan, 2014.

Gaines, K.K. *American Africans in Ghana: Black Expatriates and the Civil Rights Era*. Chapel Hill, NC: University of North Carolina Press, 2006.

Galison, Peter Louis. *Image and Logic: A Material Culture of Microphysics*. Chicago: University of Chicago Press, 1997.

García-Gorena, V. *Mothers and the Mexican Antinuclear Power Movement*. Tucson, AZ: University of Arizona Press, 1999.

Report of the Committee Appointed to Investigate the Health Needs of Ghana. Accra-Tema: Ghana Publishing Corporation, 1968.

Gillon, Luc. *Servir: En Actes Et En Vérité*. Kinshasa: Éditions Centre de Recherches Pédagogiques, 1995.

Glover, E.T. *Implementation of Borehold Disposal Concept in Ghana-Status*. Vienna: IAEA Nuclear Safety and Security. Powerpoint presentation. www-ns.iaea.org/downloads/rw/code-conduct/waste-code/presentations/tuesday/ghana.pdf (June 27, 2018).

Goodman, Michael S. *Spying on the Nuclear Bear: Anglo-American Intelligence and the Soviet Bomb*. Stanford, CA: Stanford University Press, 2007.

Gordin, Michael D. *Scientific Babel: How Science Was Done before and after Global English*. Chicago: University of Chicago Press, 2015.

Grove, Richard H. *Green Imperialism: Colonial Expansion, Tropical Island Edens and the Origins of Environmentalism, 1600–1860*. Studies in Environment and History. Edited by Donald Worster and Alfred W. Crosby. Cambridge: Cambridge University Press, 1995.

Gullahorn-Holecek, Barbara. *The Doctors of Nigeria*. Boston, MA: WGBH Boston, 1981.

Gupta, Akhil. *Postcolonial Developments: Agriculture in the Making of Modern India*. Durham, NC: Duke University Press, 1998.

Gusterson, Hugh. *Nuclear Rites: A Weapons Laboratory at the End of the Cold War*. Berkeley, CA: University of California Press, 1996.

People of the Bomb: Portraits of America's Nuclear Complex. Minneapolis, MN: University of Minnesota Press, 2004.

Gyekye, Kwame. *An Essay on African Philosophical Thought: The Akan Conceptual Scheme*. Cambridge; New York: Cambridge University Press, 1987.

Tradition and Modernity: Philosophical Reflections on the African Experience. New York: Oxford University Press, 1997.

Hart, J. *Ghana on the Go: African Mobility in the Age of Motor Transportation*. Bloomington, IN: Indiana University Press, 2016.

Hawkins, Sean. *Writing and Colonialism in Northern Ghana: The Encounter between the Lodagaa and 'the World on Paper'*. Anthropological Horizons. Toronto: University of Toronto Press, 2002.

Hayden, Cori. *When Nature Goes Public: The Making and Unmaking of Bioprospecting in Mexico*. Princeton, NJ: Princeton University, 2003.

Hecht, David and A.M. Simone. *Invisible Governance: The Art of African Micro-Politics*. Brooklyn, NY: Autonomedia, 1994.

Hecht, Gabrielle. *The Radiance of France: Nuclear Power and National Identity after World War II*. Inside Technology. Edited by Wiebe E.

Bijker, W. Bernard Carlson, and Trevor Pinch. Cambridge, MA: The MIT Press, 1998.

Hecht, Gabrielle. *Being Nuclear: Africans and the Global Uranium Trade.* Cambridge, MA: MIT Press, 2012.

Horton, Roy E. *Out of (South) Africa: Pretoria's Nuclear Weapons Experience.* Champaign, IL: University of Illinois, 2000.

IAEA. *Project and Supply Agreement: The Text of the Agreement of 14 October 1994 among the International Atomic Energy Agency and the Governments of the Republic of Ghana and the People's Republic of China Concerning the Transfer of a Miniature Neutron Research Reactor and Enriched Uranium.* Vienna: The Agency, 1995.

Project and Supply Agrement: The Text of the Agreement of 29 August 1996 among the International Atomic Energy Agency and the Governments of the Republic of Nigeria and the People's Republic of China Concerning the Transfer of a Miniature Neutron Research Reactor and Enriched Uranium. Vienna: The Agency, 1996.

Research Reactors in Africa. 2011.

Iliffe, John. *Honour in African History.* Cambridge; New York: Cambridge University Press, 2005.

Africans: The History of a Continent. Cambridge; New York: Cambridge University Press, 2007.

East African Doctors: A History of the Modern Profession. Cambridge: Cambridge University Press, 1998.

Intondi, V. *African Americans against the Bomb: Nuclear Weapons, Colonialism, and the Black Freedom Movement.* Palo Alto, CA: Stanford University Press, 2015.

Isenberg, Andrew C. *The Nature of Cities.* Rochester, NY: University of Rochester Press, 2006.

Jacobs, Nancy Joy. *Environment, Power, and Injustice: A South African History.* Studies in Environment and History. Cambridge; New York: Cambridge University Press, 2003.

Jasanoff, Shelia. *The Fifth Branch: Science Advisers as Policymakers.* Cambridge, MA: Harvard University Press, 1990.

Designs on Nature: Science and Democracy in Europe and the United States. Princeton, NJ: Princeton University Press, 2005.

Jenkins, Philip. *The Next Christendom: The Coming of Global Christianity.* Oxford; New York: Oxford University Press, 2002.

Josephson, Paul R. *Red Atom: Russia's Nuclear Power Program from Stalin to Today.* Pittsburgh, PA: University of Pittsburgh Press, 2005.

Kasanga, Kasim and Nii Ashie Kotey. *Land Management in Ghana: Building on Tradition and Modernity.* London: International Institute for Environment and Development, 2001.

Khan, F. *Eating Grass: The Making of the Pakistani Bomb*. Palo Alto, CA: Stanford University Press, 2012.

Kilson, Marion. *African Urban Kinsmen: The Ga of Central Accra*. New York: St. Martin's Press, 1974.

Kreike, Emmanuel, Allen Isaacman, and Jean Allman. *Re-Creating Eden: Land Use, Environment, and Society in Southern Angola and Northern Namibia*. Social History of Africa Series. Portsmouth, NH: Greenwood Publishing Group, Inc., 2004.

Kuchinskaya, Olga. *The Politics of Invisibility: Public Knowledge about Radiation Health Effects after Chernobyl*. Cambridge, MA: MIT Press, 2014.

Langewiesche, William. *The Atomic Bazaar: The Rise of the Nuclear Poor*. New York: Farrar, Straus and Giroux, 2007.

Lindqvist, Svante. *Center on the Periphery: Historical Aspects of 20th-Century Swedish Physics*. Canton, MA: Science History Publications, 1993.

Livingston, Julie. *Improvising Medicine: An African Oncology Ward in an Emerging Cancer Epidemic*. Durham, NC: Duke University Press, 2012.

MacKenzie, D.A. *Knowing Machines: Essays on Technical Change*. Cambridge, MA: MIT Press, 1998.

Mavhunga, Clapperton Chakanetsa. *Transient Workspaces: Technologies of Everyday Innovation in Zimbabwe* Cambridge, MA: MIT Press, 2014.

Mamdani, Mahmood. *Citizen and Subject: Contemporary Africa and the Legacy of Late Capitalism*. Princeton, NJ: Princeton University Press, 1996.

Masco, Joseph. *The Nuclear Borderlands: The Manhattan Project in Post-Cold War New Mexico*. Princeton, NJ: Princeton University Press, 2006.

Matusevich, Maxim. *No Easy Row for a Russian Hoe: Ideology and Pragmatism in Nigerian-Soviet Relations, 1960–1991*. Trenton, NJ: Africa World Press, 2003.

May, Allan Nunn. *The Atomic Nature of Matter: An Inaugural Lecture Delivered on 29th January, 1970 at the University of Ghana, Legon*. Accra: Ghana Universities Press, 1971.

Mazuri, Ali A. *Niger-Saki: Does Nigeria Have a Nuclear Option?* Lagos: The Nigerian Institute of International Affairs, 1981.

McRae, Ian. *The Test of Leadership: 50 Years in the Electricity Supply Industry of South Africa*. Muldersdrift: EE Publishers, 2006.

Mindell, David. *Between Human and Machine: Feedback, Control, and Computing before Cybernetics*. Baltimore, MD: The Johns Hopkins Press, 2002.

Mutsaers, H.J.W. *Peasants, Farmers and Scientists: A Chronicle of Tropical Agricultural Science in the Twentieth Century*. Dordrecht: Springer, 2007.

Nelson, Alondra. *Body and Soul: The Black Panther Party and the Fight against Medical Discrimination*. Minneapolis, MN: University of Minnesota Press, 2011.

   The Social Life of D.N.A.: Race, Reparations, and Reconciliation after the Genome. Boston, MA: Beacon Press, 2016.

Nyerere, Julius Kambarage. *The Second Scramble*. Dar es Salaam: Tanganyika Standard, 1962.

Obeng, Letitia. *A Silent Heritage: An Autobiography*. Surrey: Goldsear, 2008.

Odoi, H.C., R.G. Abrefah, I.J.K. Aboh, J.K. Gbadago, S.A. Birikorang, and Edward Oscar Amponsah-Abu. *Implementation of Reactor Core Conversion Program of GHARR-1*. 36th International Meeting on Reduced Enrichment for Research and Test Reactors, 2015.

Okorafor, Nnedi. *Lagoon*. London: Hodder & Stoughton Ltd, 2016.

Omitoogun, Wuyi. *Military Expenditure Data in Africa: A Survey of Cameroon, Ethiopia, Ghana, Kenya, Nigeria and Uganda*. Sipri Research Report. Oxford; New York: Oxford University Press, 2003.

Osseo-Asare, Abena Dove. *Bitter Roots: The Search for Healing Plants in Africa*. Chicago: The University of Chicago Press, 2014.

Patton, Adell. *Physicians, Colonial Racism, and Diaspora in West Africa*. Gainesville, FL: University Press of Florida, 1996.

Perkovich, George. *India's Nuclear Bomb*. Berkeley, CA; London: University of California Press, 1999.

Petryna, Adriana. *Life Exposed: Biological Citizens after Chernobyl*. Princeton, NJ: Princeton University Press, 2002.

Pickering, Andrew. *Constucting Quarks: A Sociological History of Particle Physics*. Chicago: University of Chicago Press, 1984.

Pink, Sarah. *Doing Visual Ethnography: Images, Media and Representation in Research*. London: Sage, 2007.

Plummer, B.G. *In Search of Power: African Americans in the Era of Decolonization, 1956–1974*. New York: Cambridge University Press, 2013.

Preeg, Ernest H. *India and China: An Advanced Technology Race and How the United States Should Respond*. Manufacturers Alliance/MAPI and CSIS, 2008.

Quartey, J.A.K. *Reactor Report*. 1966.

Quartey, S. *Missionary Practices on the Gold Coast, 1832–1895*. Youngstown, NY: Cambria Press, 2007.

Quayson, Ato. *Oxford Street, Accra: City Life and the Itineraries of Transnationalism*. Durham, NC: Duke University Press, 2014.

Ramana, M.V. *The Power of Promise: Examining Nuclear Energy in India*. New Delhi: Penguin, 2012.

Redfield, Peter. *Space in the Tropics: From Convicts to Rockets in French Guiana*. Berkeley, CA: University of California Press, 2000.

Reindorf, C.C. *History of the Gold Coast and Asante*. Accra: Ghana Universities Press, 2007.

Rodney, Walter. *How Europe Underdeveloped Africa*. Washington, DC: Howard University Press, 1981.

Sackeyfio, Naaborle. *Energy Politics and Rural Development in Sub-Saharan Africa*. Cham: Palgrave Macmillan, 2018.

Sackeyfio-Lenoch, Naaborko. *The Politics of Chieftaincy: Authority and Property in Colonial Ghana, 1920–1950*. Rochester Studies in African History and the Diaspora. Rochester, NY: University of Rochester Press, 2014.

Scott, James C. *Seeing Like a State: How Certain Schemes to Improve the Human Condition Have Failed*. Yale Agrarian Studies. New Haven, CT; London: Yale University Press, 1999.

Seaborg, Glenn T., States United, Aec, and U.S. National Commission for UNESCO. *Science in a World of Widening Horizons*. Washington, DC: United States Atomic Energy Commission, 1966.

Selim, Tarek H. *On the Economic Feasibility of Nuclear Power Generation in Egypt*. Cairo: The Egyptian Center for Economic Studies, 2009.

Shin, David H. and Joshua Eisenman. *China and Africa: A Century of Engagement*. Philadelphia, PA: University of Pennsylvania Press, 2012.

Singh, Naunihal. *Seizing Power: The Strategic Logic of Military Coups*. Baltimore, MD: Johns Hopkins University Press, 2014.

Stephenson, G. *Atom*. Edited by Ghana Bureau of Languages. London: Longmans, Green and Co., Ltd., 1964, 1966.

Steyn, Hannes, Richardt Van Der Walt, and Jan Van Loggerenberg. *Nuclear Armament and Disarmament: South Africa's Nuclear Experience*. Lincoln, NE: iUniverse, 2005.

Sur, Abha. *Dispersed Radiance: Caste, Gender, and Modern Science in India*. New Delhi: Navayana Publishing, 2011.

Sutherland, Bill and Matt Meyer. *Guns and Gandhi in Africa: Pan African Insights on Nonviolence, Armed Struggle and Liberation in Africa*. Trenton, NJ: Africa World Press, 2000.

Swann, John Patrick. *Academic Scientists and the Pharmaceutical Industry: Cooperative Research in Twentieth-Century America*. Baltimore, MD: Johns Hopkins University Press, 1988.

Thiong'o, Ngũgĩ wa. *Decolonising the Mind: The Politics of Language in African Literature*. London: James Currey, 1992.

Tilley, Helen. *Africa as a Living Laboratory: Empire, Development, and the Problem of Scientific Knowledge, 1870–1950*. Chicago: University of Chicago Press, 2011.

Tousignant, Noémi. *Edges of Exposure: Toxicology and the Problem of Capacity in Postcolonial Senegal*. Durham, NC: Duke University Press, 2018.

Traweek, Sharon. *Beamtimes and Lifetimes: The World of High Energy Physicists*. Cambridge, MA: Harvard University Press, 1988.

United States. Congress. Senate. Committee on Foreign Relations. *The International Claims Settlement Act: Hearing before a Subcommittee, Eighty-Sixth Congress, First Session, on S. 706. May 29, 1959*. US Government Printing Office, 1959.

United States. Congress. House. Committee on Foreign Affairs. *Approving the Proposed Agreement for Nuclear Cooperation with Egypt: Report (to Accompany H. Con. Res. 176)*. Washington, DC: US Government Printing Office, 1981.

United Nations Scientific Committee on the Effects of Atomic Radiation. *Sources and Effects of Ionizing Radiation: Sources*.Vienna: UN, 2000.

Walters, Ronald W. *South Africa and the Bomb: Responsibility and Deterrence*. Lexington, MA: Lexington Books, 1987.

Weart, Spencer R. *Nuclear Fear: A History of Images*. Cambridge, MA: Harvard University Press, 1988.

Wendland, Claire L. *A Heart for the Work: Journeys through an African Medical School*. Chicago, IL: The University of Chicago Press, 2010.

Wizarat, al-Kharijiyah. *Egypt and the Peaceful Uses of Nuclear Energy*. Cairo: The Ministry, 1984.

Thesis

Jessee, Emory Jerry. "Radiation Ecologies: Bombs, Bodies, and Environment During the Atmospheric Nuclear Weapons Testing Period, 1942–1965." PhD Thesis. Montana State University, 2013.

Multimedia

"Academic Staff, Department of Physics and Engineering Physics, Obafemi Awolowo University." https://phy.oauife.edu.ng/academic-staff-2/ (April 2, 2018).

"Ademola Amusa, Consultant, Nuclear Science Educator, Researcher." https://prabook.com/web/ademola.amusa/473412 (April 2, 2018).

"GAST [Ghana Association of Science Teachers]: The Association." www .ghanaweb.com/GhanaHomePage/blogs/blog.article.php?blog=1463 &ID=1000001762.

Gbeddy, Gustav. "Radioactive Waste Management in Ghana; a Country Currently without Nuclear Power Plant." Powerpoint presentation, 2015.

"Pioneer and Retired Staff, Department of Physics and Engineering Physics, Obafemi Awolowo University." https://phy.oauife.edu.ng/pioneer-and-retired-staff/.

Arthur, Lawrence. "History of Radiography in Ghana." Ghana Society of Radiographers, http://ghanasor.org/history-of-radiography-in-ghana/ (July 13, 2017).

Kuti, Fela. "Colo Mentality." *Sorrow Tears and Blood*. Kalakuta, 1977.

Marley, Bob. "Redemption Song." *Uprising*. Chris Blackwell, producer. Island Records, 1980.

Nkrumah, Kwame. *The World without the Bomb [Sound Recording]*. Berkeley, CA: Bancroft Library Phonotape 3667A, 1962.

Index